To the memory of
A.A.D.

Understanding Miracles

Zsolt Aradi

Understanding Miracles

How to Know if They Are from God, the Devil, or the Imagination

Sophia Institute Press
Manchester, NH

Understanding Miracles was first published under the title
The Book of Miracles by Farrar, Straus and Cudahy, New York: 1956.
© Zsolt Aradi 1956.

Sophia Institute Press
Box 5284, Manchester, NH 03108
1-800-888-9344
www.SophiaInstitute.com
Sophia Institute Press® is a registered trademark of Sophia Institute.

Cover design by Carolyn McKinney.

Art credit: The Marriage at Cana, 1819 (oil on canvas),
Schnorr von Carolsfeld, Julius (1794-1872) /
Hamburger Kunsthalle, Hamburg, Germany /
The Bridgeman Art Library.

Printed in the United States of America.

Nihil Obstat: John A. Goodwine, *Censor Librorum.*
Imprimatur: Francis Cardinal Spellman, *Archbishop of New York.*

Library of Congress Cataloging-in-Publication Data

Aradi, Zsolt, Dr.
  The book of miracles / by Zsolt Aradi.
    p. cm.
  Originally published: New York : Farrar, Straus and Cudahy, 1956.
  "An ARKive edition."
  Includes bibliographical references (p.   ) and index.
  ISBN 978-1-933184-78-4 (ppbk : alk. paper) 1. Miracles. I. Title.
  BT97.3.A73 2010
  231.7'3—dc22

                                                              2010029895

Author's Note

I express my particular gratitude and appreciation to the following persons for their generous help during my research work and during the writing of the book. To the Very Reverend Monsignor Orazio Cocchetti, Archivist of the Sacred Congregation of Rites, Rome; to the Reverend Mother Geraldina of the Sisters of Divine Love, Rome; to Prof. Cesidio Lolli, Editor of the *Osservatore Romano*, Vatican City.

To the Very Reverend Monsignor Michael Schmaus, Professor of Dogma at the University of Munich, Germany, for his invaluable advice.

To Mr. Salvator Attanasio, New York City, for his editorial assistance.

Contents

Preface

THE LESSON OF LOURDES

It seems to me that nothing could be more appropriate as an introduction to a book on the meaning and value of miracles than some remarks on the miracles which the Lord deigns to perform in Lourdes through the Blessed Virgin. Soon we shall be celebrating the centenary of the apparition of the Virgin to St. Bernadette. In this our time, so pagan, rationalistic and blasphemous, in which the most diverse ideologies and social systems have made use of subtle and all-pervading means to rob men of the patrimony of the Faith; God, through Lourdes, has wished to demonstrate that He is our Lord and Creator who controls the forces of nature. The miracles of Lourdes are a call to mankind to recognize God in all His omnipotence and mercy. For this purpose the Lord has availed Himself of the Immaculate Virgin in order to make manifest to the peoples of our time, victims of impurity, the pristine and beautiful purity of the Immaculate Virgin, and to demonstrate the power of her intercessions at the throne of God. The Madonna is the one creature, above all others, preferred by God because she issued directly from His hands.

There is, however, another aspect of Lourdes which is necessary to mention because it is rich in lesson for Christians. Anyone who has witnessed the processions in the name of the Holy Sacrament that take place on the piazza of the basilica has found the spectacle of throngs of people publicly imploring the assistance of the Almighty a deeply moving religious experience. This fact is a recognition of the role that the Blessed Virgin plays in the life of the Church and in the supernatural life of every individual. It is evidence that the Divine word not only chose to become flesh among men by being born of woman, but that it also seeks to draw mankind to itself through a woman.

Per Mariam ad Iesum. This is the motto which today resounds through Lourdes. On the one hand the Blessed Virgin, by drawing the masses of people to Jesus in the form of the Holy Sacrament, sheds light on the value and the efficacy of eucharistic pity. And on the other hand, she provides a supernatural sanction for that eucharistic movement to which all the Popes, from Pius X to Pius XIII, have given such solemn and active support; just as she gave a similar sanction to the dogma of the Immaculate Conception when she appeared before Bernadette Soubirous. The throngs of pilgrims render homage to Mary in a thousand forms, always as eloquent as they are varied, imploring graces from her. And the Blessed Virgin responds with miracles that bear witness to Jesus Christ.

It is this dual aspect of Lourdes that I would like to discuss here. It will permit us to understand why the crowds of pilgrims that visit Lourdes return to their daily labors in homes, factories, offices and private studies, bringing to their arduous tasks the vigor of a rekindled faith.

First let it be said that it is a fact that Lourdes presents a completely unique spiritual configuration, the importance of which can escape no observer and which merits our examination. This spiritual phenomenon presents a characteristic that I would call one of *excessiveness,* not in the etymological sense of the word but in its psychological sense. By this I mean that it is like an effervescent liquid that cannot be contained in the vessel out of which it flows.

For those who judge Lourdes without having ever visited the shrine the most salient fact is the miracle, the healing act. But for those who study Lourdes through its throngs of pilgrims, its rites and its ceremonies, the miracle ceases to be the central phenomenon. In other words, it ceases to be something in itself and which is incomprehensible; instead it enters into the order of all the other events that transpire in Lourdes, and becomes thereby a kind of warning that is most important for us to heed: the Virgin is calling us to a Christian life. Men accustomed to the mere gloss of human respect, literally dragged to the shrine by the piety of a mother, sister or wife, suddenly forget themselves and their own prejudices; they become Christians and approach the sacraments with a feeling infinitely deeper than mere respect. Women, timid in their religious practices, take on a physiognomy illuminated by Christian courage. And young people who show the effects of a shakened faith accept with closed eyes what was formerly repugnant to their intellect.

The Christian piety at Lourdes is a eucharistic piety *par excellence*. When the Eucharist is carried in processions by the crowds, when the crowds keep vigil for entire nights over the Eucharist, when the Holy Sacrament seeks out, so to speak, all the sick and consoles them one by one, the homage to Jesus assumes so solemn a form that it brings to mind the most sublime pages of the Gospels. How many times have I had to rub my eyes and ask myself: "Am I really alive? And do I see these things with my own eyes? Have I not been a witness to scenes out of the New Testament?"

During the unforgettable benediction on the piazza of the basilica, the crowds of pilgrims gradually get the upper hand over the austerity of the rites; they break and surge through the dikes of the solemn forms of the liturgy and in its place they substitute their own invocations which are the moving manifestations of their own richer, more genuine and simple faith.

At such moments the crowd, in response to the suggestions of its own explosive faith, performs acts that elsewhere might be judged to be irreverent. People throw themselves on their knees, and open wide their arms in gestures of supplication; they pray, lament, weep and intone hymns. Each individual supplicant in his own way unites his prayer and his invocation with those of the others, and the voices raised in different tongues and accents merge and fuse into a single supplication. Only in such moments is it possible to understand how a father dares to raise his child aloft and how the child can manage to kiss the *ostensorium;* only in this way is it possible to understand how the bishops manage to place the *ostensorium* on the heads of the sick; only in such an atmosphere is it possible to understand how, on occasion, the pilgrims can abjectly throw themselves to the ground and present such a great spectacle of faith by reciting that sublime prayer, the *confiteor*.

The invocations that pour forth from the throats of the faithful on the immense piazza, when the Holy Sacrament is displayed in front of the Church of the Rosary, are not to be found in any book of the liturgy. Yet they are naught else but a repetition of the cries of love, faith and pity which the Saviour Himself aroused during His wanderings in Gallilee. They are the expressions preserved in the Gospels, they are the spontaneous explosion of many long-suffering souls who see in Him the only salvation. And this correspondence of words and feelings is the spontaneous demonstration of the fact that Jesus Christ alone is the luminous center toward which humanity must aspire. "Lord, just say one word and I shall be cured," "Lord, let me walk again," "Lord, let me see," "Lord, let me hear once more." These exclamations in the vernacular are, to be sure, evangelical expressions. But they are also expressions of fundamental, inextinguishable and indelible sentiments of the human spirit. They are not the collective cry of sick bodies, languishing under the pressure of physical pain; they are, the cry of the Christian soul which sighs for eternal light and which feels the total imperfection and incompleteness of earthly life. It is the cry of the creature to his Creator Who alone can understand and satisfy his needs.

It must not be thought, however, that things have always been so at Lourdes. In the beginning, as is well known, it seemed that the supernatural in Lourdes converged toward only one point: to give a confirmation of the words that the Blessed Virgin had pronounced there on her seventh apparition: "I am the Immaculate Conception."

After 1888 the devotion in Lourdes assumed a new orientation, thus inaugurating a new phase in its history. It is well known that in these times of a deep and widespread religious crisis there is also a noticeable parallel movement among the faithful to intensify their devotion to the Eucharist. This phenomenon, noticed in all countries by those who minister to souls, seems to tell us that the disciples of Christ, caught in the maelstrom of the anti-religious activity which seemingly overwhelms everything about them, feel a great need to rally more fraternally than ever around the Divine Master. It can be said that what Christianity has lost in extension, it has gained in intensity. There is also felt a need for a more active demonstration of faith in order to resist the blows of the enemies of the Church. At first sight it might appear that the religious enthusiasms at Lourdes might easily degenerate into distortions of true religious feeling—dangerous distortions, indeed, because they would be due more to fevered imaginations than to anything else. Instead it can be pointed out that the religious feeling at Lourdes has been guided by a mysterious instinct, in such a manner that it seeks those very forms of expression peculiar to the Church herself. Rather than speak of instinct one should say, perhaps, that the people let themselves be guided by their pastors along lines that are in beautiful harmony with everything that is transpiring within the Church. And just as there is noticeable within the Church an intensification of the cult of the Eucharist, so Lourdes, without ever ceasing to be the center of the Marian cult, has also noticeably become a center of devotion to the Most Holy Sacrament.

In August 1880 a simple priest conceived a bold idea. His idea was to revive the scenes of the New Testament in Lourdes itself by having Jesus Christ, in the form of the Eucharist, walk among the multitudes of the sick, the halt and the blind who came to the shrine imploring to be healed. Thus began this wondrous spectacle on the piazza of the shrine which I feel so powerless to describe adequately and which, as I have said, moves one to tears, so movingly akin is it to the scenes that once took place in Palestine. From the thousands of sick stretched out on their beds and from the thousands of persons who accompany them pour forth the very same exclamations that once were cried out by the blind, the deaf and the paralytics whom Jesus healed. And by His healing Jesus, present under the veils of the Eucharist, loves to show that He accepts the homage and answers them who pray and implore for His mercy.

Thus are the two great objects of Catholic devotion, Jesus and Mary, united intimately at Lourdes. Thus on the very ground where the apparitions of Mary first took place do we now have eucharistic manifestations. The cures which are begun in the waters are completed during the procession of the Holy Sacrament, and the healings that are invoked at the grotto, where the Virgin Mary first appeared to Bernadette Soubirous, are obtained when Jesus passes by, in the form of the Blessed Sacrament. Thus it becomes impossible to separate the two objects of the cult, and we see realized in life itself the doctrine of St. Bernard, according to which the Virgin is the co-redeemer of the world, and the intermediary between the Saviour and us. It is in this way that the eucharistic manifestations in Lourdes, religiously colored and enhanced by the beauty of the Most Holy Virgin, acquire a physiognomy peculiar to them.

The fruit of this eucharistic piety is the transformation of souls. Lourdes itself offers no special natural attractions. In fact, more than other towns in southern France, it possesses those negative features common to the countryside between France and Spain, so devoid of natural beauties or works of art. The sky over Lourdes is frequently cloudy, and there is nothing inviting about its environs. And yet when you are there you have a feeling of joy, as though present at a feast of the heart. And the mystery of this feeling of well being is explained the moment you share the intimate life of the pilgrims. You see them fraternize among themselves, you approach them and they bare their souls to you, rich with a sublime ingenuousness which excludes any thought of smiling over their manner of speech. If in you they see a good-hearted person, they will tell you about their troubles and misfortunes. They confide in one another, they help each other, providing marvelous examples of pity and charity. Lourdes is like a corner of the world in which egotism has been banished; it is a world in which the spirit of the Christian community lives and thrives.

Lourdes is a prodigy of piety. To be fully appreciated, the signs of this piety, expressed by souls hungering for religious peace, must be observed by the simple in heart. He who looks for them with the cold analysis that kills finds only words without sense, puerilities, insignificance. But he who studies Lourdes with the intellect of love finds there a veritable paradise of piety, to employ an expression used by the pilgrims themselves, who truly abandon themselves to the spontaneity of faith. The preachers at Lourdes do not strain for colorful images and carefully wrought phrases, yet they move their listeners to tears. The sick may at first offend you with their shameless exhibition of diseases and infirmities; the crowd presses against you and suffocates you and seems to break the enchantment of your spiritual solitude and your colloquies with God. Still he who has faith and lives in the faith feels at peace. It is as though a sense of spiritual lightness were communicated to the body and you feel yourself being literally dragged to the feet of Jesus in the form of the Blessed Sacrament. In the nights of vigil and adoration that every pilgrim keeps, the priests gather the fruit of all this intense spiritual activity that the Blessed Virgin effects in us without our knowledge. Only a priest who has sat in the confessional on such nights can attest to the profound changes that take place in many souls, changes that constitute the most beautiful miracle and which find their confirmation in a communion with others that renews the enchantments of the Last Supper. After a day spent in the practice of piety and in the procession, after the last strains of the religious hymns are lost in the darkness of early evening, and after the last torches are extinguished, the doors of the Church of the Rosary are opened for the pilgrims who want to spend the night before the tabernacle. All of them are tired after hours in crowded trains, but despite their fatigue they wish to bear Jesus testimony of their love, and with their penitence and adoration they wish to atone for the outrages that others commit against Him.

Among the numerous sick persons that I have accompanied to Lourdes and whom I have helped there, I have seen spiritual transformations of much greater value than the material benefits for which they implored the Virgin of Lourdes. They were unhappy creatures, inexorably condemned to live in wheelchairs, or in beds; poor souls truncated in members and in their most legitimate aspirations as well; wretched broken bodies held together by a mere thread of life. All of them, in the long days of their suffering, in the empty silence of nights devoid of expectations and consolation, had entertained one single hope: to be able to go to Lourdes, to feel, perhaps, the blood flow once again to their hearts and from there revitalize the rest of their bodies so they could once again feel the joy of life. But in Lourdes a complete change would take place. Many times I remember bending over the sick in the hospital trains in order to console them or to render them a small service. The only desire that I ever heard them express was to have their health restored, and thereby life itself! It was difficult for me to restrain such sentiments and to do no more than suggest gently that the Christian must bow before the designs of Providence. But, as if by enchantment, a deep and amazing change would come over all of them once they were assigned to a bed in the hospital of Seven Sorrows, or immediately after their first visit to the grotto, or to the spring. It was a change that came over all of them, even among those who were the least spiritually prepared. The change was the result of witnessing the diseases and the distress of others, of living in an atmosphere saturated with the Christian spirit, so that little by little these persons, sick as they were, began to see and evaluate their own misfortunes in a different light.

How deeply moved I was one day when a poor woman, whose legs had been amputated below the knee, and to whom I was trying to say a few words of encouragement, looked up at me and said: "Father, I no longer seek to be healed. Instead, I ask for it only for the many souls who suffer more than me." One year, while the nurses were preparing to move a group of invalids from the hospital of Seven Sorrows to the hospital trains (they numbered about one hundred and not one had shown the slightest improvement), I addressed a few words to them, the tenor of which was that as Christians they should resign themselves to the mysterious designs of God. When I had finished speaking, those that could rose to their feet and gathered around me, kissing my hands, while the rest from their stretchers reached out their arms toward me. With one voice all of them were saying: "Father, it is not necessary that you tell us this. Here we have come to understand that our misfortunes are not the worst and that our crosses are not the heaviest. We renounce the graces for which we petitioned so that the Madonna may grant them to others more in need and more worthy than ourselves." And among these poor souls were several upon whom the sentence of death had already been pronounced.

I have spoken of the marvelous flowering of piety that takes place in Lourdes. This is not completely comprehensible, however, unless

I refer to another fact correlative to it and intimately linked with it: the eucharistic miracle.

The Jesuit priest, Tonquedoc, has already carefully noted that at Lourdes there is no continuity between piety and a miracle. The latter is prepared by acts of faith, hope and charity; it, in turn, gives rise to new acts of similar virtue around itself. The miracle is suddenly seized, so to speak, by means of persistent prayer and, in its turn, it arouses and reanimates other prayers.

It is truly edifying to observe what happens when a sick person is cured; the story of his cure spreads quickly by word of mouth to all around him. Here the critical spirit should not insinuate that one should separate that which is true from that which is added by fantasy and the legends formed around the invalid. Even the unbeliever feels the influence of the action that radiates from the invalid and is then translated into works of mercy, and into the sudden conversion of other hearts. The invalid is surrounded by many persons who ask only one thing of him: to get closer to God. They feel that they are touching something which is of God when they are in contact with this creature in whom God has wished to show His power and mercy.

In my opinion this particular atmosphere that surrounds the miracle in Lourdes cannot be considered apart from the miracle itself, if the intimate significance of the miracle is to be really understood. I have affirmed this on several occasions during my discussions of the events of Lourdes.

If we take an animal, kill it and then make a minute anatomical study of it we shall learn all about its most intimate inner structure. But we cannot grasp the phenomenon of life in all its palpitant reality because we no longer have it under hand, as it were. In order to know what life is we must study it among the living, in its marvelous manifestations, and in those secret connections which adapt the living organism to the milieu in which it lives, and to its needs.

Thus is it with the miracle. If we wish to understand it we must not analyze it with the instruments of criticism. By such a method we shall learn to know only the pathological elements, or that which constitutes the physical condition. The essential element will escape us. In Lourdes this very element is given by the intimate nexus that exists between the Eucharist and the manifestations of the mercy of Jesus Christ. It is necessary, therefore, to study the miracle in its own atmosphere. Such a statement should occasion no wonder. The poor widow or the poor blind man of the Gospels understood the miracles of Jesus Christ much better than did the Pharisees who with their casuistic subtleties lost sight of the essential element of the miracle. At Lourdes, to cite but one example among a thousand, a poor, ignorant woman, named Rouchel, was able to make the following serene reply to a commission of incredulous doctors indulging in subtle, scientific probing: "How I came to be healed I do not know. Nor do I know what was the nature of my disease. I know only that I have been healed because the Most Holy Virgin has interceded for me with her Divine Son. And for me this is enough. From now on I must love Jesus, in the form of the Holy Eucharist, more and more." On the one hand we have a wondrous wisdom under the humble appearance of ignorance, and on the other a gross ignorance hidden behind the trappings of modern science.

By this I do not mean that there must be no scientific research on the miracles of Lourdes. On the contrary such scientific research should be carried out with the utmost meticulousness, because it places in our hands a precious element for demonstrating the existence of supernatural fact at Lourdes. But let us not delude ourselves. My personal experience there permits me to make an important observation with respect to this. If we wish to understand the miracles of Lourdes, or any other miracles in the true sense of the word, we must not remove them from their ambience. We must study them on that holy ground, blessed by God. Only then will we be able to understand this intimate nexus that exists between the miracle performed through the intercession of the Virgin and the eucharistic manifestations.

fr. AGOSTINO GEMELLI, O.F.M.

Understanding Miracles

". . . Flesh fade, and mortal trash Fall
to the residuary worm; world's wildfire,
leave but ash:

In a flash, at a trumpet crash, I am
all at once what Christ is, since he was
what I am, and This Jack, joke, poor,
potsherd, patch, matchwood, immortal
diamond,

       Is immortal diamond."

Gerard Manley Hopkins, from "That
Nature is a Heraclitean Fire and of the
Comfort of the Resurrection," *Poems.*

CHAPTER 1

Meeting the Miracle

"Let us doubt without unbelief of
things to be believed."
(St. Augustine, *De Trinitate*)

Belief in God requires no miracles. I did not write this book to demonstrate or justify my faith. Should it help anyone on the way to belief, I would be pleased, although I could not take any credit myself. My own faith is mine by the grace of God, nourished and strengthened by deeply religious parents who took seriously the injunction "Love thy God and neighbor." Though this book is not an evidence of faith, I feel that without this faith it would have been impossible for me to write a single word on miracles.

Save for the miracles of revelation as contained in the Old and the New Testaments, one is free to believe or doubt any miracle. Great saints, says Jean Hellé, "have often given an example of extreme skepticism. Most of them, especially the mystics, reveal themselves to those who study them as men or women of great common sense who have their two feet firmly on the ground and are not easily hoaxed."[1]

At the same time, assent to miracles has never constituted a problem for me. Since I do not doubt the existence of an omnipotent God, the source of all being, how could I challenge Him and delimit His infinite power? But easy credulity and the reasonable willingness to accept the existence of a world beyond one's reach are two different things. I realize that it was my thorough religious education, and my belief in and obedience to the Church, that enabled me to make this distinction. The Church grants the greatest possible freedom to search for meanings in things and events, even the freedom to make mistakes in the search. But we know that in the Church we have an authority upon whom we can and should rely. Thus, I was not unusually preoccupied with the invisible world, though I could not avoid meeting it.

I was only seven when my piano teacher, an amiable old maid, tied a large old-fashioned door key to the pages of a prayerbook. If the shank of the key were held, the prayerbook revolved, swinging sometimes to the right and sometimes to the left. Smiling gently but with a mysterious air, the old piano teacher asked me to hold the key. Then she called her sister, also an old maid. Together they mumbled some words and then they made the Sign of the Cross—in reverse. I did not know what was on their minds until both stared at me penetratingly and announced that they would get in touch with their recently deceased brother. I was told that the prayerbook, which hung on the key held by my fingers, would revolve; two gyrations to the left would mean that the ghost of the brother was saying Yes, two to the right, No. Furthermore, the ghost might even touch me.

I never found out whether they succeeded in communicating with their yellow-bearded, crippled brother (whom I remembered because he died only the week before). All I know is that I was seized with a sudden terror, dropped what to me was a devilish device, and ran away.

Many years later, in 1927, I lived in the vicinity of the Tatra mountains in Czechoslovakia, a region literally soaked in lore and legend of all kinds. Every castle—and there were hundreds, every ruin—and there were thousands of them, had its particular "house ghost." I lived in many of those castles and often roamed amid the ruins. I knew all about the eleventh-century *seigneur* who once a week, at midnight, walked down from the tower-dungeon, his feet chained to his arms, and his left hand holding aloft his own head. And I knew about the beautiful white lady of Levoca, who for the last four hundred years had been retiring nightly to the room where she had killed her unfaithful lover. The sudden opening of locked windows during windless nights of total silence, peasant ghosts enfolded in white sheets and crouched in the branches of apple trees, and the rest of the mysterious folklore, so much a part of the daily life of the people there, did not bother me. But one day while walking back from a fishing trip through a neighboring village, I had to give some thought to this invisible world. It was a coal and mercury mining town, quite unromantic, and at least half the labor force was organized in unions hostile to any religion. Superstition remained the pastime of a few old women. It was daylight when my uncle and I stopped at an inn for a cup of coffee. After a few minutes the innkeeper excitedly tapped my uncle on the shoulder and through the window pointed to a young boy of about thirteen walking on the other side of the street. "That is young T. They don't know what to do with him. Stones fall, heavy objects travel through glass windows wherever he goes. It all started three days ago. T. went fishing with his father, when suddenly stones started to fall upon them, some of them as large as a man's head. When they ran away in fright, the stone shower followed them with the density and rapidity of machine gun fire. But neither the boy nor his father was hurt when the stones touched them."

My uncle—always interested in adventure—paid the check and we followed young T. He was the son of a forester whom my uncle knew; so we were received as friends at their house. Young T. looked completely normal except that his eyes would horrify anybody not prepared for such a sight; his black eyes looked only one way; inward! When young T. went into the other room we talked with his father. Suddenly we all froze into a statuesque rigidity. A four-inch figurine on a shelf began to move; it rose up into the air, and then like in a slow-motion film it ambled over to the other corner of the room, and without being damaged it settled itself on the floor. Before we could recover our senses, a marble inkstand, filled with ink and holding three pens, lifted itself from the desk, shot up into the air, then literally fell on its side without spilling the ink, and ended its antics by rolling to another corner of the room. This was enough for me. I took my uncle's hand, gasped a hasty good-bye, and then we both ran away. As we left the house a stone about the size of an apple fell at our feet. It was a piece from the ore collection of the forester. They had not thrown it at us; it came from somewhere above.

The case of young T. became world-famous and the story has been reported in many scientific journals. Since I was not a scientist, I decided I would do no further personal research into the cause of this strange phenomenon. But from that time on I have not ridiculed those who, though lacking my kind of faith, indulged in lengthy discussions about the possibility of communicating with the invisible world. I realized that their approach was not mine, but I sensed that it did at least border on mine. Later when I read the books of the well-known English Jesuit—Scholar Herbert Thurston, I agreed with his assertion that to attribute strange or unusual physical phenomena "to fraud would be unjust and even dangerous for a sound apologetic." Both cases that I have related were harmless. It is possible that my old piano teacher might have done me harm if she had succeeded in passing on her spiritualistic superstition to me. But upon looking back to these first brief encounters with the "invisible," I consider them harmless. I was certainly frightened, but this was my own inner attitude; the phenonmena did not give rise to any public scandal and had no evil effect upon the community.

Then one night in August, 1933, a man from Roumania, entered the Hungarian border police station at L. and immediately collapsed on the floor. The man was searched immediately, but it appeared that the assistance of a doctor was more necessary than detective work to determine his identity. He was bleeding from at least five bullet wounds. After treatment by the doctors it was learned that he was a member of a fanatical religious sect known as the Legion of St. Michael. He had been shot at by his fellow "legionnaires," who intended to kill him because he had balked at carrying out a mission of some importance—to kill a nationally known Roumanian politician. Members of this group were not merely political terrorists: they acted on the impetus of a deeply-felt religious conviction. (The Legion of St. Michael later became a full-fledged political party, called the Iron Guard. It organized pogroms, killing thousands of people, Jews and non-Jews alike, and it helped to deliver the country to Hitler.) When later I met this man as he sat on his hospital bed, I had no idea that I would have to descend with him into the most sinister depths of the invisible world.

The origins of the Legion of St. Michael can be traced to the great veneration for St. Michael held by all Eastern Christians, including the Catholics of Oriental rites. The archangel Michael is the head of the "celestial armies who fight Satan." Throughout history he has been considered the defender against the attacks of diabolical forces. The Orthodox churches, each of which is nationally and independently organized, have sometimes given an arbitrary explanation of what they consider diabolical. Thus the imagination of their communicants has often been excited by an ill-digested mysticism. Constant oppression, social and political, intensified their desire for a joint earthly and heavenly salvation so as to liberate themselves from the utter depravity and misery in which they lived. The founder of the Legion of St. Michael, Zelea Codreanu, came from such an environment, being the son of very poor Roumanian peasants. Zelea Codreanu was less than twenty years old when he suddenly had a vision of St. Michael and allegedly received a message from him. Already psychologically conditioned to the occult, the inhabitants of the little village near Jassy in Roumania became as aroused over the vision as Codreanu himself. Soon thousands and thousands of persons from all over the country made a pilgramage to the site where St. Michael had allegedly appeared to Codreanu. Half-educated and credulous priests gave ecclesiastical support to the story of the apparition, in which St. Michael is said to have told the young man to form a legion and fight the oppressors with fire and iron. The oppressors were identified as anybody who opposed the legion, particularly the capitalists, the government and the Jews.

Young Zelea Codreanu lost no time in carrying out the message. In 1923, when he was but twenty, he killed the police chief of the city of Jassy, because he had attempted to maintain public order in the face of mounting excitement. Although (or perhaps because) Codreanu was arrested and jailed, the movement grew apace, becoming rapidly something of a national menace. The authorities viewed it as an expression of mass hysteria based on the alleged vision. It is certain that Codreanu was not a "faker," and that he had "seen" something in a trance. His vision was of course not a miracle but clearly a symptom of psychiatric disorder, hysteria.

The members of the Legion formed a semi-secret society. They not only terrorized villages, small cities, and the countryside, but also threatened politicians. They concentrated on destroying the shops and houses of Jews and burning their synagogues. In 1933 Codreanu was freed. Acting as "ordered by St. Michael," in that year he assassinated the head of the Roumanian government, Coriolan Duca. As the movement grew, a political party called the Iron Guard was formed in accordance with St. Michael's "instructions" to Codreanu that he should use "fire and iron" to achieve his aims.

In effect the Iron Guard was a uniformed private militia. It occupied the streets, marched on the highways; wherever it appeared murders were committed. By 1933 the toll of victims ran into several hundreds. Eventually Codreanu himself was killed, but his lieutenants and the Guard, now numbering hundreds of thousands, carried on.

Now, these people were not unbelievers. They were deeply "religious" persons who really believed in God, and their cruel and bloody fanaticism was fed by the so-called apparitions that Codreanu claimed to have seen in 1923.

The man on the hospital bed who talked to me was a member of this group. He considered himself a traitor, a weakling; he regretted that he had survived because, as he said, "I did not deserve other treatment for faltering before the orders of St. Michael the Archangel." As he spoke, his eyes gleamed fanatically.

A few months later, in January, 1934, while enroute to England, I stopped in Belgium to study a new political movement. But as soon as I arrived in Brussels my friends insisted that Belgium had far more interesting events to offer than a survey of the effect of Hitler's coming to power upon this industrious and charming little country. My friends offered me nothing less than *two* miracles, two apparitions.

The experience of the Iron Guard being still fresh in my mind, I had no desire even to listen to the story of the apparitions that had allegedly occurred in Beauraing and Banneux. I dreaded the idea of encountering hysterical crowds, shouting men and weeping women; seeing people being trampled upon by a mob calling itself religious; and I certainly did not wish to witness scenes of police and soldiers using violence in order to disperse people whose morbid curiosity is sometimes far greater than their reverence for an apparition which, even though unconfirmed, partakes of the holy. I went to Beauraing, nevertheless.

To my surprise I found no crowds. The village was calm, the religious-article stands around the church were empty, and people went about their business as though nothing had happened. When I stopped a middle-aged worker and asked him what he could tell me about the "miracle," he shrugged his shoulders and told me to go see the pastor. Some people in the inn were more talkative. They informed me that since November of 1932 five children, ranging in ages from nine to 15, sons of hard-working, sane, and healthy families, had received a total of thirty-three visions, and that at these apparitions the Blessed Virgin showed herself to them and told them to be good, to sacrifice themselves, and to love Christ and their neighbor. Some of my fellow guests in the inn loudly criticized the bishop of the diocese for having prohibited any pilgrimages, any cult, and even any gatherings in connection with these miracles. The criticism became shrill when some others present accused the doctors and the French Carmelite Fathers, who were expert in psychiatry themselves and members of the Church's investigation committee, of behaving "as if they did not believe a word."

"The French won't let us have our Madonna, though they have so many," complained an old man sadly. "They do not want to believe that the Blessed Virgin meant what she said during the apparitions. She said quite clearly: 'I have come for the glory of Belgium and to defend the country against the invader.' Is not that clear enough?" But the rest of the guests silenced the old man: "Be still, Maurice, the Blessed Virgin said nothing of the sort to the children. It's just that old man boasting about a new vision. But who is going to believe him?"

The pastor confirmed what I had heard. The matter of the apparitions was in the hands of the ecclesiastical authorities. The investigation was now in full swing; doctors, priests, psychologists, psychiatrists, theologians were busily at work. "Do you believe it was a miracle?" I asked the pastor.

He did not answer but put his hand on my shoulder. "Come and see the children," he suggested.

When I met them one after the other and looked into their eyes, clear and sincere, I felt reluctant to ask questions. These children were not afraid, but, in fact, rather curious to meet someone who came from thousands of miles away. In their childlike curiosity they were unaware of their effect upon me.

If the apparitions had been authentic, then I was looking into eyes that had actually seen a figure come from a far greater distance, from quite another dimension of life. Their calm and casual behavior was to me the greatest surprise. These children, I thought, are either the most accomplished actors or the innocent victims of some vicious mass-suggestion. Otherwise how would it be possible for them to maintain so quiet and peaceful a composure? Here we just talked about trivial subjects—the weather, the ocean and trains. And the more I looked into their eyes, the deeper became my realization that their unconcerned and normal behavior, their very lack of pretension and euphoric excitement, *might* be an indication that they really were chosen by God. Otherwise how could they bear the burden of their revelation?

I asked myself many questions while driving back to Brussels. The children's story was strange, and yet it seemed to me to be a simple enough matter to accept it. But why did it happen in Beauraing, and not somewhere else? Was it possible, I said to myself, that I and the children I had just seen were walking the same earth? If so, the wonders of the old saints and the miracles of Christ are no longer nebulous, anachronistic events out of my reach and experience; not merely pious beliefs transmitted, each time more hazily, by the narrative of successive generations. Here was a *contemporary* wonder! I still don't know whether this is authentic or not, I said to myself, but if it is I certainly have encountered a miracle. . . .

For ten long years there was silence about Beauraing. There were battles, too, though quite different from the battles of the Iron Guard. There were those who tried to exploit the apparitions for economic aims; others suspected the children of mischievous deception and some people actually accused the Church of encouraging superstition. All this, however, was to the good, helping as it did to clarify the situation.

Finally in 1943 the Bishop of Namur in Belgium authorized the cult of Our Lady of Beauraing.

The children who had seen her grew up, married, and now have their own children. All are as normal as ever. They have not started any movements or enjoyed any material gains as a result of their experiences. Beauraing has reaped no profits from expanded tourist trade. Nor has anyone been killed or even harmed. On the contrary, "The Lady of the Golden Heart," during her 33 appearances, always asked for more and more prayers and love. And the prayers of the faithful have created works of love and charity and understanding. The apparitions have greatly promoted the spiritual welfare of the whole community and of its members as individuals.

After all this, I could hardly hesitate to accept the events in Beauraing as being truly miraculous. Still, when in the spirit of St. Augustine I accepted the decision as most probably a just one, I could not help wondering about those who are either unable to go even so far as a *doubting* acceptance or else dismiss any contact with the marvelous with an air of superiority. In the first category—the skeptics—belong persons who are extremely proud of sheer human effort and creativeness and their visible results in the world of art, science and technology. In their daily contact they are so continually involved with the material universe that without any sort of reflection—a priori, so to speak—they believe in no other world. According to them, material achievement does not occur in a vacuum; nothing happens without human effort—the labor of hand and brain. If we stop working, the production of material things cease also. No one would be miraculously fed, sheltered, or clothed. These are sound, authentic objections; they are also totally and completely false. Such persons reckon only on their own actions and the actions of those within their immediate social circle, trade, or profession. Of course, human effort is most essential in the world, but the world itself is a miracle, and human history, viewed in a series of events in time, past and present, is certainly not controllable by the individual. No philosopher, sociologist, or historian has ever given a satisfactory answer to the question: What happens to man, *homo faber,* who has made such brilliant use of matter, from skyscrapers and tanks to household gadgets and surgical instruments—what happens to him when he leaves this world?

It is better to accept the possibility, even if only hypothetically, of the beyond, of an unseen world, of miracles, than to reject without fair investigation the validity of events that bring us in touch with this unseen world.

I have written this book for everyone, including unbelievers and the skeptics among them. I have written it even for those who repudiate these ideas with hatred and contempt—the dialectical materialists, and those others whose hearts have hardened because of their worldly power and possessions with which they think they can shore up defenses even against death.

We live in a world whose citizens have lost all sense of proportion, meaning, purpose. This situation has created, on the one hand, an attitude of extreme credulity amounting almost to superstition, and on the other, a belief in the exclusiveness and totality of matter. One such extreme has led to the nonsense that technology should be suppressed; the other, to the position that belief in the supernatural should be liquidated once and for all. There are some among us who preach that we are only creatures of this earth and that there is no world beyond ourselves. And there are again those who would have it that we must abjure the material world because only the spiritual is important and matter has no bearing on it.

The truth is that man is both spiritual and material at the same time. To ignore this unity can be fatal both for the individual and society.

The purpose of this book is to show what the miraculous is, its meaning and function in human life, its ever-existing reality. The idea was born three years ago when I was asked to write a book on the great miracles of saints. But as I examined the material my curiosity increased, and I decided to embark upon a discussion of the reality of miracles themselves and all questions relating to them in their proper context.

I am neither a theologian nor a scholar in the research of the unseen world. My purpose was not to make discoveries but to convey to the reader the principles that should be kept in mind when dealing with these questions, principles based on the findings of those great men who have dedicated their lives to the study of these questions.

In the bibliography at the end of this book readers will find listed certain works that provide detailed answers to the phenomena described here in more general terms.

CHAPTER 2

The Principles

Miracles are possible only by virtue of the existence of a personal and supernatural God. Pantheism, holding as it does that the Godhead and the world of nature are identical, cannot recognize the possibility of a miracle, for to do so would imply that the deity could destroy its very being.

This objection, raised as well by others than Pantheists, states that if a miracle occurs it means that God, who exists eternally and is unchangeable, changes His mind. The answer to this objection is that the capacity to reveal Himself through miracles, i.e., by interfering with his own order, is an inherent attribute of God, and all miracles were foreseen by Him.

Other critics suggest that the natural order, i.e., the creation of God, must be imperfect if He interferes to "correct" it through miracles. Such critics overlook the difference between the natural and the supernatural order. Nature can be considered perfect in its own sphere, but miracles come not from the natural but from the supernatural order—i.e., from grace. Grace but fulfills and perfects nature.

The philosophical objections to the possibility of miracles are summarized in the rationalist argument that miracles are impossible because physical laws are as immutable as they are necessary. According to Catholic belief, physical laws are contingent and not at all necessary. Therefore, exceptions to them are not impossible. All philosophical objections to miracles stress one principal point, namely, the a priori impossibility of miracles.

Modern scientists, as a result of a series of revolutions, particularly in modern physics and chemistry, find themselves in a difficult position. Instead of offering evidence of the immutability of nature, some scientists admit that they are now confronted with questions that may never be resolved. Other scientists have clearly stated that these questions are beyond the scope of the tasks science sets for itself. The militant negation of miracles by the adherents of dialectical materialism cannot be considered as a negation on the philosophical level. For dialectical materialism is not a philosophical system, but a series of ideological arguments dogmatically expressed and applied according to the exigencies of the Communist revolutionary movement.

The latest objections against miracles are crystallized around the principle of the uniformity of nature. It is stated that miracles cannot be proved because the universal experience that established the aforementioned principle provides no evidence of the reality of miracles. To this we answer that if universal human experience was, and is, able to discover natural laws, the same human experience can establish the facts of miracles and declare what in them is miraculous. In other words, the human experience that bears witness to miraculous events is part of the universal human experience that established the principle of the uniformity of nature.

A personal and supernatural God who is omnipotent Creator and Lord is able to intervene in the events of nature created by Him. If any limits are imposed on His mode of action, this would be tantamount to a denial of His divine independence and, by implication, to deny His very existence. Creation was an act of the will of God. And just as He set creation in motion and maintains its unceasing course, so is He free and able to produce effects that nature, whether in the form of individual human beings or in its totality, is unable to produce.

If, according to Catholic belief, miracles are possible, how can we define and discern a miracle? One of the best definitions is given by Donald Attwater, who describes a miracle as "an effect wrought in nature directly by God. It is not necessarily a breach of the laws of nature, or even a suspension of these laws, but an effect wrought independently of natural powers and laws and of such a character that man reasonably concludes that God Himself who alone is above and beyond nature, is the immediate and direct cause of the effect, without having acted, as normal, through the series of intermediate causes we call nature."[1]

The decisions of the Vatican Council held in 1870 are binding for Catholics in the matter of miracles. These decisions were sanctioned by the current Pope (Pius IX) in an infallible way. The Vatican Council declared:

> "If anyone shall say that divine revelation cannot be made credible by external signs, but that man must be moved to believe solely by the internal experience or private inspiration of each one, let him be anathema."

A Catholic Commentary on Holy Scripture[2] sums up the relation between revelation and miracles in the following way. The Vatican Council obviously viewed miracles as "external proofs of revelation." This does not exclude the possibility that miracles might occur for other purposes than to prove revelation. The Vatican Council, however, mentions them only in connection with revelation. It should be noted that this Council made no mention of any miracles before the age of Moses, it neither denied nor affirmed their authenticity. The Council was concerned with four groups of miracles: two groups in the Old Testament and two groups in the New Testament, i.e., Moses and the Prophets, and Christ and the Apostles. This means that the Council desired to stress the connection between miracles and revelation, because many miracles occurred during the divine revelation on Mount Sinai, and at the founding of the Mosaic religion, as well as under the monarchy. As for the New Testament, the Council did not specify any particular miracle of Christ or of the Apostles.

"Of course the enumeration of two particular miracles in the Creeds—the virginal Conception and Birth, and the resurrection of Our Lord—shows that these must specifically be accepted as of faith. Belief in other Scriptural miracles, taken individually, does not stand on the same footing. It is not precisely part of the defined Catholic Faith that every single marvelous event narrated in the Old and New Testaments was in fact a miracle."[3]

According to St. Thomas Aquinas, "A miracle must be evident to the senses, and therein lies its power." . . . "It is natural to man to arrive at the intelligible truth through its sensible effects. Wherefore . . . he is brought to a certain degree of supernatural knowledge of the objects of faith by certain supernatural effects which are called miracles."[4]

The Church admits that even outside the Catholic Church God may manifest Himself in miracles, and that the cause of a miracle could be attributed to other powers than God. But the difference between a true miracle and a diabolical or pernicious or merely prodigious event is immediately discernible.

The Christian miracle is a manifestation of God, who wishes to enlighten, to warn and help man, and who through such an event desires to elevate and unite man to Himself. The Christian miracle is religious in nature, and its significance is immediately understandable. In contrast, the prodigious event is a happening devoid of meaning; it is lost in chaos. The grotesque, the vulgar, the useless, the pointless cannot be considered to be miraculous in the sacred Christian sense.

For this reason genuine miracles do not occur often. The Christian God is no Jupiter, seated on a mountain, launching thunderbolts. He lives and breathes in the smallest particle of the universe, and if He manifests Himself through a miracle, it is for a clear and spiritual purpose. No material benefits are realized as the result of an apparition. The Christian miracle always brings general or individual welfare in its train. Christ restores sight to the blind, He cures the servant of the Roman centurion, and feeds the multitude.

The diabolical or the prodigious is pointless, useless and often vulgar. It has no spiritual purpose and brings destruction instead of individual or general welfare. The effects of the alleged apparition of St. Michael described in the previous chapter were death, misery, destruction, and scandal. Since God is infinitely good, He cannot be the cause of such sensational events. When Moses and Aaron, at God's command, talked to the Pharaoh and showed proofs of their divine commission, "Aaron took the rod before the Pharaoh and his servant and it was turned into a serpent. And Pharaoh called the wise men and the magicians and they, also by Egyptian enchantments and certain secrets, did in like manner . . ." (Exod. 7:10, 11). Whenever Moses and Aaron performed a miracle upon command of the Lord, the Pharaoh's magicians did exactly the same. Why were the miracles of Moses and Aaron true, while those of the magicians of diabolical origin were not? Because the purpose of the signs given through Moses and Aaron was entirely religious, and aimed at the spiritual welfare of individuals and the whole people: to soften the heart of the Pharaoh and liberate the Jewish people who were held in captivity. The answer given through the magicians, on the other hand, had no spiritual intent at all; it hardened the heart of the Pharaoh and foisted even more misery upon the Jews and upon the people of Egypt.

How can we know when a wonder, a sign, a power or a work (expressions used by the Gospels to characterize the miracles of Christ) is really miraculous and not merely an extraordinary, inexplicable event or coincidence that in time will be explained in *natural causes*. It is quite possible that such an occurrence may have been religious in nature and in significance; that it procured general or individual welfare, and was of morally innocent character, and yet not be a miracle wrought by God. Many people asserted that they saw the statue of Our Lady of Assisi move and smile (1948). Later, however, the Church declared that there had been no apparition in Assisi. Theresa Neumann has been receiving the stigmata of Our Lord since 1920 and apparently has not consumed any food for the last 30 years. Her spiritual influence on individuals and on the community is highly praised, yet the Church has not made any announcement on this phenomenon, and great theologians as well as competent doctors doubt that there is anything miraculous in her case.

We have quoted the decision of the Vatican Council (1870) decreeing excommunication for Catholics who reject in principle the possibility of miracles: "Christ promised the continuance of miracles in His Church, and the Catholic Church has always and does now display them and will always do so." Yet acceptance of the principle, and belief in each isolated miracle, are two different things. "Though a Catholic is bound to accept the principle as a matter of faith, the miraculous character of each individual occurrence must be settled by evidence. Hence no individual miracle, except those mentioned in the Holy Scripture, is of faith."

How is it possible to doubt the miracles that occurred after the closing of revelation when the Church declares that these were manifestations of the divine power? Did not the Church declare that certain of the cures of Lourdes are miraculous, did not the Church accept the miracles of St. Francis of Assisi, the apparitions at Fatima, La Salette, and other places?

The answer is a qualified Yes. The supreme authority of the Church rests in the Pope. His word is final, but not all his final decisions concern questions of faith. The infallibility of the Pope usually applies to statements on matters of faith and morals made in solemn *ex cathedra* declarations—i.e., when the Pope declares that he will make an infallible pronouncement. These *ex cathedra* declarations on faith and morals are held to be infallible by the whole Catholic world. But there have been very few infallible papal declarations.

Some Popes have died without having made even one *ex cathedra* pronouncement. Other papal utterances are regarded by the faithful with respect because of the Pope's function as supreme teacher. Any Catholic who does not accept *ex cathedra* declarations as infallible falls into heresy. It is not heresy, however, if one can not accept an ordinary or routine papal declaration. To resist openly papal pronouncements would be an act of contempt against the discipline of the magisterium of the Church.

On the question of post-revelation miracles, visions, or apparitions, there have been no *ex cathedra* declarations of the Popes, and so it is not heretical to doubt the validity of these miracles. On the other hand, if the doubt extends to a denial of the principle of miracles itself, then the Catholic is confronted with an article of faith.

Thus, when it is said that the Church has pronounced upon this or that miracle or apparition (always a post-revelation miracle), we mean that the Church by virtue of its teaching office, entrusted to her by the Divine Master, has explored all possible means of ascertaining whether there is any natural explanation for an extraordinary event claimed as a miracle. When all possibilities are exhausted, then the Church, i.e., the Pope or a bishop, declares that there is no reasonable doubt of their authenticity, yet he does not give the faithful a total, unqualified assurance. While the Church at large and millions of faithful accept the apparitions of Lourdes and Fatima, and believe in the miracles of Don Bosco or in the miraculous healings effected by Mother Cabrini, there are deeply religious monks, priests, and laymen who remain skeptical. This attitude does not exclude them from the Church, for they still remain obedient to its rules.

Anyone who knows how scrupulous are the investigations that precede a declaration about an allegedly miraculous event will see that "the Church does not seek to derive any utilitarian advantage from miraculous phenomena." Actually this thorough, conscientious procedure is in itself a reason for credibility. One who doubts is free to doubt, since faith is a matter of grace and conscience; but such a one should at least recognize the accumulated facts assembled by experts of great intellectual and spiritual integrity, though they are not necessarily infallible.

Most of the accepted miracles were performed by saints either during their lifetime or after their death. These miracles were proved and accredited at their canonization proceedings—which sometimes last for centuries. The process for canonization begins at the diocesan level—usually, through the bishop in whose diocese the "servant of God" died. After certain conditions are fulfilled, the case goes before the Sacred Congregation of Rites, which makes the final decision and submits the "cause" for approval to the Pope. A detailed description of the procedure will be found in the Appendix.

In the case of apparitions, or any other miraculous case not connected with a saint or with a canonization process, the diocesan bishop in whose territory the miraculous event occurred judges in full competence. The authenticity of the phenomenon at Lourdes was pronounced by the Bishop of Lourdes and Tarbes and that of events of Fatima by the Bishop of Coimbra. Reportedly miraculous cures at Lourdes are declared miraculous—after careful examination—not by the Vatican nor by the Bishop of Lourdes, but by the bishop of the diocese to which the miraculously cured person belongs.

The bishops make their decisions in close co-operation with the Supreme Sacred Congregation of the Holy Office, which very seldom makes any *direct* positive pronouncements on an alleged apparition or vision.

Cardinal Ottaviani, Secretary of the Congregation of Holy Office, has rightly said: "The Church certainly does not desire to keep hidden the miraculous occurrences performed by God; the Church does desire, however, to open the eyes of the faithful and to show what comes from God and what does not come from God, because often it could come from His adversary. The Church is an enemy of the false miracle."[5]

All these objections (or seeming objections) and cautionary statements, as we said, should not constitute an obstacle to our belief that the miracle is possible. We may now safely define the miracle as a perceptible fact that occurs outside of the laws of nature. But beyond this minimal definition, what makes a miracle a miracle?

According to the definitions of Cardinal Lépicier quoted by almost everyone who has written about miracles since his book[6] appeared, the characteristics of the miracle are the following:

1. The phenomenon should occur with relative infrequency. God did not create the world in order to interfere continually with His own laws.
2. Since the miracle is of divine origin, the event should be reasonable and of moral character, and not a phantasy or prodigy of dubious merit.
3. There is always an evident spiritual motivation in it.
4. It procures general or individual welfare.
5. It is most frequently *instantaneous*, although it may be *progressive* in its unfolding.
6. Its effects should be *persistent*, but this is not an indispensable condition. Some miracles because of their nature are limited in time. A healing could be permitted to manifest the existence of God, to demonstrate the efficacy of the prayer.
7. The miracle generally occurs as an answer to prayer.

Miracles classified according to their modality:

1. *Material miracles:* physical, astronomical miracles in which the earth, the sun, moon, and stars are involved; or those in which matter is involved, e.g., the multiplication of food. One miracle took place at the Battle of Gabaon (13th century B.C., when upon the prayer of Joshua "the sun and the moon stood still, till the people revenged themselves of their enemies," and "the Lord cast down upon them great stones from heaven . . ." (Josh. 10:10-13).

The apparitions at Fatima in 1917 may be classed as a material miracle, for at the end of the sixth and last apparition "the dark sky opened, and the sun appearing in a clear, blue sky, suddenly began to tremble and shake, and then turn about swiftly like a great wheel of fire casting off long shafts of light which colored the sky and earth."[7]

Other material miracles were the passage of the Jews through the Red Sea, which opened before them (Exod. 14:21-22), and the first plague of Egypt when the waters became blood (Exod. 7:20, 21). Christ's first "sign," the changing of the water into wine (John 2:3-10), was also a material miracle, as was His multiplication of bread. We will see other multiplications of food in the lives of St. John Vianney, St. Andre Hubert Fournet, St. John Bosco, St. Joseph Cottolengo, and others.

2. *Miracles involving living beings.* The Old Testament furnishes several instances, particularly during the plagues of Egypt, where we read of the multiplication of the locust, the flies, the beetles, the frogs, the cattle plague. In the plague of locusts God makes use of an auxiliary agent, a strong wind to bring on the plague and to remove it (Exod. 10:12-20). The miraculous character of the cattle plague is shown in the fact that this disease struck all the cattle of the Egyptians one night, whereas the cattle of the Jews in the same place remained untouched.

3. *Miracles concerning the human body:* resurrection of the dead, healing and curing of disease. Most of the miracles of Christ, and certainly all the miraculous cures in history up to modern times, belong in this category.

4. *Intellectual and spiritual miracles:* direct and extraordinary

interventions of God in the human spirit and mind. The conversion of St. Paul belongs in this category, as does the sudden change of heart in Alfred Ratisbon in Rome, 1840. Shortly after visiting the church of St. Andrea delle Fratte in Rome, this atheist, son of a wealthy Alsatian Jewish family, had a vision of the Miraculous Medal as it occurred to Catherine Labouré in Paris. After this vision Alfred and his brother Adolph became ardent believers and later Catholic priests. They were founders of the religious congregation Notre Dame de Sion.

All visions belong in this category. According to Attwater's definition in *A Catholic Dictionary,* a vision is "a supernatural perception. It may be: (a) a bodily or sensible vision, i.e., an apparition in which something naturally invisible is seen with the bodily eye." All the apparitions that have occurred—such as in the Rue du Bac, La Salette, Lourdes, Fatima, Beauraing, Banneux, and Syracuse, among others—were bodily or sensible visions.

In December, 1955, it was reported that Pope Pius XII received a vision in which Our Lord appeared to him during the night of December 3, 1954. Should this vision be confirmed after due process by the Church, it will be classified as a sensible vision.

Sensible visions have been recorded in the Old Testament. Such were the burning bush or the writing hand that wrote "Mane, Thecel, Phares," during King Baltasar's profane banquet, read and interpreted by the Prophet Daniel (Dan. 5:5).

Attwater further classifies visions as: (b) "An imaginative vision, produced in the imagination during sleep, or when awake; such was the angel who appeared to St. Joseph." (c) "An intellectual vision in which the mind perceives a spiritual truth, without any sense image"[8] (like St. Teresa of Avila's vision of the Holy Trinity). St. Teresa describes one such vision in the following way: ". . . on St. Augustine's Day (August 28, 1575), I had just communicated, when I was enabled to learn, and almost to see—in what way I cannot tell, unless it was by an intellectual vision which passed quickly—how the Three Persons of the Most Holy Trinity, whom I bear engraven on my soul, are one. This truth I was enabled to learn by means of so remarkable a picture, and so clear a light, that it has worked upon

me very differently than if I had merely known it by faith. Since that
time I have been unable to think of any One of the Three Divine
Persons without realizing that They are Three, so that today, when
I was considering how, though They are all One, the Son alone hath
taken human flesh, the Lord showed me how, though One, they are
distinct."[9]

Although the Church has accepted certain of the visions and apparitions occurring after the death of the last of the Apostles, these
visions and apparitions, as we already stated, are not articles of faith
like the visions narrated in the Old and the New Testaments.

In addition to the visions classified above, we can also describe
supernatural locutions. These are, in Attwater's definition, "words
heard by the ear but produced supernaturally; words produced supernaturally in the imagination or thoughts communicated directly to
the intellect."

All these miracles, apparitions, visions, and locutions are extraordinary graces given by God, and because of this they are of the
highest value. In spite of this, all mystics and teachers of mysticism
urge the greatest possible reservation and most thorough inquiry in
such matters, stressing always that they are not essential to the
spiritual life. There have been many saints who never underwent an
ecstasy or any kind of supernatural experience, among them St.
Thomas More, or modern saints such as St. Thérèse of the Infant
Jesus (Lisieux), St. Maria Goretti, St. Conrad Parzham, and many
others.

The Church conducts severe and rigorous investigations to determine the possible authenticity of a vision, apparition, or locution.
Cardinal Ottaviani, in his important article cited above, said: "For
a number of years, we have witnessed a recrudescence of popular
enthusiasm for the miraculous (meraviglioso) even in religious matters. Great masses of faithful rush to visit the places of 'pretended'
visions and alleged miracles, while they neglect the sacraments and
the sermons . . ."

Because of these feigned visions it is of extreme importance to understand the usual procedure of the Church in the case of reported
visions, apparitions, or locutions.

Divine revelation ended with the death of the last of the Apostles. The Church, nevertheless, admits the possibility of apparitions and other supernatural manifestations, not because they could reveal or teach anything *new*, but because they might call the attention of the faithful to the revealed truth that is already known, and could at the same time serve to stir the conscience of the lukewarm in faith. The Church reserves for herself exclusive authority to judge the authenticity of these manifestations, examining them with extreme prudence. If, in certain cases, the Church has not intervened, this happened only because the "visions" in question were obviously ridiculous, and the Church was confident that both time and the faithful would judge them properly. The Church, however, has often intervened; and sometimes her intervention has provoked rebellious demonstrations from those who insisted upon the veracity of their vision. And the Church's decision has more often been negative than positive.

The first task of the Church is to ascertain the authenticity of the account made by the person or persons who claim to have a vision. This inquiry is initiated on the diocesan level by the bishop's commission, composed of theologians and physicians. In many a case a simple interrogation of the visionary and some of the witnesses has sufficed to prove that it was a matter of autosuggestion. In addition, all circumstantial evidence must be searched, and the visionary must undergo a careful psychophysical and moral examination to determine whether there were any satanic or psychotic elements present. It is inconceivable that, for instance, the Madonna should appear to a person lacking in Christian virtue; or if the recipient did in fact lack such virtue, that he should not be transformed into a more virtuous person as a result of the vision.

St. Bernadette of Lourdes and the children of Fatima could not continue to live mediocre lives after seeing the Blessed Virgin. Furthermore, no one who lacks genuine humility can have an apparition. All theologians concur in maintaining that no one who has had an apparition has ever looked for any material or lucrative advantage from it. The investigations employ all the techniques of modern science, especially psychiatry. One single symptom of hysteria discovered in the personality structure of the visionary immediately puts the authenticity of the visionary in doubt. Another element in the judgment of an apparition is the evaluation of its "message." If the content of the message contradicts the Faith, or contains ridiculous and incongruous elements, the apparition is fraudulent and false. Whether it involves the Madonna or any other saintly person, an apparition must always be characterized by dignity, and the message be worthy of the supernatural messenger. Moreover, the aim of the apparition must be the sanctification of the visionary and the faithful. Otherwise it is false.

Characteristics of a genuine vision, as attested by those who have experienced them in the past, are the following:

A real vision arrives suddenly.

At first it stirs and agitates the soul, but immediately floods it with a sense of peace.

It does not last long.

It leaves a strong desire for perfection and abundant gifts with which to practice the Christian virtues.

It remains impressed for a long time on the mind of the recipient.

The true vision cannot be provoked or sought—and it is followed by miracles as confirmation of the apparition.

5. Now we have arrived at the last category in our classification of miracles—namely, *the miracles of faith.* These are the miracles that totally escape the control of our senses. Actually they are mysteries of faith.

The miracles of faith are certified by Christ and by the teachings of the Church; the Christian only adds his faith to them. The miracle of faith *par excellence*—the greatest miracle of all—is the mystery of the Eucharist, the presence of Christ under the appearances of bread and wine during Mass. The visible appearance of the bread and wine remains the same but their substance is no longer the substance of bread and wine, but has become the substance of the body and blood of Christ. Many miracles are related to the Eucharist. In one that occurred at the Church of Bolsena in Italy in 1263, a priest who did not believe that Christ was actually in the host while he celebrated Mass, suddenly saw the blood drop from the host upon the altar cloth and upon the corporal during the elevation of the host. This and other miracles involving the Eucharist will be dealt with further.

We should raise here the question of the possibility of diabolical "miracles" and prodigies, and what we are to think about the group of still unexplained occurrences known as occult phenomena (spiritism, telepathy, telekinesis, telesthesy, extrasensory perception). Are they of diabolical or of divine origin, or are they natural phenomena that may eventually be explained?

Diabolical "miracles" are possible in principle, but their effect is limited. On the other hand, a great deal of magic can be reduced to natural causes. Occult phenomena cannot be judged in a general manner, but each phenomenon, and within each phenomenon each individual case, must be evaluated on its own merits.

Theoretically it is possible for God to permit genuine miracles to occur outside of the Church. It can also be assumed that such miracles actually do happen. Although these are isolated cases, they cannot be considered extraordinary *per se*, for their aim is always identical with that of the Church, of the true religion. According to Cardinal Lépicier, "miracles may take place outside of the body of the Catholic Church but never outside of the spirit of the Church. As a systematic fundamental fact, as a system in harmony with those immutable principles and fixed laws, the miracle exists only in that religion which calls itself universal or Catholic because it was founded by the First Cause, which unites everything and in whose favor even the miracles of the Old Testament were wrought."[11]

Holy Scripture itself gives testimony to this effect. St. John the Apostle reported to Christ: "Master, we saw one casting out devils in thy name, who followeth not us, and we forbade him." But Jesus said: "Do not forbid him. For there is no man that doth a miracle in my name and can soon speak ill of me. For he that is not against you, is for you" (Mark 9:37, 39). There is also reference to miracles performed by those not adhering to the group of Moses: "Now there remained in the camp two of the men, of whom one was called Eldad, and the other Medad, upon whom the spirit rested for they also had been enrolled, but were not gone forth to the Tabernacle.

And when they prophesied in the camp, there ran a young man, and told Moses, saying: Eldad and Medad prophesy in the camp. Forthwith Josue, the son of Nun, the minister of Moses, and chosen out of many said: My Lord Moses forbid them. But he said: Why hast thou emulation for me? O that all the people might prophesy, and that the Lord would give them spirit!" (Numbers 11:26–29).

It is, however, very difficult to determine which miracles have occurred "outside of the body but not outside of the spirit of the Church." Lépicier tells the story of a Russian Orthodox priest, Ivan Serguief, a man of great piety, to whom the people attributed the gift of miracles. Ivan Serguief was pastor of the principal Orthodox church in Kronstadt. He enjoyed such widespread fame that in October, 1894, Tsar Alexander III called this saintly priest to his deathbed, hoping to be relieved of his suffering through his intercession.

It is even more problematical with miracles within Islam, Buddhism, or other religions. Doubtless there were, and are, genuine mystics in Islam whose ascetical and mystical ideal is of the highest value. Mohammed himself accepted certain Christian miracles, and the idea of prophethood plays a decisive role in his religion. Although the Koran is considered by Islam to be the ultimate revelation of the word of God, the prophets of the Old Testament are also from God, and the signs of the prophets are miracles. One of the greatest mystics in the history of Islam was al-Hallag, an exponent of Islam's system of spirituality, the Sufism. Al-Hallag lived the life of an ascetic and a mystic, having advanced through all the prescribed phases. The last phase, the mystical union with God, as interpreted by him, led to the divinization of the mystic himself. For this notion he was crucified in Bagdad in 922. A critical investigation of the "miracles" of al-Hallag did not confirm their authenticity.

As for the miracles of the Greco-Roman world, these are mostly legendary. The healings achieved by Serapis, Asclepius, and Epidauros are legends which, in certain cases, can be attributed to demonic or diabolical forces or explained through telepathy, hyperesthesia, or similar means.

A case in point is Apollonius of Tyana, whose historical existence cannot be stated with absolute certainty. According to a biography attributed to Philostratos, Apollonius was born some years before Christ in Tyana in Cappadocia in the Taurus mountains in Asia Minor, and was persecuted under Nero and Diocletian—by Diocletian because he had prophesied his death. It is said that he traveled in many countries of the East and the West and that Vespasius and Titus knew him. Philostratos describes several ecstasies of Apollonius and claims that this magician could liberate himself from chains, halt earthquakes, and raise the dead. The biographer of Emperor Aurelianus states that Apollonius in A.D. 97 appeared in a vision to the Emperor.

Whether or not Apollonius of Tyana actually existed or was a product of the imagination, it is evident that the ideas surrounding him represented a reaction of the Greco-Roman ideology against the advent of Christ and the rapid spread of Christianity. The "miracles" of Apollonius (assuming his real existence) were but prodigies to be explained by natural causes or by diabolical intervention. But not even the facts as given can be accepted, since Philostratos was a notorious liar, with a wild imagination. In addition, he put everything he could find into his biography, taken mostly from the Apocryphal scriptures. His immediate aim was to please Empress Julia, the wife of Severus.

Most of the prodigious events to be found in great Eastern religions, or among the primitive religions of the Indians, in North and South America, are not preternatural but explainable by natural causes. In some cases, however, diabolical origin is not to be excluded, as is likewise the case with primitive religions among African tribes today.

The Church does not recognize the miracles of Buddha and Krishna, or those related by the Apocryphal scriptures. Nor does the Church accept the late Rabbinical miracles as elements or continuations of the Old Testament tradition. Rather, they are considered to be products of the imagination or explainable, at best, as occult phenomena. Nevertheless, the principle of the possibility that God performs miracles outside of the body of the Church remains. St. Augustine, referring to the already quoted passage taken from the

Gospel of St. Mark, observes that the statement of Christ, "Those who are not against you are with you," does not contradict the Gospel of St. Matthew (12:30), where it is written, "Who is not with me is against me." According to St. Augustine, the man involved in the first case, while not belonging to the Apostles, was not against them, since his cures were wrought in the name of Christ.

All this becomes evident in the light of the doctrine of the Church. On this question—what is the body of the Church and who belongs to its spirit—it is relevant to cite the controversy that arose in Boston, Mass., in 1952 around Father Feeney, who erroneously asserted that there is no salvation outside the body of the Catholic Church. The answer was promptly given by the Supreme Sacred Congregation of the Holy Office, which condemned the error. This decision quotes, among others, the encyclical letter of Pope Pius XII, issued June 29, 1943, "On the Mystical Body of Jesus Christ." The Holy Office declared that ". . . in this letter the Sovereign Pontiff clearly distinguishes between those who are actually incorporated into the Church as members, and those who are united to the Church only by desire. . . . Toward the end of this . . . Encyclical Letter, when most affectionately inviting to unity those who do not belong to the body of the Catholic Church, he mentions those who 'are related to the mystical body of the Redeemer by a certain unconscious yearning and desire,' and these he by no means excludes from eternal salvation, but on the other hand states that they are in a condition 'in which they cannot be sure of their salvation' since 'they still remain deprived of those many heavenly gifts and helps which can only be enjoyed in the Catholic Church.' . . . it must not be taught that any kind of desire of entering the Church suffices that one may be saved. It is necessary that the desire by which one is related to the Church be animated by perfect charity. Nor can an implicit desire produce its effect, unless a person has supernatural faith."

The possibility that true miracles may be wrought outside the body of the Catholic Church must be approached and understood in this spirit.

CHAPTER 3

Satan's Powers

The chapel off to the right of the Cathedral of Orvieto in Italy contains one of the world's most famous frescoes, that of the Last Judgment, by Luca Signorelli. This gigantic composition contains hundreds of figures—angels, fantastic flying devils, men rising from death. The condemned in this Dantesque fresco are seen being pursued toward hell, and the saved, their faces reflecting a beatified vision, head heavenward. But the whole composition is grouped around two central figures: the Christ, victor and judge, and the Anti-Christ, who already stands among those who will march with the condemned. In this austere and awe-inspiring work the artist, a Renaissance painter, gave vivid expression to his truly medieval sensibility. The greatest achievement and the most striking feature of this fresco lies in the artist's ability to convey to us precisely that quality which is satanic in Satan, and that which makes the Anti-Christ, Anti-Christ. The face of Signorelli's Anti-Christ actually expresses and demonstrates what theologians and religious philosophers have discussed for centuries.

From a distance the Anti-Christ looks exactly like Christ, but if one studies his eyes the difference between Christ and the Anti-Christ becomes as clear as night and day. With incomparable talent the artist Signorelli created a face, that of Anti-Christ, whose total expression is neither monstrous nor ugly, yet it is an evil face, poisonously jealous and hateful and hating though with a smile. One senses at once that these eyes and these features express the essence of diabolical negation, deception, and evil.

Although modern society may reject the idea of a personified Anti-Christ, as it rejects Christ Himself, it cannot deny the existence of evil. Save for those who reduce evil to some form of psychopathology expressed in action, there is a general belief in the existence of evil. Some have a definite, articulated conception of evil; others accept the existence of a principle of evil on the basis of faith, but without intellectual perception; and there are still others who content themselves with the most nebulous ideas about God and His adversary. Yet almost everyone prefers not to think that this principle of evil operates actively in the world, that it can take the form of a person or persons one might meet on the street, on a train, or in a plane. One shudders to think that Satan, a pure spiritual being like the angels, exists.

Satan, or the devil—whatever the name given to him—is not the invention of the Judaeo-Christian Bible. If the teaching of the Church concerning the continuous revelation that began with the creation of man is accepted, it follows that the belief in Satan is hundreds of thousands years old (according to paleontologists man appeared on earth 600,000 years ago). The most ancient phase of human civilization, the age of the hunter, left its mark on the civilization of the primitive natives of Central Africa, Australia, and the Americas. When their civilization is studied in the light of paleontological and prehistorical research, one finds that in many religious myths of the American Indian and the Central African primitive, Satan is represented by a wolf. Among California Indian tribes Satan takes the form of a coyote, the name of the prairie wolf.

Among the primitive Ural-Altai, who led a pastoral life, the figure of the devil was gradually transformed from a fiery wild horse to an anthropomorphic image. In a myth of the Altai Tartars, God says to Erlik (the name given to the devil): "Now, you are in sin. You wanted to do me evil. Your name will be Erlik, and those people who will be full of evil sentiments shall be your people; those persons who are good shall be my people." The etymological meaning of the word Erlik is unsolved. In a similar Asiatic myth, this adversary of God is called Ngaa, and he is personified as death.

The word *Satan* comes from the Central Asian word *chaitan*. These ancient primitive peoples, who believed in the existence of the Supreme Being and in His infinite goodness, were unable to explain the deficiencies of the created world otherwise than by attributing them to the intervention of an evil being; they were unclear, however, about his origin.

The idea and the figure of Satan became much clearer in the religion of the prophet Zarathustra, the founder of Mazdaism. This religion, flourishing in Persia around 600 b.c., was based upon the equality of the principle of goodness and the principle of evil. The principle of good is called *Ormuzd*; the principle of evil, *Ahriman*, meaning a tormenting and evil-working spirit. In the *Avesta*, the most ancient sacred books of the Persians, Ormuzd and Ahriman are twins, and both co-exist equally from eternity. It is interesting to note that the adjectival form of Ahriman is *druj*, which means a lie, a falsehood, just as is the case with Satan in the Judaeo-Christian tradition, though it has been scientifically established that no contact was ever established between the Persian and the Judaeo-Christian tradition.

Divine revelation, as established in the Old and New Testaments and in Christian tradition, provides clear notions about Satan. Almost immediately after the narration of the creation of the universe and its inhabitants, we meet the Tempter in the Bible. Acquaintance with Satan in the Bible begins in the third chapter of Genesis, where he appears in the form of a serpent. This serpent argues provocatively and makes subtle suggestions, but what is most important, he lies: "For God doth know that in what day soever you shall eat thereof [the fruit of the tree], your eyes shall be opened; and you shall be as gods, knowing good and evil" (Gen. 3:5).

All the elements of Satan are discernible in these few lines. He lied when he declared that man through disobedience will become like God; he is wicked because he makes promises that he cannot fulfill or that are contingent upon circumstances over which he has no influence. He is the spirit of negation, that is, of revolt. The revolt against a duly constituted authority is always negative, it being the negation of a positive principle. The appearance of Satan coincides with this first act of denial and defiance, and it will persist until the end of the world.

The Christian religion does not accept this dualism. It believes in One God Who exists from all eternity. Satan is not His equal and does not exist from eternity. Satan was created, and created good, like all the other angels. The angel who later became Satan had free will and great intelligence. He had in his "angelic nature beauty, perfection, goodness." (He) refused to "look beyond the angelic perfection to its divine source. . . . As is the way of pride Lucifer isolated himself even from God."[1] It is his very pride that made Satan the prince of the rebellious. As a result he was driven out of Heaven together with his insurgent army, but he remained and remains a pure spirit. Since then he flashes through the world with his demons endeavoring to enslave and ensnare by every conceivable means the creature man. It is understandable that he despises anything that is human. God whom he lost became man. In his very controversial book on the devil, Giovanni Papini asserts that the devil is envious of man because God loves man and created him out of pure love.[2]

Satan has tremendous power; the question is, how far-reaching is this power? If we were to accept the equality of God and Satan we would have to accept the idea of co-eternity, too; thus man would be absolutely helpless and unable to defend himself against Satan. The great teaching of the Judaeo-Christian tradition is that man not only is able to defend himself against Satan but can also defeat him.

One of the most significant assurances of this alliance of God and man appears in the Book of Job, written about 500 b.c. Since Satan can operate only with God's permission, God allows Satan to tempt Job, a good, Godfearing man. It seems at first glance that God has delivered one of His best friends into the hands of His greatest enemy. But Job is only being tested: God wanted to prove, not so much to Satan as to Job, that Satan is not omnipotent; that his power is but the remnant of the power bestowed upon him when he was created an angel. From the Book of Job comes the pristine evidence and hope that man is mightier than Satan because man can ally himself with God. This Satan cannot do. The end is thus complete salvation from the grip of any satanic force that might attack the human being, for

God, who became man, makes it possible for man to keep the alliance viable until the end of the world. And we know from Sacred Scripture that the struggle between humanity and Satan will last until the end of the world.

If it be true that this fight for the soul of man has been going on since the beginning, then it is understandable that Satan should have attacked and tempted Christ in His human nature. Christ came to redeem mankind from original sin and through this redemption destroy Satan's empire. Satan knew this because he had been warned by God about the coming of Jesus. In his relation with Christ, Satan (whose name means "adversary") is the Anti-Christ in his clearest form. The word Anti-Christ, mentioned four times in the New Testament, is reserved for the adversary of Christ who will tempt and will succeed in seducing many Christians during the coming centuries. Sacred Scripture provides more than ample evidence that, despite the promise of his ultimate defeat, Satan is a formidable adversary who desperately fights in spectacular battles. Such, for example, was the battle of the angels in which St. Michael and the "celestial armies" remained victors, and Satan and his hordes plunged into the abyss. And such was the battle in the Garden of Eden, which decided the destiny of mankind. Both are events of such magnitude and significance—we would minimize them by adding the adjective cosmic—that the greatest happenings of human history diminish in importance by comparison. Such was, too, the struggle of Satan with Christ. The fact that Satan tried again and again proves that he did not fear approaching even the purest, noblest embodiment of the human race—one who was God and man at the same time.

The first encounter of Jesus with Satan on earth took place in the desert. After John had baptized Jesus in the waters of the Jordan, Jesus retired into the desert fastness for contemplation before continuing His public mission. But Christ was actually "driven" out into the desert by the Spirit following His baptism. Matthew (4:1) clearly points out the purpose: "Jesus was led by the Spirit into the desert *to be tempted by the devil*." It was the will of God that while Christ went to commune, face to face, with the divine Father, he should be strengthened by undergoing a trial, in his human nature.

The triple temptation is most significant. Christ was hungry, and Satan tempted him, by suggesting that as the Son of God he should make bread out of the stones of the desert. The second time, when "the devil took him up to Jerusalem and set him up on the pinnacle of the temple," the trial is of higher nature: it is a challenge to exploit His own power and God's promise for His own glorification.

During these two temptations of Satan, Christ remained steadfast; He refused calmly and gave the devil adequate answer. The cynicism and measureless pride of Satan, the prince of the world, betrayed itself in the third temptation. In a vision he shows the whole world to Christ and promises power—earthly power, material power—above all things, "if falling down thou wilt adore me." This time the refusal of Christ is not a simple, calm denial; it is a solemn statement, reiterating the first and greatest commandment of the true religion. But Christ acts as well as speaks: He puts Satan to flight in the first exorcism of human history. "Then Jesus said to him, 'Begone, Satan! for it is written, *The Lord thy* God shalt thou worship and Him only shalt thou serve' " (Matt. 4:10).

Here it should be remembered that the baptism rite of the Catholic Church contains a minor form of exorcism. The priest does not deal with the devil. He orders him to leave.

Who is this Satan, this devil, who tempted Christ and whom Christ drove out from the bodies of the diabolically possessed? We can answer with Christ Himself. When the Scribes and the Pharisees brought a woman before Jesus and told him that "this woman was even now taken in adultery. . . . Moses in the law commanded us to stone such a one. But what sayest thou?" (John 8:4–5). What follows this question is one of the most beautiful passages of the Gospel: "He that is without sin among you, let him first cast a stone at her." But no one does so, and all the accusers leave. "Hath no man condemned thee?" And the woman answered: "No man, Lord." And Jesus said: "Neither will I condemn thee. Go, and now sin no more" (John 8:7–11).

This episode led to a discussion between Christ and the Scribes and Pharisees, in which the wickedness of the accusers became more and more evident. Refusing to accept the true meaning of purity as taught to the children of Abraham and the children of God, they hoped to set a trap for Christ. They wanted glory for themselves. The answer of Christ reveals the abyss between the influence of Satan and the power of God: between the world of self-glorification, self-righteousness, and that constant desire and readiness to forgive which characterizes the Christian. How could they ever understand why Christ forgave the adulteress? There is only one answer: "Jesus therefore saith to them: if God were your father you would indeed love me. For from God I proceeded, and came; for I came not of myself but He sent me . . . Why do you not know my speech? Because you cannot hear my words. You are of *your* father the devil, and the desires of your father you will do. He was a murderer from the beginning, and he stood not in the truth; because truth is not in him. When he speaketh a lie, he speaketh *of his own:* (italics author's) for he is a liar, and a father thereof." (John 8:42–44)

Christ himself then defined Satan as father of the lie, father of falsehood, murderer from the beginning because he brought death into the world. Inspirer of all that is contrary to the *one* ever-existing Truth that was incarnate in Christ.

But Jesus went even further and deeper in telling the truth about Satan, explaining the precise nature of a lie.

The Pharisees understood very well that they had to counteract the influence of Christ and particularly the effect of the miracles performed by Him. They could not deny that these were true miracles. The only way out for them was to accuse Christ of chasing the demons with the help of Beelzebub. (Matt. 12: 22–23). It was an accusation worthy of the father of the lie but this gave Christ an opportunity to point to the heart of the matter. First He destroyed their argumentation with logic: "Every kingdom divided against itself shall be made desolate: and every city or house divided against itself shall not stand. And if Satan cast out Satan, he is divided against himself: how shall then his kingdom stand? And if I by Beelzebub cast out devils, by whom do your children cast them out? Therefore they shall be your judges. But if I by the Spirit of God cast out devils, then is the kingdom of God upon you. . . . Therefore I say to you: Every sin and blasphemy shall be forgiven men, but the blasphemy of the Spirit shall not be forgiven. And whosoever shall speak a word against the Son of man, it shall be forgiven him; but he that shall speak against the Holy Ghost, it shall not be forgiven him, neither in this world, nor in the world to come" (Matt. 12:25–32).

This is the sin against the Holy Ghost. In particular it is the "deliberate resistance to the known truth," which so hardens the soul against the inspiration of grace that repentance is unlikely. Deliberate resistance to the known truth is the supreme lie.

The other encounters of Christ with Satan occurred during the numerous occasions when demons were cast out from the possessed. Certain critics of Christianity, notably the materialists, take strong exception to these exorcisms, asserting that most of these possessions were not diabolical at all, but pure and simple cases of hysteria. Modern science, they say, is well equipped to deal with the pseudo-possessed. At best these critics concede that during the time of Christ people understandingly enough attributed all mental illness to dia-bolical intervention. These objections only sound reasonable; actually they are not. The Gospels distinguish among those possessed by the demon, the mentally ill, and paralytics. When Jesus commanded the Apostles to go and preach in Galilee, he was precise in his instructions and about the powers he had invested in them. Jesus told them to heal the sick, to raise the dead, to purify the lepers, and cast out devils. And in several cases the Gospels record the very answers of the demon while Jesus was performing the act of exorcism. "And in the synagogue there was a man who had an unclean devil, and he cried out with a loud voice, saying: Let us alone, what have we to do with thee, Jesus of Nazareth? Art thou come to destroy us? I know thee, who thou art, the holy one of God. And Jesus rebuked him, saying: Hold thy peace, and go out of him. And when the devil had thrown him into the midst, he went out of him, and hurt him not at all" (Luke 4:33–35).

It is most significant that there is no report, no hint in the Gospels that any person once exorcised ever became possessed again. It is significant because exorcism does not help in hysterical (mental) cases—a problem to be dealt with later.

If we accept as given the supreme intelligence, the purity and infallible judgment of Jesus, and if we further accept the view that Jesus, being God, possessed the power and the knowledge to distinguish between mental illness and diabolical possession, it follows that we must accept the descriptions as true. Christ did not use the popular language of the times to describe the mentally ill as being possessed, for He was a man apart from the ignorant mass of that age. His language, the language of the Gospels, is clear and comprehensible to and for all ages. It is possible that some of these diabolically possessed persons were in fact neurotics or psychotics, but if Christ Himself says they were possessed, then this was the form of their obsession. The tendency to reduce everything to the simple explanation of mental illness is unacceptable, even to an honest non-believer. Indeed, the great number of highly-trained, responsible psychiatrists know quite well that while they can cure a man's mind, they are ill-advised to interfere with his soul. Co-operation between psychiatrists and priests, of late, has brought forth additional evidence to indicate that it is possible for the same patient to be both mentally ill and possessed.

The existence of Satan was further confirmed by the Apostles when they received the order to preach the Gospel to all people. The Acts of the Apostles and the Epistles contain an abundance of evidence. Christ had called Satan the prince of this world; St. Paul called him the god of this world, and with this he points to the essential feature of Satan. St. Paul confronts his listeners several times with the terrible choice. In his letter to the Ephesians, he says, resist the machinations of Satan, fight against the world of darkness, against the evil spirit. And St. Peter, in his first letter, warns the faithful to remain vigilant: "Be sober and watch: because your adversary the devil, as a roaring lion, goeth about seeking whom he may devour" (I Peter 5:8). St. James recommends that we submit ourselves to God and resist Satan. If we do so, the devil will flee. When we ourselves approach God He comes nearer to us.

Manicheism, the heretical religion that caused so much division and disunity during the first centuries of Christendom, is probably the most demon-ridden of all mythologies. Since popular phantasy in the Western World has been greatly influenced by the demon-image of Manicheism, we will describe the demonology of this sect. Mani, or Manes, the founder of Manicheism, was born in A.D. 216 in Babylonia. His father, Patek, belonged to the Mede dynasty of the Arsacides. According to Mani, there are two eternal first principles: God, the cause of all good, and matter, the cause of all evil. The distinctive teaching of Manicheism, borrowed from the Gnostics, is that all matter is evil and consequently the primal source of evil. When he was about 24 years old, Mani traveled in India and in Beligistan. He converted the ruler of that country, who saw in him a reincarnation of Buddha. After two years of preaching, Mani was recalled to Persia and commissioned by King Sapor to teach his own people. The successor to King Sapor, King Bahram, arrested him, the chief accusers being Mazda priests. Mani died after 26 days of jail and suffering, and his followers looked upon his death as the "crucifixion of Mani."

Many heresies and religious movements of the early Christian period slowly faded out, but the doctrine of Mani lived on, sometimes manifesting itself in most interesting forms even when it seemed nonexistent. In the 12th century it had a most fanatical revival in Albigensianism. The Albigenses, so called from Albi, a town in Italy and once their stronghold, professed the usual Manichean doctrine, rejected the sacraments (especially marriage, which was forbidden), and encouraged suicide (usually by starvation). This, however, was the code of the elite leadership of the movement, the "perfects." But the masses of their adherents indulged in magic and all manner of licentious and immoral practices.

Because of its rejection of matter as evil, the mythology of Manicheism is replete with demons hierarchically constituted. The king of the demons is the Prince of Darkness. He is the head of an infernal territory, with five "provinces" ruled by other princes. These are the prince of the world of fire, the prince of the world of wind, the prince of the world of water, the prince of the world of cloud and the prince of the world of smoke. Besides these princes, there were other ruler-demons in Manicheism. The ruler of bipeds, the ruler of reptiles, the ruler of quadrupeds, the ruler of winged animals, and the ruler of fishes. All these "kingdoms," however, constituted one large empire: the kingdom of evil as opposed to the kingdom of light.

This Prince of Darkness is identified in Western Christianity and in the Moslem world with Satan, in the Persian mythology with Ahriman, in China with Tan-mo, the demon of covetousness, and in Central Asia with Samnu. One of the chief characteristics of this Manichean Prince of Darkness is that he ignores and denies everything that is outside of himself; he sees only what is close, present. He is without principle and without aim, preoccupied only with the present, never thinking of the antecedents or consequences of the present. All these characteristics are also the characteristics, the very essence, of sin. He is a vivid counterpart of the sinner who does not want to perceive, understand, or see anything outside himself or the present.

The Manichean Prince of Darkness, then, is Satan personified: man filled only with himself, reduced to himself, taken out from the context of past and future, cut off from contact with God and, therefore, with other men.

"... the Prince of Darkness, who reigns by terror of his voice, or by the startling character of his apparitions over this empire, heaving with latent rebellion and devastated by endless sedition, is himself the incarnation of all the fury of this disorder, all the senseless violence of his appetite for destruction, never at peace with himself, inflamed against all the others and against himself. He is made up of ill-temper, anger, rage, envy, moved by nothing but the rancour and gall that inflames his yellow visage. . . . He is hungry for flesh, thirsty for blood, carried away in his turn in a kind of revolt against his own subjects and preying on his own offspring, a revolt which in the end is turned against his own substance. As an image of desire which feeds, like care, on itself, self-consummated, self-consumed, the Manichean devil . . . finding nothing more for his insatiable greed to devour, finally devours himself."[3]

The prophet Isaias, in his parable against the Babylonians, used the word *Lucifer* in order to speak about this fallen angel. Lucifer is a Latin word meaning "bearer of light." In the Hebrew original, he is not called Lucifer but *Day-Star*—the name of the morning star, Venus; and the word Lucifer was used later on in that context by Cicero and Tibellus. Isaias writes: "How art thou fallen from heaven, O Lucifer, who didst rise in the morning? How art thou fallen to the earth, that didst wound the nations? And thou saidst in thy heart: I will ascend into heaven, I will exalt my throne above the stars of God, I will sit in the mountain of the covenant, in the sides of the north. I will ascend above the height of the clouds, I will be like the most High. But yet thou shalt be brought down to hell, into the depth of the pit" (Isa. 14:12–15).

The early Church fathers, too—Origen, Tertullian, St. Cyprian, and the others—use the word *Lucifer* when writing about Satan.

The descriptions of saints about their struggles with Satan always form the most interesting pages of their lives. The ceaseless battles of St. Anthony the Hermit are more than spectacular. Born A.D. 251, Anthony was the son of a merchant in Egypt, and he became very rich at the death of his parents when he was only 20 years old. Deeply influenced by the words of the Gospel, however, he distributed his entire wealth among the poor and retired to the desert. Anthony realized that the devil dwells among people, but he did not know that Satan lives not only in the world but also in the heart of man. Thus rather than flee from him (which is often impossible), Anthony decided that the way to overcome his assaults is to meet them head on.

During the long years of his hermit's life Anthony saw Satan in many forms; St. Anthony was surrounded by fantastic apish faces, horrible claws clutched at him, many sleepless nights were filled with such terrifying visions that he prayed on his knees to dispel them. Once he imagined that angels were lifting him into the air just as diabolical figures approached him and started to enumerate all sins that Anthony had committed in worldly deeds or thoughts. The angels sang: "We do not remember his sins because God's mercy has erased them all." When Satan saw that young Anthony resisted, he tried to overcome him with new visions and new attacks. First he drove him into states of depression and desperation, then he haunted him with obscene visions, and at last he played on Anthony's pride; but all this was in vain because Anthony fully understood the significance of doing battle with Satan. The Legend says that he was old when he left the desert, yet looked like a young man.

In his biography of St. Anthony the Hermit, St. Athanasius wrote that Satan, who thought himself equal with God, was defeated by a young man. Satan the ruler of all flesh and blood, was brought down by a man who let his flesh die. By making the presence of Satan a reality, and prayer and battle against him a constant necessity, St. Anthony has been a most important influence on the formation and development of Christian spirituality.

The question of magic is usually raised in any discussion of Satan. According to Attwater's definition, magic is "the power or practice of producing marvelous physical effects, either through the invocation of evil spirits (Black Magic), or by means which are generally thought to be disproportionate to the effects they produce (White Magic)" (*A Catholic Dictionary*). The word itself is of Turanian-Iranian origin and means "profound." The old Iranian-Persian word *magus* means sorcerer. The Magi were one of the six tribes of the Medes, most of them being priests of the religion of Zarathustra. They were great astronomers and enjoyed enormous prestige. At the time of Christ, the term *magus* was not necessarily connected with any evil practices. Those Magi who came from the Orient to find out about the birth of Christ were such that the Church honors them among its saints. Later the name was linked with suspiciously evil supernatural practices, and in the New Testament we read about a Simon Magus who is identified as one who sold himself to the devil.

On the island of Cyprus St. Paul met another *magus* called Elymas, who was trying to undo all the Apostle's good work.

The practice of magic is found among the most ancient people, the Chaldeans, an extremely superstitious tribe who believed that the natural processes of our bodies are caused and directed by spirits. According to them, demons could and did enter the human body. They fought this intrusion with practices similar to exorcism. But they fought also mental disturbances, nightmare, plague, in the same manner.

In Egypt the magicians wielded great power. They were given freedom to evoke good or evil spirits and to make use of them. Their word meant life or death for the persons on whom they conducted their experiments.

The Chinese were also addicted to magic. Before the appearance of Confucius, the priests called Wu had an important position in the social hierarchy that determined the position of each inhabitant of the Empire. These Wu were sorcerers, and their magic rites consisted of special dances that ended in a state of trance. They had secret, mystical formulae by means of which they evoked spirits, foretold the future, and blessed family groups and individuals.

Similarly, the Greeks and the Romans were familiar with magic practices. Hecate, a Greek deity, was the goddess of sorcerers, but very often Greek magicians turned to foreign (usually Oriental) deities to test or strengthen their own magic power. The golden age of sorcerers in Rome came during Imperial times when magicians from all over the world made Rome their own special capital. Here they earned lucrative fees by exploiting the fears and anxieties of a slowly decaying, superstitious society.

In the primitive Church there was no problem of sorcerers. All idols, and pagan gods were considered to be images of Satan and his demons. Although the Christian fought Satan, it was not necessary for him to fight sorcerers among his own people. The fight against Satan took the form of benedictions. All these legitimate liturgical ceremonies are still practiced. The Church has not changed in doctrine or practice; to the Christian the best defense against Satan is still the pure heart of man with his free will and the power to invoke the grace and help of God. This is the reason for blessing water, oil, seeds, crops, food, boats, automobiles, public monuments, and almost any article one can think of. The satanic danger ever exists, and the blessing signifies an urgent appeal to God for protection against it. From the most ancient times to the present, the outward sign of the struggle against Satan is the Sign of the Cross (if invoked with faith). The Church has always taught that in order to fight diabolical influences the Christian should be armed with this weapon. No liturgical act is performed nowadays without making the Sign of the Cross or invoking God with the prayer, "Our help is in the name of the Lord"—*Adjutorium nostrum in nomine Domini.* . . .

Weakened human nature, however, very soon left the path pre-scribed by the Church, and in the sixth century the Church was com-pelled to make its first solemn declarations against belief in magic. This was the beginning of a long series of events culminating in or-ganized witch-hunts, i.e., in legal condemnation of those who were found guilty of sorcery. (It should be mentioned that the Romans themselves punished with death by fire magicians whose practices resulted in the death of a human being.) In 563 the Council of Braga (Portugal) declared anathema against those who believed that the demon had power over atmospheric phenomena like light-ning or thunder. Bishops and Popes warned Christian Europe against naïve superstitions. In the meantime, however, probably under Oriental influence, the popular imagination became more and more excited over the alleged diabolical meetings and orgies of witches and sorcerers in the Hartz mountains in Germany, Benevento in Italy, and elsewhere.

No age can boast of being entirely immune to superstition, and every age has taken measures for the violent suppression of diabolism under the form of heresy, witchcraft, or whatever. It was in the 13th century that the violent repression of sorcerers and witches began. This was the time when such sects as the Cathari, at base a revival of Manicheism, with ramifications both in the West and the East, made their appearance. The western branch, called Albigensians, and the eastern branch, the Bogomili, taught that the material world was created by an evil principle coexistent with God. The ideas of the Albigensians and the Bogomili caused much trouble and disorder in Europe for about four hundred years and resulted in great popular disturbances. The Albigensians, with the support of the Count of Toulouse, exerted a widespread and pernicious influence. Although they fiercely defended their beliefs they were almost entirely ex-terminated in a war that lasted about twenty years.

It was a tragic turn of history. The first Christians did not believe in witchcraft and they had compassion for those who prayed to idols. Later, the Christian belief in God's mercy and eternal justice (which would manifest itself in God's own inscrutable way) was weakened by a fear of sorcery and witchcraft. So instead of invoking God's name and believing in His power, certain medieval Christians in a mood of self-righteousness and spiritual pride exercised rights which were the prerogative of God alone, to take the lives of those allegedly culpable. St. Martin of Tours protested against the execution of an apostate priest, yet this first blood sentence by Christians was carried out in 385 A.D., shortly after the persecution of the Christians ended. The first trial against witchcraft was held in 1258 under the auspices of the Inquisition. The first condemnation to death at the stake was pronounced in 1275 by the Bishop of Toulouse against a woman who "confessed" to having had carnal intercourse with a demon and of having fed him with the flesh of little children whom she kidnapped at night. This seemed clearly to be a case for psychiatry; nevertheless, her confession excited the populace to anger. The judges themselves were often subject to bias. Moreover, as Thurston writes, "That such a thing as witchcraft exists or has existed in the world, no Christian can deny who believes his Bible to be the inspired word of God. It is impossible to suppose that the story of the witch of Endor (I Kings, 28), of Simon Magus (Acts VIII, 9), or of the girl with the pythonical spirit (Acts XVI, 16) are to be understood merely as allegories."[4]

The explanation for the frequency of witch-hunts, so often accompanied by violent and barbarous trials, is to be found not in the belief in witches but in mass hysteria. No community, no religious grouping can accuse another of having been solely responsible for the witch-hunts of the past. It is significant that the first hysterically violent cases began in and around Toulouse, which had already been enveloped in a mist of superstitions because of the stress laid by Manicheism on the power of Satan. In 1335, at a trial in Toulouse, 63 people were accused of having participated in so-called Witches' Sabbaths, and all of them confessed their "crimes" under torture. Eight were burned at the stake, eleven condemned to lifelong prison, and the rest to twenty-years' imprisonment. But the same hunt for witches went on in Germanic countries, too. The Sachsenspiegel and the Schwabenspiegel (1225, 1275) punished with death anyone connected with sorcery. From 1400 on mass executions took place in Switzerland. In Wallis alone from January 14, 1428, to June, 1429, two hundred persons were burned at the stake. Finally in 1486,

Pope Innocent VIII published his bull *Summis Desiderantes Affectibus*, which in good faith gave almost exclusive power to Henry Institoris and Jacob Sprenger, two German Dominican priests, to act against sorcery. The bull did not speak about Witches' Sabbaths, about "flights with the devil," or the transformation of human beings into beasts. It simply deplored the fact that many people had left the Christian Faith and were in contact with Satan. Thus the Bull cannot be blamed for magnifying the witch problem. The Archbishop of Brixen in South Tyrol, the most important ecclesiastical authority in German-speaking territory, wanted to put an end to the extremist activity of the two priests. The two friars replied with a book, *Malleus Maleficarum* (The Hammer of the Sorcerers), in which they vividly described the horrors of alleged witch practices and gave instructions to the inquisitors on techniques of dealing with such people.

In the course of the 16th century this became the handbook of hysteria, followed by a long series of other books of demonology, which were not only theoretical treatises on Satan or demons, but also anthologies of stories on witchcraft. They added enormously to the popular tensions and excitement. The extent of the popular concern with witches is expressed in the art of these times. It is enough to cite the two great names of Peter Breughel and Hieronymus Bosch. Their works are filled with a "morbid unrest," scenes of Witches' Sabbaths, figures of part-beasts, part-angels, part-men, a flourishing of diabolical imagination never surpassed since then. The 16th century was obsessed with the idea of hell, the devil, and death (consider the popularity of the *danse macabre*). It was also the age of astrology, and people expected to be cured of disease and rescued from the plague by the constellation of stars rather than by medicine, primitive as it was. No sickness can really be cured, said the astrologers, because sickness is an outcome of original sin. Epilepsy was considered diabolical, alchemy was practiced on a large scale in most variegated forms. Some alchemists tried to change base metals into gold, others hoped to find a mixture of the spiritual and material which would express the principle of life; and the most ambitious among them were convinced that spontaneous generation was possible by which a so-called *homunculus* could be produced. Typical of the age was Paracelsus, philosopher, astrologer, alchemist, and doctor. "All intellectual activity tended towards a mysterious unknown," says Emil Brouette.[5] Thus on the one hand society was interested in finding occult means to penetrate secrets of the universe and, on the other, it took steps to suppress these same efforts.

The Councils of the Church dealt constantly with problems of sorcery.

This was the age of the greatest religious crisis of the Western world, the so-called Reformation. But the Reformation was as obsessed by Satanism as certain people in the Church itself. "Luther, Melanchton, and Calvin believed in Satanism, and the fanatical preaching of their disciples aggravated the natural credulity of the nations who accepted the New Gospel" (Brouette, in *Satan*). Protestant assemblies and synods also dealt constantly with the same subject and thus the persecution of sorcerers went on from both sides. It is sufficient to remember the iron rule of Calvin in Geneva, the sentencing to death of Farrell and later of Castellio. The climate of the times has been admirably portrayed by Thurston:

"When we calmly review the data of this intricate problem of witchcraft and witch-persecution, the only sane conclusion seems to be that nine-tenths, perhaps ninety-nine hundredths, of the trouble was due to the morbid and hysterical mental conditions engendered among a number of superstitious and very imperfectly educated people by an atmosphere of suspicion, terror, and mystery. No doubt there were here and there persons of intelligence, like Gilles de Rais for example, who believed in these things, and who for mercenary or evil ends did deliberately seek to put themselves in communication with the spirit of all evil, and who, having become desperate, stopped short at no kind of crime, blasphemy, or sacrilege. But the immense majority had probably been guilty of little more than a curious or sometimes malicious dabbling in the occult and dangerous. Wherever persecution and a great sensation occurred and set all the world a-talking, witches began to be manufactured and to multiply, until the judges, Protestant and Catholic alike, found they dared not proceed further and follow up all the supposed clues."[6]

Under the title "Il Diavolo in Italia" (The Devil in Italy), an Italian weekly, *Il Borghese*, published the story of a diabolical possession case, the true story (as the weekly declared) of Caterina Brandellero, "victim of the demon in 1955. . . ." According to the account, the possession began in May, 1951, when Caterina, a 34-year-old housewife with four children, living in a hamlet in the mountainous, legend-haunted country north of Vicenza, heard an inner voice say to her, "Today I will be with you, prepare yourself." The woman, being pious and God-fearing, recited the *Ave Maria* in answer. She said nothing to her relatives. Suddenly at sunset of the same day, she underwent a complete transformation before the eyes of the children and her husband. "The skin of the face became dark, her teeth protruded, the forehead became full of deep lines and she started to scream in a voice that was not her own, unrelated and disconnected sentences, obscene phrases, sometimes in Italian and sometimes in a language unknown to the horrified on-lookers. These shrieks were interrupted by seemingly improvised songs and then again by shouts that were more like the barking of dogs than any human sound."

Then, according to the newspaper, "ecclesiastical authorities were consulted," and soon a priest and a doctor arrived. After several days and weeks of investigation the woman underwent a solemn exorcism that put her at ease. But after some months the possession returned, and again she was exorcised. In 1954, when the obsession alternated with a normal state, she was taken by a priest to the sanctuary of Loretto, where she again was exorcised. The Italian newspaper reported that she seemed to be healed, but on the first day of Lent in 1955 the apparent obsession began to manifest itself in a violent form such as she had never before experienced. The same priest who had performed the exorcism in Loretto exorcised her again; at this time "fifteen demons left her."

The description of the Italian newspaper seemed to be so exact (it even described the details of the medical treatment which had proved futile) that I did not doubt that this was a case of a genuine possession. In November, 1955, I went to Vicenza to ask the permission of the bishop of the diocese to visit the woman. To my great surprise, the bishop told me that the incident was a classic case of sensational journalism. According to the rules of the Church no exorcism can be undertaken without the specific authorization of the bishop of the diocese. Despite this very strict rule, the bishop said, he was not asked to give his authorization. The ecclesiastical authority mentioned in the newspaper report was not an authority, for only the bishop possesses that power. The ensuing calamity resulted from this initial error. The bishop told me that the head of the psychiatric ward in Vicenza had examined the woman and investigated her background and family history, and had discovered that the woman's family had a history of mental illness; a brother, in fact, had been committed to a Vicenza hospital.

This story of Caterina Brandellero shows clearly what immense caution is necessary in such cases, and how easily impressed people are by certain signs they consider diabolical. If it were not so tragic, one might dismiss as amusing the comments of a woman who witnessed the "possession" of Caterina. She claimed to have seen the lines on her forehead, and later she testified that two small horns were visible there—"a sure sign of the devil's presence."

But what is the law of the Church with regard to exorcism? Here is a brief account of her legislation, based upon the explanatory notes of Joseph de Tonquedec, S.J.

Two kinds of exorcism are known in the Church, the ordinary and the solemn. The ordinary is directed against temptation; in its best-known form it is found in the Catholic baptismal rite; the solemn exorcism is directed against actual diabolical obsession. Although every candidate for the priesthood receives the office of exorcist as one of the minor orders, very few persons are authorized to practice exorcism. In each case the permission of the bishop is required. The Roman Ritual prescribes, with painstaking precision, under what circumstances exorcism is allowed, the duties of the priest before exorcism, how the priest can distinguish diabolical possession from mental disorder, and the formula for exorcising.

First of all, the Roman Ritual says: *"In primis ne facile credat aliquem a daemonis obsessum esse"* (He should not at the outset allow himself to believe in obsession too easily). This is not a new

God creating the sun and the moon. Fresco by Michelangelo in the
Sistine Chapel of the Vatican.

The vision of the Prophet Ezechiel. Painting by Raffael in the Pitti Gallery, Florence, Italy.

Christ walking on the water and carrying St. Peter. Painting by Cigoli in the Gallery of Ancient and Modern Art, Florence, Italy.

Detail of the Last Judgment. Fresco by Signorelli in the Cathedral of Orvieto.

Lucifer expelled from heaven. Painting by L. Lotto.

A saint chasing demons. Painting, artist unknown, in the Vatican.

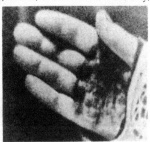

Padre Pio, the stigmatized Italian
Capuchin, during Mass.

The wound marks on the hand of
Padre Pio.

Saint Gregory the Great and the miracle of the bleeding Host.
Painting by Andrea Sacchi in the Vatican.

The fourteen saints, helpers in emergencies. Painting by N. Schat in the Municipal Museum, Frankfort/Main, Germany.

rule in the Church. In 1583 the national Synod of Rheims prescribed that the life conditions, reputation, health, and other circumstances of the allegedly possessed should be investigated and that the priest should discuss the problem of the person with well-balanced, intelligent people. As Bruno de Jésu-Marie observes, "Melancholics, lunatics, and persons bewitched often declare themselves to be possessed and tormented by the devil and these people nevertheless are more in need of a doctor than of an exorcist."[7]

In other words, the exorcist must be sure that he is not deceived by some symptom of hysteria, epilepsy, or other disturbance (these pseudo-obsessional signs will be dealt with in another chapter). At the same time, the priest must arm himself against the judgment of unbelieving doctors who are determined to explain everything by natural causes. The exorcist, however, cannot rely on faith in judging the attitude or veracity of the diagnosis of such doctors. As Tonquedec rightly points out, the Church really distinguishes between essential of supernatural and the modal supernatural.

"... The distinction [between the two] is capital and governs the whole problem of the marvellous. . . . Only the essential supernatural is the supernatural properly so-called, the supernatural simply. It points to a reality that surpasses nature. It is totally inaccesible to science, unknowable by natural means. . . . The study of the essential supernatural belongs exclusively to the sphere of faith and theology."[8]

The marvelous, the miraculous, is an observable phenomenon, subject to scientific examination. Thus, a diabolical possession belonging in the category of the modal or marvelous supernatural is detectable, and, like any other marvelous phenomenon, displays *signs* having a "probative value."

As the Roman Ritual insists, *"Nota habeat ea signa quibus obsessus dignoscitur ab iis qui vel atrabile, vel morbo aliquo laborent"* (He [the exorcist] must recognize signs to diagnose the obsessed distinguishing him from melancholics or suffering from other disorders). For this reason the help of psychiatrists or neurologists must be employed, but the exorcist should be prudent in evaluating the medical diagnosis. He "should complete the psychiatric or neurological examination with another, not of course to check the medical value of the first, but to find out whether the resulting diagnosis covers all the facts. . . . There is no question of superimposing a preternatural explanation on top of the natural one; . . . The exorcist will simply be careful to see that none of the manifestations presented, or indications of behavior, is left unaccounted for."

The signs common to genuine obsession and to neurasthenia, hysteria, and epilepsy will be dealt with later. The Roman Ritual speaks of three specific signs of possession: "*Signa autem obsidentis daemonis sunt: ignota lingua loqui pluribus verbis, vel loquentem intelligere; distantia et occulta patefacere; vires supra aetatis seu conditionis naturam ostendere*" (Use or understanding of an unknown tongue; knowledge of distant or hidden facts; and exhibitions of physical powers exceeding the age or condition of the subject).

This is, however, one of the most intricate problems facing the exorcist, because he has to apply all his knowledge of theology, psychology, and the so-called occult forces. The use of an unknown language does not necessarily mean that the patient has a speaking knowledge of the language. In such a case it could be cryptomnesia, the reappearance of buried linguistic recollection. This could mean that the patient's ancestors knew the language that reappears in him. According to ecclesiastical experts on the subject, this is unlikely. It is also unlikely that the patient had absorbed the same language through telepathy. This is also impossible because even though it may be possible to read the thoughts or certain words in another persons' mind, it is impossible to learn an entire language through telepathy, because the structure of language is something abstract. Tonquedec, Thurston, Bruno de Jésu-Marie, and many others are now inclined to admit the reality and purely natural character of telepathy.

It is therefore something of importance that the exorcist and his assistants should talk to the patient during the inquiry, in a language that they do not understand. The answers are translated after the interrogation. These questions, carefully prepared by someone else, are read to the patient. The reason for this precaution is that if the exorcist knows the meaning of what he asks, he will formulate the answer in his unconscious and by telepathy the very same answer will be perceived by the patient and returned to the questioner. The same precaution is valid for the second sign of true diabolical possession, namely the knowledge of distant or hidden facts. The exorcist must determine whether the patient has been a thought-reader since birth or had acquired this gift later. If he has had it since birth, he certainly used it before. Whether it was acquired later is more difficult, but still possible, to determine. In the absence of thought reading or telepathic gift, the probability of genuine possession increases. The same is true for other phenomena, such as the case of levitation, which falls into the category of telekinesis. There are sufficient authorities who admit the possibility that levitation, like telekinesis, has natural causes based upon the fluids that emanate from every human being.

Tonquedec quotes a still unauthenticated case reported by a missionary some years ago. The missionary was faced with a case of alleged possession. He and his assistants carried the patient to the center of the church and laid him down close to a pillar. While they were carrying him his body became rigid. Then the missionary in Latin commanded the demon to carry the possessed to the ceiling feet first, head downward. In a split second the patient was lifted up into the air and remained thus suspended head downward for more than a half-hour. Again in Latin the missionary then commanded the demon to put the patient down unharmed. The command was carried out immediately. Of course there is no natural explanation for this case.

But even in such cases when a natural explanation somehow would seem possible, the exorcist must use other methods of deduction than that of the unbeliever. If such occult, metapsychical phenomena as levitation or thought-reading seem to be used in connection with truly evil purposes, the theologian has a right to suppose that these otherwise explainable phenomena are employed by the devil.

The conversation and answers of the patient must be evaluated very carefully. If the answers of the patient are along the same line of thought or at least show the same tendency he manifests during his normal states, there is reason to doubt the possession. "In genuine possession, the action of the demon doubtless dominates the body, seizes on its organs and uses them as if they were his own, actuates the nervous system and produces movements and gesticulations in the limbs, speaking for example through the patient's mouth," writes Tonquedec. But these movements and postures are not mechanical: "they proceed from a subjacent mental state but one which remains in a way exterior to his own personality."[9]

The aspects of possession are manifold. Physical signs consist in bodily and facial changes: the complexion alters, the features assume angry expressions, full of hatred. Headaches and dizziness set in, cramps are felt, and all the bodily functions and instincts are thrown into disorder. Very often a cold wind emanates from the walls. Those who practice exorcism list among the intellectual signs the state of tension and a tendency to prophesy. It is important to note that pride, the original sin of Satan, does not play an important role in cases of possession. Possession does not occur immediately; each truly possessed has a history of his possession during which the devil has prepared the ground, and as does the grace of God, building upon the nature of the person in question. In other words, it can be only one step from the psychiatric case to one of true possession. A person obsessed by loneliness, by guilt, by pride, inferiority, who lives without organic links to life, could be worked into a state where real possession by the demon takes place. (In most cases such possessions do not develop into a full-fledged diabolical obsession, if the afflicted consults both a priest and a doctor.) These are forces of evil resulting from modern conditions of life, as other forces of evil worked in other ages, adapting themselves to the material conditions of the period.

Among the famous unexplained historical cases, one of the most spectacular is that of the Ursulines of Loudun. A convent of the Ursuline nuns was founded in 1626 in Loudun, near Poitiers, France. There were about 17 nuns in the community, most of them from the French aristocracy, and a school for girls was attached to the convent. The ecclesiastical authorities appointed one Abbé Mignon as spiritual director of the institute, although this post was coveted by another priest, named Grandier. Grandier's reputation was not too savory, and once indeed his enemies had succeeded in obtaining his removal from the city of Loudun. In 1632, however, he returned. At this moment, the prioress of the convent, Mother Jeanne-des-Anges betrayed the first signs of diabolical possession. Very soon all the nuns of the convent exhibited the same strange behavior. Their faces sometimes burned black, they had horrible visions, they spoke in seemingly unknown languages. One of the sisters, in a possessive trance, told the interrogators that the cause of their bewitchment was the priest Grandier. Later, other nuns described alleged sorcery cases that occurred in the parish to which Grandier had previously ministered. He was accused of having thrown a bewitched bouquet of roses into the garden of the convent. This was, they said, the way their possession started.

Since the signs of possession did not subside, Abbé Mignon began to exorcise the nuns. In the meantime the whole city was already terrorized, and the news about the demons reigning in Loudun had spread all over France. The exorcism was carried out in public, and people went to watch it as though it were a theatrical spectacle or wrestling match. (Executions were carried out in public until the end of the 19th century.) Not too prudently, the exorcists asked questions that increasingly involved the Abbé Grandier. When the Archbishop of Bordeaux became aware of what was happening, he sent his own doctors to Loudun; and when they reported no evidence of diabolical obsession, he prohibited further exorcism. The priest obeyed, and the strange phenomena ceased at once. In 1633, however, Cardinal Richelieu appointed a new military chief to the district—Jean Martin, a violent, vulgar man full of superstitions. He made a new report to Richelieu, who then ordered the reopening of the process. With this, all Loudun seemed to become possessed. First the nuns, then the students of the institute, and finally some inhabitants and even the children of Loudun. The trial lasted less than a year and ended with the condemnation of Grandier, who was subsequently burned at the stake. Strangely enough, the nuns at the convent were not liberated from their pitiable state after the death of Grandier. To put an end to the seemingly interminable ordeal, Jean Martin invited the Jesuits, among them the famous

Father Surin, to deal with the case. Father Surin's memoirs tell the story from there on.

Although Father Surin was one of the exorcists, for a while, he says, he himself was possessed. When the demon left Mother Jeanne-des-Anges, he entered Surin. Since this was witnessed by many great personalities, among them Gaston d'Orleans, brother of the King of France, Father Surin's reliability is beyond question. During all this time fear and terror reigned in Loudun and its environs. The years passed, and still the devil ruled in the convent. Finally in 1638, Richelieu, like the Archbishop of Bordeaux some years before, ordered the suspension of the exorcisms. After this interdiction, calm and peace returned to the city and the convent.

Exorcisms were less frequent during the 17th, 18th, and 19th centuries, but there was no reason to change one's view of them since the Church believes in the reality of the devil. But there is more caution about these matters in our times. Exorcists are priests who have psychiatric training and employ the assistance of other psychiatrists.

People still come up with reports about alleged possessions and apparitions. One established and proved case of diabolical possession, however, occurred in 1920 in Piacenza, Italy.[10] One day a woman entered the sacristy of the Franciscan church of Santa Maria in Campagna. She told one of the priests there that for some time she had the feeling that her body and soul were in the possession of an unknown power. She was able to sing opera arias she had never heard. The power possessing her talked with her in foreign languages. She tore shirts and sheets to pieces with her teeth, she danced until exhausted; moreover, she saw things that happened a great distance away and were unknown to anyone else. For instance, she told of participating at the funeral of a young woman. After an investigation the details and data given by her proved to be exact.

Since the Franciscan who listened to the woman's confession served as chaplain for the psychiatric ward, at first he concluded that the woman was hysterical or insane. At the moment this was going through his mind, the woman began to reassure him that she was neither an hysteric nor insane. She wanted to liberate herself, she had prayed much, but without success. She did not want to be considered a psychotic, she wanted to be helped. The priest told the woman to return after a few days. When she returned he started to bless her in the church. While he was administering the blessing (not exorcism), the woman first began to bay like a dog at the moon, then her voice turned into a beautiful and passionate soprano singing an extremely beautiful song; then suddenly she began to talk in an unknown language as though she were engaged in conversation with an invisible person. Finally, after a violent outburst, she began to cry.

The next day the Franciscan, who had seen so many pathological cases during his service in the psychiatric hospital, was still unconvinced. He reported the case to the bishop. The bishop ordered him to perform the exorcism, but the Franciscan tried to convince the bishop that it should not be performed, and, if so, then someone else should be the exorcist, because he had his doubts about the case. The first exorcism took place on May 21, 1920, at 2 P.M. in the presence of another Franciscan and a doctor Lupi, a psychiatrist of Piacenza, the mother and the husband, and two women friends of the possessed. The exorcism always starts with the following words: *"Exorcizio te, immundissime spiritus, omne phantasma, omnis Legio. . . ."* (I exocise thee, most unclean spirit who are all phantasm . . .).

At this moment the woman jumped into the air and then with great ease she fell into the center of the room. Then turning to the exorcist as if she wanted to attack him, she shouted: "But who are you, who dare to measure yourself with me? Don't you know that I am Isabo, and that I have long claws and a strong fist."

The priest, shaken for a moment, felt as though he were being destroyed. But he regained his courage as if an unknown force had been infused into him, and he addressed the demon with authority:

"I am a priest of Jesus Christ. And I give orders to you, whoever you are, through the mysteries of the Incarnation, of the Passion and the Resurrection of Jesus Christ, through His ascension into heaven, and through his promise to return at the Last Judgment, that you should do no evil to this creature of God, neither to those who assist her here in this room nor to all her goods and possessions—but do all that I command you to do."

From this moment on, a dialogue started between the priest and the demon through the mouth of the possessed.

"Where do you come from?" asked the priest.

"But you order me as if I were your slave," answered the woman.

The priest again demanded: "Tell me, where from do you come?"

The demon answered, simply, "No."

Then the priest said: "In the name of God, God whom you know well, tell me from where you come!"

At this moment the possessed fell into convulsions, her face distorted.

The priest repeated his demand: "In the name of God, by His Blood, by His Death, tell me where you come from."

The demon answered, "From far distant deserts."

The priest: "Are you alone or do you have companions?"

The demon: "I have companions."

The priest: "How many?"

The demon: "Seven."

The priest: "Why did you enter this body?"

The demon: "Because of a violent love, unreciprocated."

The priest: "Unreciprocated by whom?"

The demon: "You are an idiot."

The priest: "Answer, who is the person who did not respond to this love?"

The demon: "This body."

And saying this, the demon invisibly grasped the possessed and struck her on her chest.

The priest: "And why did she not want to respond?"

The demon: "Because it is not just."

These last words were pronounced in a mocking tone, as if to imply that the resistance of the woman was ridiculous.

After many sessions, the demon said that he would leave on June 23. In the meantime the exorcist wanted to know how the demon had got possession of this woman. Whatever the demon said was to be doubted since he was "the father of lies." At any rate, the demon explained that the cause of his coming was a man who practiced occultism and wanted to convert the woman to occult practices and take her into his possession.

The priest: "Are there actually any sorcerers?"

The demon: "Yes."

The priest: "What are they doing?"

The demon: "These are people who are capable of doing evil to others."

The priest: "Do they have power over the demon?"

The demon: "Yes."

The priest: "Do they have direct communication with the demon?"

The demon: "Yes."

The priest: "Is the sorcerer always an evil man or could he be a good man?"

The demon: "He could be both good and evil."

The priest: "Good, in what sense?"

The demon: "Good in appearance, but not in his innermost being."

The priest: "Did these sorcerers sell their soul to the demon?"

The demon: "Almost."

The report of this dialogue is not complete and it does not completely reflect what went on during the exorcism. The answers were not given promptly, each answer was preceded by convulsions and reticent, recalcitrant movements. In other words, the replies were given only after great resistance. It was a struggle to the end. The demon had to be defeated at each question.

The last exorcism was carried out on June 23, 1920. As has been said, Doctor Lupi, psychiatrist of the city of Piacenza, participated in all these sessions. He became ever more curious as to what would happen to the possessed after the demon left her. If the demon left her and there were no further signs of obsession, then the woman could be considered cured or curable, but if the demon left her and the signs of possession returned the conclusion could be drawn that she was not diabolically possessed but mentally sick. If a patient suffers from hysteria or a pathological neurosis, no exorcism, no holy water, no orders given to the devil can ever make the patient healthy. According to the documents the patient herself awaited the last exorcism, on June 23, with a frantic tension. The priest, in Latin, again ordered the devil to obey him:

"In the name of God, I order you to obey me in all that I am going to command."

There was no answer and the tension increased, becoming more and more oppressive.

The priest: "Did you understand?"

No sound broke the tense silence.

The priest: "I command you in the name of God and of the Holy Virgin."

No answer.

The priest: "If you understood what I told you, lift one arm. If you did not, two . . ."

At this moment the possessed, very slowly and with seeming reluctance, lifted one arm.

Then finally, the priest's voice broke the silence again in a most solemn manner. He commanded the demon to leave the possessed at once. A weak, broken, lamenting voice answered: "I am going. . . ."

The possessed then threw herself into the middle of the room, and in the midst of convulsions began to vomit up an enormous quantity of mysterious objects. The priest continued his commands with increasing fervor and joy: "Leave her, leave her, go. . . ."

Suddenly the possessed stood up. She smiled, and in her most natural manner and voice, the soft, pleasant voice of a young woman, she cried out:

"I am cured."

During the exorcism the demon, Isabo, talked several times about a small pellet that he had forced her to swallow seven years before. The psychiatrist, Dr. Lupi, examined with a little stick the basin the patient had used. Curiously, all that she had regurgitated a few seconds before could be lifted by the stick as though it were a piece of cloth. In fact, when it was laid on the floor it became a large and beautiful veil, bordered with the colors of the rainbow. But at the bottom of the basin they found the completely hard and dry little ball so often described by Isabo. This was a small piece of salt pork, the size of a hazelnut, with seven pointed protrusions.

The patient never became possessed or ill again, and at this writing she is still alive and living in the same village in the neighborhood of Piacenza. And she is now a happy grandmother.

Diabolical possessions such as described in the preceding pages are very rare. The demon can manifest himself, however, in less aggressive forms. One may ask, Why does God permit, even rarely, these full diabolical possessions? The answer might be that He permits them because He wants to give an example, to warn people from time to time about the reality of Satan. Though the less aggressive diabolical manifestations do not have such terrifying accompanying effects, they are no less serious. These are called diabolical infestations. Such was the nature of the troubles caused by the devil which was inflicted upon St. John Vianney, the Curé of Ars. These were all exterior attacks and not temptations. St. John Vianney suffered most of these attacks during the winter of 1824–25, when he was 38 years old. Most of the manifestations were grotesque and bizarre, but none the less quite frightening. Over a long period the curtain of his bed was torn to pieces at night. Then the demon knocked on the door or yelled loudly in the courtyard of the parish. Sometimes several voices were heard, and there were times when the shouts and the conversations sounded as though a whole army were camped in the courtyard, talking in an unknown language. There was an instant when the demon made his presence felt in the very room where the saint slept. The demon moved the furniture around and cried with a terrifying voice: "Vianney, Vianney, you truffle eater, you! Are you still alive, haven't you died yet? I will get you!"

It is interesting to note that on February 19, 1858, when Bernadette Soubirous had received her fourth apparition at the Grotto of Massabielle, she, and those who were with her, suddenly heard an outburst of quarreling, as though an excited crowd were disputing. Bernadette was particularly frightened when she heard an angry voice cry out, "Go away, get out!"

Bernadette, who was then about fourteen years old, did exactly what the saintly Curé d'Ars (whom she did not know and of whom she had never heard) had done under similar circumstances. She looked up, with absolute confidence, at the face of the Madonna; and at that very moment the sound and fury ceased.

Napoleon's mother, Madame Letitia, who outlived her famous son, had a mysterious experience in Rome in 1821. Madame Letitia, lived in Rome in a palace donated to her by her son. The Pope, whom her son had humiliated on more than one occasion, guaranteed the safety of the mother. She still entertained the hope of seeing Napoleon again, completely unaware of the grave illness that afflicted him in his exile on the Island of St. Helena.

On January 26, 1821, a man presented himself at the entrance of Madame Letitia's palace. He said that he wished to speak to Madame Letitia alone, and that he could not identify himself or explain the reason for his visit to anyone but her. The servants, fearing for her safety, refused him entry; but he insisted. After a long parley at the gate, Madame Letitia was informed, and she decided to receive him in the presence of two close relatives. The stranger was led into the room, but there he refused to disclose his identity or to disclose the purpose of his visit unless he was left alone with Madame Letitia; whereupon the two relatives left. The servants and relatives, however, remained close by the entrance of the room. Once alone the stranger approached the mother and announced: "Madame, at this moment, while I am talking to you, your son has been relieved of his sufferings and has passed away from this earth."

Madame Letitia, stricken with sudden grief, closed her eyes for a second. When she opened them again, the man was no longer in the room. No one had seen him leaving either the room or the palace. A thorough search of the immediate neighborhood and the whole city of Rome failed to reveal any trace of him. He seemed to be a spirit.

This story is told by Cardinal Lépicier, who is not easily given to believing similar stories.[11] The eminent author cited it in order to illustrate his explanation about the nature of angels. This stranger might have been a good angel or an evil angel—that is, one of the demons. Ever since the Fourth Lateran Council, and most recently since the Vatican Council (1870), it has been an article of faith that angels are pure, spiritual beings, created by God at the beginning of time (i.e., they do not exist from eternity). Angels have no bodies. They differ from each other, have free will, and live constantly in the state of grace. One doctrine declares that each of the faithful has a personal guardian angel. At their creation all angels were good, even Satan. The demons became evil through their revolt. Satan and the demons thus have the same characteristics as the angels—except, of course, for the constant state of grace. Both angels and demons can assume the corporeal form and features of a human being, and function in his stead. Thus it is possible that Madame Letitia was informed by an angel or by a demon about the death of her son.

In the preceding chapter we "met the devil" in the various forms he has assumed through history and in the mythology of other religions. The purpose of our study was to become acquainted with the nature of Satan and with his capacity to conjure up prodigies, and to mislead and ensnare the strong or the weak with the aim of snatching their souls for eternal damnation. It is difficult to believe that there is eternal damnation. In recent times, the great Italian writer Papini contradicted this dogma in his highly controversial book on the devil, though he accepted the existence of Satan. We know that many saints are in heaven, but we do not know with certainty that anyone is in hell. Yet we believe in the existence of hell. It is related that in the 17th century the cause of an eminently saintly priest was brought up for canonization. He had lived an exemplary virtuous life and the chances of his elevation to sainthood seemed to be great. Nevertheless, his canonization process was stopped at a certain point and shelved forever. The reason given was that once this priest had accompanied a convicted murderer on his walk to the gallows. The murderer refused to accept the consolation of religion, he refused to kiss the Crucifix; and he was hanged without repenting. When the criminal's death was officially confirmed, the priest turned to the onlookers and told them that they had just witnessed a most unique event, that of a man going straight to hell, to his eternal damnation.[12]

This statement lost the otherwise virtuous priest his canonization forever. No one knows the ways of God, and no one should dare put himself in the place of God by talking in His name.

We know that Satan is damned. We know that he leads the war

against God, that he craves souls. What we do not know is the identity of those who give themselves completely into his power, thereby turning away from God and damning themselves for eternity.

In his book, *The Devil's Share*,[13] Denis de Rougemont says that the devil "by nature, will never be clearly and honestly definable . . . vulgar and seductive, pharasian and holigan, both a hypocrite and a cynic, repulsive but none the less fascinating, he is undoubtedly the most *poetic* creature in the world. He is handsome in the eyes of the naïve who believe that evil must always be ugly; and he is of an irresistibly attractive ugliness in the eyes of the disillusioned or the refined."

The devil is everywhere in all ages and in all professions. True, diabolical possessions or infatuations are exceptional phenomena; still he manifests himself everywhere—and woe to a society that forgets that the devil exists! De Rougemont calls the devil and his band of demons "the fifth column of all ages." The devil infiltrates everywhere, the church as well as philanthropic institutions. Assuming many forms he can become the man of the world, the busy businessman. When necessary he becomes a fortuneteller, an author, even a lover. He creates the boredom of the modern age, instills the love of money, and encourages the wildest passions. In short, he is in the real god men worship. Writes De Rougemont: "The devil prevents us from recognizing God in Jesus Christ," but inversely he prevents us also from recognizing ourselves in our idols. This is how men chained themselves to the gods they create." These are the gods of nation, race, class, and the ego. The devil is at home mostly in places where people are depersonalized, where there is a lack of responsibility—in those places, that is, where the individual or his shadow, the man of the mass, instead of worshiping the one true God worships those gods whom he has created. "The gods of men are merciless. They are devils."

De Rougemont is right to remind us that "it was in the desert that the demon tempted Christ; it is always in the desert that he dwells, deserts of sand, of acrid waters or of rocks, deserts of crowds or those that the heart denuded of love and hope bears within itself."

How does the devil exercise his power in this world? Always by deceit, literally by the big lie. "Germany awake! (*Deutschland erwache!*) Hitler shouted at the very moment he was plunging his people into the nightmare of collective hypnosis" (De Rougemont, *ibid.*). The Bolsheviks in Russia and in all the satellite countries mouth the slogans of freedom while annihilating all true freedoms. The same Bolsheviks sing hosannahs to peace and use the olive branch and the dove as its symbol while preparing enslavement of people and the most atrocious wars. The devil paints pictures of happiness and freedom to the thief, to the gangster, while he knows that in the end the misery of damnation will engulf them, and he encourages even wilder dreams of legitimate expansion and self-interest, power, and glory to those obsessed by money.

We have to be careful. St. Thomas Aquinas reminds us that not all the evil in the world has been committed at the instigation of the devil, and not all ills of the world can be attributed to his direct work. In this connection Tonquedec, observes that: "it is true that most, if not all, of the scriptural and patristic texts in question are capable of a less precise interpretation; namely, that Satan is the first rebel, is the ancestor of all sinners, and that having brought about original sin and thereby introduced disorder and concupiscence into human nature he is, indirectly, the cause of all faults arising out of it. We may, then, leave the question open."

But Tonquedec makes it very clear that one should not make Satan into a rival of God as the Manicheans did. "Pure and total evil does not exist . . . nor is Satan the unique and universal originator of all the evil committed in this world. . . . One would simply be deluding oneself if one were to seek the ultimate answer to the problem of evil in diabolical interventions on earth. . . . We have seen that in addition to him, and only too often collaborating with him, there is human freedom, fallible by nature and as capable of giving way to the attraction of evil as of resisting it. Moreover, in the moral field, demoniacal influence is not compelling, in the last analysis man himself is always responsible for his sin."[14]

In all the childish stories about evil, in all the popular superstitions and beliefs, there is always a grain of truth. They are "remnants of Christian doctrines in a strange mixture." Theologians warn us not to go to extremes. "It would be madness to rely solely on prayers and religious rites to obviate all else—for example, to treat illnesses with exclusively supernatural remedies. . . . Even if diabolical influences do have a part in some event, that does not mean that other causes—normal, human, natural—cease to function" (Tonquedec, *ibid.*).

But it certainly should give us pause to think that we live in an age in which, for the first time in history, the nonexistence, the death of God is preached openly in public places all over the world. This at a time in which we also have more ways and means than were available to the societies of the Middle Ages, the Renaissance, and other periods to permeate society and the life of the individual with the spirit of God. Despite this we have the dubious privilege of witnessing the public spectacle of His dethronement. I, for one, do not suggest or think that this is a more diabolical age than any other, but centuries to come might justifiably arrive at such a conclusion.

CHAPTER 4

Occultism and its Problems

To believe in the miracles that are articles of faith and to accept unconditionally any other miracle or miraculous event are two quite different things, as we have seen. But in which category should the believer, the man of common sense, place those phenomena which do not involve saints and, in most cases, not even religion? And what are we to think about magic? Does it exist or not? Can we really communicate with the dead, and is it possible that some people really possess the gift of divination, that they can foresee the future and put themselves or be put into a state in which they can recount the past secrets of persons long dead about whom they had no prior knowledge?

"There are things between heaven and earth, Horatio, of which your scholarly wisdom has no thought," Shakespeare has Hamlet tell his good friend. And this is exactly what has excited mankind ever since its history began, those things "between heaven and earth." Although man is unable to penetrate heaven, he has attempted to meet the unknown, the unexplainable—the occult—those things half-way "between heaven and earth." But are these actually any phenomena, spirits, things between heaven and earth? Is there an in-between? Can the so-called occult phenomena be explained as occurrences peculiar to this twilight atmosphere? Was Nietzsche correct when he wrote, *"Die Welt ist tief und tiefer als der Tag gedacht"* (The world is deep, and deeper than the daylight might unveil)? Can we say that the unseen world and occult phenomena are only a yet unexplained aspect of the visible world? Or are these phenomena indeed caused by the actions of departed souls and good and evil spirits—that is, by angels and devils?

First, a word of caution is in order. Many volumes have been written on this subject by eminent experts. The author of this book cannot treat it exhaustively because the subject is a vast one, with many ramifications. In a brief chapter we shall attempt only to enumerate the occult phenomena and give explanations that are accepted by competent and objective scholars; Catholic and non-Catholic. Before doing so we shall give a brief history of occultism, and finally, we shall discuss the attitude of the Church with regard to these matters at the present time.

We are about to enter a field where precision, honesty, and our filial faith in God should be our most important companions. An unshakeable faith in Christ who redeemed the world has not hindered great scientists in their technical research. This is the attitude that must be ours while searching this seemingly twilight area of the unknown.

When dealing with these occult phenomena the following points of view should be borne in mind:

1. Modern science, particularly medical research in the fields of psychology, psychiatry, neurology, and neurosurgery, has revealed, and is constantly revealing, more and more unknown facts about the indescribably delicate mental-nervous system of the human being. Popular belief, however, generally still focuses on one aspect of this vast field—psychoanalysis. With all respect for the genius of Sigmund Freud, and without minimizing the importance of his theory and practice, one has to be reminded that psychoanalysis is only one branch of the great tree of psychological research. Nevertheless, medical science, including depth psychology, is able to provide answers, as we shall see, to many so-called occult phenomena. In our study we cannot go into the details of each specific case. Thus, when it is indicated that the answer is found in hypnosis, hysteria, or other phenomena, we are referring to the proven results of medical science.

2. While admitting the above, there is still a vast field that remains unexplained at present but can perhaps be explained eventually. And there is hope that science will find the explanation.

3. There are, however, many cases which cannot be classified as eventually explainable. These fall into the category of genuine occult events. This should occasion no surprise, for, the teaching of the Church makes it perfectly clear that certain kinds of preternatural forces can produce such phenomena. In other words, we do not, a priori, deny that such forces might interfere. At the end of our chapter the reader will find the directives and the unequivocal views of the Catholic Church with respect to occult phenomena. Here we shall only indicate that the Church, despite the unscientific attitude of past centuries, has never admitted occult phenomena in a canonization process.

The term *occultism* comes from the Latin *occultus*, meaning secret, hidden. Occultism is an ancient practice about whose origins and nature we are not yet fully informed. For about fifty years, the term *parapsychology* has been employed to describe spiritual or near-spiritual occurrences that are beyond the limits of ordinary psychology, thereby avoiding the superstitious overtones associated with the word occultism.

Questions of parapsychology and spiritism are so clearly related that it is only one step from parapsychology to those occult practices that are severely prohibited by the Church. Despite the fact that there are many societies honestly dedicated to the scientific research of these questions, the whole problem remains in a sphere of limited and sometimes vulgar empiricism linked to spiritism. The most important societies are the National Laboratory of Psychical Research attached to the University of London, the Society for Psychical Research, also organized in London in 1882, the American Society for Psychical Research, founded in Boston in 1885, and the Institut Metapsychique International, established in Paris in 1919.

The phenomena of parapsychology are usually divided into physical and psychical, despite the fact that they all possess psychical characteristics, since they always occur only in the presence of a human person, thereby involving him through his conscious or unconscious activity.

Among the physical phenomena the following may be listed: knocks, noises, percussions of unknown origin; variations of temperature within the objects of research as well as in the room where the experiment takes place (particularly the waves of cold air in the presence of a medium); chemical, electrical and magnetical phenomena, i.e., sudden changes in electrical current; variations of weight, with respect primarily to the medium who loses or gains considerable weight during the experiments.

Among the psychical phenomena is xenoglossy, which is the speaking of foreign languages unknown to the medium in his normal state. Only when the medium is capable of engaging in any kind of conversation at any length can the phenomenon be considered xenoglossy, and not when the medium simply repeats the same text several times. Changes in personality which cannot be caused by hysteria are also considered psychical phenomena. It is absolutely necessary in such cases that the medium should reveal a completely new personality.

Among the several hypotheses offered one that is largely accepted attributes all this phenomena to spiritism. It is true that certain disclosures may emerge through the invocation of a dead person. But up until now it has been impossible to furnish any scientific proof of this hypothesis. Most of the proofs brought forward are childish. The hypothesis based upon the discovery of Albert Einstein is also gravely erroneous. In our chapter on Science and Miracles, it will be seen how Einstein's concept of time and space and his explanation of the fourth dimension should be evaluated. Certain researchers in the field of parapsychology assert that objects are capable of moving from the third to the fourth dimension. These investigators forget, however, that the fourth dimension is time. Their error consists in the assumption that the fourth dimension has the same nature as the third one in which we live. The formula of Einstein is mathematical and has nothing to do with the physical reality of things.

The Catholic Church has formulated precise directives in connection with spiritism and related phenomena. On March 10, 1898, the Supreme Sacred Congregation of the Holy Office issued a decree answering the question whether it is permissible to evoke the souls of the dead. The question also included a description of the method to be employed—that is, to ask God's permission to communicate with the spirit of a certain deceased person. The answer of the Holy Office was clear and final, *"Uti exponitur non licere* (It is forbidden); it was negative, prohibitive. Pope Leo XIII confirmed this decision.

About twenty years later another question was forwarded to the Congregation of the Holy Office asking whether it was permissible to participate in experiments in which communication or manifestation of spiritistic nature is sought. It was further asked whether it made any difference if such experiments were carried out through a medium, or without a medium, or by use of hypnotism, assuming that all participants are persons of sincere piety. In short, was it permissible or not to communicate with the spirits of the dead; was it permissible to participate in such experiments as a mere observer?

The answer again was a decisive No. And Pope Benedict XV confirmed the decision on April 26, 1917. These decisions mean that Catholics can never participate in such sessions as described here.

Superstitious people tend to attribute to human beings powers that can be exercised only by God. There are many examples of this, fortunetelling or prognostications about the future being the most familiar. Astrologists deceive themselves that they can predict the future of a person from the constellation of stars at the moment of his birth, and dream interpreters see in dreams the signs of coming events. Other forms of predicting the future are associated with ordinary playing cards, special cards of the deck being endowed with portentous meaning. From a certain point of view the Church considers spiritualism as a superstition, though many of its aspects are not yet clear and remain unexplained. It is considered a superstition when the sessions are used for material gain, as a means of consoling bereaved persons, or as a form of spiritual direction. The use of otherwise legitimate supernatural means could also degenerate into superstition when one uses sacraments and prayer for unworthy purposes, or if any special significance is attributed to an arbitrary number of prayers and devotion or to a specific church or shrine to obtain supernatural help.

The history of occultism is really as old as mankind itself. The first human beings after the Fall began to feel that they were surrounded by mysterious powers, and they assumed that the inner structure of these mysterious powers was similar to their own. This is the way the belief in spirits was generated, without any other cause. This belief in spirits persists in the world today. For about a century now the whole problem has been demanding admittance into the halls of science. It has been a long road from the primitive oracles to present-day research. The deeper the past is penetrated the more oracles and magic are found, and the tendency is to regard them either as frauds or examples of boundless naïveté. This, however, is an untenable attitude. The Old Testament and the New are full of proofs to this effect. The Pharaohs' magicians were able to duplicate the results of some of the plagues in Egypt. In the New Testament there is the case of Simon Magus, who deceived many by his sorceries. Yet there are limits, and the magicians themselves were forced to recognize the power of God in the miracles of Moses. And Simon Magus "wondered to see the signs and exceeding great miracles" worked by the Apostles. There is much room for speculation as to the means whereby the magicians and Simon Magus worked their own marvels. Probably causative natural powers would account for much, if not all of their sorcery.

Attempts to commune with the inhabitants of the unseen were common in India and Chaldea and had taken place from time immemorial among the Chinese and Egyptians. The Greeks consulted Apollo in his temple at Delphi and the Romans petitioned the Sybilline oracles at Cumae and at Tibur for signs and favors. Poseidonios of Apameia, a Greek philosopher (2nd century B.C.), wrote that "Prophecies are based on the existence of God and the laws of nature and nature." The soothsayer is able to see the future, he says, "because all that will happen in the future does not happen suddenly; it is similar to the uncoiling of a ship's ropes; the course of time does not bring anything new." How is it possible that the soothsayer foretell something still lying in the womb of time? According to Chrysippos (278–240 B.C.), the answer is, by "natural sympathy." This is the mysterious force that makes things distant in time and space present and actual for us. John Tritheim, Abbot of Trier, Germany, expressed himself much more clearly in the 15th century. He claimed that he could communicate his thoughts to people who lived at a

distance of more than a hundred miles if those persons were familiar
with the art of this kind of communication. He wrote that he could
communicate his thoughts without words, signs, or any other media,
as clearly and detailed as required in a completely natural way without the help of spirits or other superstitious practices.

The problem of witchcraft and the mass phenomena resulting from
a witch mania that swept 16th and 17th century Europe has been
dealt with in the chapter on diabolical or pseudodiabolical forces. The
questions of interest here are telepathy, telekinesis (the self-move-
ment, chiefly of heavy objects, from one place to another); levitation
(a medium lifts himself without external help and remains or walks in
mid-air); *apporte* (an object or person is brought from distant places
without external help); teleplasty (from the medium's body emanates
a nebulous mass that later forms itself into inanimate objects or human persons showing signs of life); dematerialization (objects disappear); telesthesy (claiming to see events happening at a great distance, e.g., Swedenborg's claim of having seen the burning of Stock-
holm in 1759 from Goteborg—250 miles); psychometry (retrospective
clairvoyance, when a medium claims that by touching a certain object
connected with an event that dates hundreds or thousands of years
back, he is able to put himself into the place and conditions of that
event); kryptoscopy (the claim that one can read a letter closed in an
envelope or see what goes on behind a wall).

There were several attempts during the last hundred fifty years
to provide an explanation of these occult phenomena. The German
Mesmer (1815) suggested that the human organism possesses a
certain power of attraction which he called "animal magnetism,"
and tried to prove that persons possessing a greater degree of this
power could perform some of the above phenomena. Although Mesmer's system proved to be wrong as a general theory, certain 20th-
century scientists (the Swedish Sydney Alrutz and the French
Barety) came to the conclusion that animal magnetism, as a theory,
had not completely played out its role. A similar theory was elaborated
by the German Von Reichenbach, who maintained that he could
produce certain radiations he called "OD rays" through magnets (the
OD theory).

In contrast to these psychophysical theories, that of animism has tried to explain these phenomena purely on the spiritual level. The most important initiative in this respect was that of Helen Petrovna Blavatsky and of Colonel Olcott, who asserted that no one can be a true occultist without being a theosophist, since the alternative is black magic even if it is unconscious. Blavatsky wrote that the divine spark that every human being possesses in its substance and essence is identical with the Universal Spirit. She further asserted that spirit and matter are the two cornerstones of life's different manifestations, and that hence there is no gap between spirit and matter, and no distance in space or time between them. According to her, the human spirit intervenes directly in creation and is able to perform most miraculous phenomena—yet there is nothing supernatural in it, because everything is well imbedded in nature. . . . Modern theosophy, in all its ramifications, is based upon this theory.

The United States in general, and New York State in particular, has played an almost historical role in the development of occult studies. In March of 1848 the two Fox sisters, Margaret, 14, and Catherine, 12, who lived in Hydesville in Wayne County, New York, asserted that they had succeeded in communicating with an unknown spirit through tapping and knocking. Within the next eight years interests in the happenings in the Fox family grew into a world movement. Spiritism became a cult. The Fox family, and later on their associates, traveled all over the country. The newspapers reported at length about them, and as a result Margaret and Catherine Fox were for about thirty years the most important and best-known mediums in the world.

The events that took place through their intervention were described as follows: clearly audible voices whose source could not be determined; furniture and objects moving by themselves; writings found on floors and in rooms that no one could enter. One of the "disciples" of the Fox family, Judge Edmonds, a man of great integrity, asserted that he received communications through mediumistic writing from Francis Bacon, Swedenborg, Benjamin Franklin, and others. Spiritism in the United States was considered by European travelers to be the country's most important movement. According to a report of H. Spicer, a British traveler, spiritism in the United States in 1854 had three million followers, 30,000 of whom were mediums. In Philadelphia alone there were 300 spiritist circles. In 1888, however, spiritism was dealt a great blow. The two Fox sisters, now married, suddenly declared that all their exhibitions had been frauds. They were too young, they said, to resist the influence of their third sister, Helen. Their mother in good faith had at first believed the phenomena and then settled back to enjoy the money-making. To prove that they were now telling the truth, the two Fox sisters in a public exhibition at Carnegie Hall gave a demonstration of how the alleged occult phenomena had been naturally produced. One year later, however, one of the sisters recanted her confession made in 1888. This second confession declared that all her accusations against spiritism were false.

Father Thurston holds that Mrs. Margaret Fox Kane was right when she denounced spiritism as a fraud but that she was equally right when she retracted, saying that not everything was a fraud.[1] Spiritism has not been and is not a complete fraud. But Margaret Fox Kane, who had become a Catholic in 1857, could not liberate herself from these practices even after conversion. The only way of escaping from her situation was to deny everything, but her honesty dictated a retraction.

These were the beginnings of modern spiritism. The question of Margaret Fox Kane has never been completely resolved. There was no doubt that as a medium she was able to produce loud sounds, taps, and knocks. She was accused of fraud. At the same time she let people believe that the knocks were produced by spirits who were in contact with her, though she had a vague inner hint that somehow these mysterious forces had their origin in herself. But there is no question about the authenticity of phenomena produced through her. Tests were made in full daylight, and people who checked them were not her friends or fellow spiritists.

Few persons did more to "rehabilitate" spiritism after the rise and fall of the Fox sisters than Sir Arthur Conan Doyle, the British novelist. It was under his leadership that a society for the study of psychic science was organized. Spiritists all over the world date the birth of modern spiritism with the appearance of the Fox sisters. This is not completely accurate, as Emmanuel Swedenborg (1688–1722) had already organized a sect in Sweden.

After the activity of the Fox sisters and the organization of the psychic science society, there was an ever-increasing interest in occult phenomena. During the course of the last half-century several experiments and tests have been conducted by these societies to prove one or the other theory by way of explaining these phenomena, but none of them is convincing.

In general, these actions are divided into lesser occult phenomena and occult phenomena proper. The lesser occult phenomena are those that can be explained for the most part by natural phenomena, and they can be either of an intellectual or of a physical variety.

Among the intellectual phenomena we find that amazing capacity of some mediums to speak several languages when in a state of trance. Of course there have been impostors, but a fraud cannot be maintained too long. In many cases the explanation for this is that such people were in a hypnotic state and sometimes remembered certain passages or even entire pages of texts in their subconscious. There have been cases in which a person in a hypnotic state created a new language that the subject declared to be a Hindu dialect. This was done subconsciously in a hypnotic state, without the intention to deceive, but it was not occult. These are cases of hyperamnesia, a state of extremely excited memory uncontrolled by the conscious self.

Another lesser occult intellectual phenomena is automatic writing, i.e., which a medium has an inner compulsion to write although his fingers are not bent and the pencil or the pen is not held by them, but is simply leaning against the finger. Before the pencil begins to write it suddenly trembles and when asked who is going to answer the questions, it writes down the name of a dead person as if that very person were writing his own signature. It is tempting to declare immediately that this is evidence of contact with the dead person. Yet the explanation is not so simple. If the medium is familiar with the handwriting of the deceased, it is almost certain that the hypnotized subconscious of the medium is able to reproduce without fraud the handwriting of that person. If the medium has not seen the handwriting of the communicant then we face a truly occult phenomenon, but one that could still be explained through telepathy. There remains the question of what or who moves the pencil. In most cases there is no doubt that the infinitely sensitive finger nerves are in a state of nervous shock produced by the trance.

Among the lesser occult phenomena we also find certain physical, material phenomena. The origin of most of these has been explained. Such are certain sudden appearances of wandering light with or without the agency of a medium. The spiritists often claimed the intervention of ghosts. The explanation, however, is much easier. Some of these lights, (mostly in open country) are created by the dissolution of organic material that generates heat and hydrogen gas. The heat then ignites the hydrogen. Often we are dealing with so-called autokinetic phenomena: looking at a lighter point in the darkness we will suddenly discover that this point changes its place, which is an optical illusion, for the viewer has no point of reference since he is in darkness.

Most of the cases in which a medium seems to burn, or in which a person standing on a wooden floor ignites it, are explained by the ever-present electricity, which plays a greater role, even in the human body, than most laymen think. As recently as 1943 in Pirano, in northern Italy, the story was told of a woman who was surrounded by light, apparently created by a radiation on the side of her body. Investigators were convinced that the woman entertained such fixed ideas about religion that they produced deep changes in her organism. The influence of the emotions upon the human organism is well known. For example, fear results in chill, a sudden shock makes hair white, and so on. The intense religious life of the woman in question and her strict fasting during Lent produced an excess of sulphides and these sulphides became luminous upon being excited by the ultra-violet radiation inherent in blood.

Pope Benedict XIV, whose treatise on miraculous phenomena in canonization processes has yet to be surpassed, admits that "it seems to be a fact that there are natural flames which at times visibly encircle the human head, and also that from a man's whole person fire may on occasion radiate naturally; not, however, like a flame which streams upward, but rather in the form of sparks which are given off all around; further, that some people are resplendent with a blaze of light. . . ."[2] This does not, however, exclude the possibility that a similar luminous radiation produced in the lives of saints was a different kind like that in the life of St. Philip Neri or St. Alfonso Liguori. It is possible, too, that in certain cases the radiance connected with the intense mystical life of the person was produced in a natural way.

Human incombustibility might fall in the same category, but this problem has not yet been solved. Thurston, in the book already quoted, does not exclude diabolical origin. He cites the case of a Mohammedan wonder-worker in the court of the Maharaja of Mysore in 1921 or 1922, and leaves in doubt whether what happened at the seance (some persons were burned, others were not) was caused by natural phenomena or by the demon. The Catholic Bishop of Mysore, who witnessed the event, attested that it was real burning fire, and said that in his opinion "no material cause can explain the occurrence."

Knocking or any other mysterious and recurrent noises in allegedly ghost-ridden houses can often be explained by the uncontrollable tricks of an excited imagination and by the fact that in the silence of night freakish acoustics can make the gentle noise made by the leap of a frog in a deserted cellar sound like the thud of an axe. There are still people who do not know how the divining rod that finds water or oil functions. This is simply due to the fact that certain persons are sensitive to the electricity created by the invisible evaporation of water. In other words, these persons react like living receivers for radar stations.

Not all the dancing tables are manifestations of supernatural forces. A table is made to "dance" by mediums in two different ways. In the first it is achieved by making a chain out of the hands of all the participants, which either rest on the table or keep clear of it. If the hands of the participants touch the table, the motion is created by the unconscious and invisible nerve convulsions of the palms and fingers, as was proved long ago by Faraday, the great physicist. If the dancing of the table is caused without hands resting on it—the second way—we are in the presence of a genuine telekinetic and occult phenomenon.

It would lead us too far afield to list and explain certain phenomena in connection with animals, which for a long time have been considered unexplainable. They are, of course, neither occult phenomena nor tricks of trained animals.

Genuinely occult cases must in turn be divided into two groups: the intellectual phenomena and the physical phenomena. This is, however, an arbitrary division—as we stated earlier—since there are phenomena which belong in both groups.

All intellectual occult phenomena can be grouped under the term *telepathy*. This word, of Greek origin, is applied to a person who is able to sense or observe something at a distance from him, although there is no communicating medium between the person and the "thing" sensed. Under the general term of telepathy other special abilities can also be grouped: telesthesy, the ability to see events happening at a great distance (e.g., Swedenborg and the burning of Goteborg); kryptoscopy, the ability to read a letter enclosed in a sealed envelope or to see what goes on behind a wall (sometimes called second sight or clairvoyance); psychometry, or retrospective clairvoyance in which by touching a certain object one can connect with an event lying in the dim and distant past. The identification of a person in a hypnotic trance with a person who lived long ago is also an example of psychometry.

Other phenomena, more physical than intellectual, which fall under the group-term of telepathy are: telekinesis, teleplasty, dematerialization, and levitation. Finally, there is the phenomenon of stigmata. This occurs when one's body, without any external cause, displays the same wounds that Christ bore from the thorns, the nails and the lance at the Crucifixion. All these phenomena may occur in the lives of saints without mediumistic intervention, as accompanying, secondary indications of sanctity. Such cases cannot be subsumed under the head of occultism, since they constitute—to use Thurston's terminology—the physical phenomena of mysticism.

The existence of telepathic phenomena cannot be denied. This has been proven by innumerable psychological experiments. In 1930 the International Congress of Psychic Research heard a report on the experiment made by a group in Athens to influence, telepathetically, other groups in Paris, Warsaw, and Vienna—with undeniably notable success. Cazzamali, professor of psychiatry and neurology at the University of Milan, made the following experiment. He locked a medium into a completely isolated room, so that he was able to control this subject only through microphones placed in the same room. At a certain moment the medium began to speak and related in detail what was taking place at the same time in the Italian Parliament.

Telepathy has nothing to do with spiritism and ghosts. According to one hypothesis, telepathy works through the subconscious. This hypothesis asserts that the subconscious is something like a spiritual receptacle, so to speak, where we automatically store everything we have seen, heard, read, and then forget all about. According to occultists, this subconscious can operate separately and independently from the conscious, and perceive radiations or waves as yet undefined or unidentifiable. Thus the subconscious gains knowledge that the conscious is incapable of perceiving, such as reading the thoughts of another or, seeing events at a distance. Though Christian philosophy admits the existence of the subconscious, the autonomous action of the subconscious is inadmissible, as denying or jeopardizing the unity of the soul. It is true, however, that one mind can influence another, and that this influence is similar to the alleged action, described by spiritists, of incorporeal spirits who come from another world.

Most theologians are of the opinion that telepathy is an established fact. By telepathy is meant the transmission or reception of thought or spiritual-mental substances (contents), without the use of ordinary means of communication. It seems, however, that a certain kind of "feeler" must be established between the sender and the receiver. A "feeler" can be a simple idea or thought about a person or a thing in which both sender and receiver are unusually interested. The telepathic impression may often be so vivid that it appears as an exterior perception. Transmission and reception of telepathic phenomena occur in the majority of cases independently of the will of the persons involved. This is why the transmission of the most secret thoughts, in the conscious or subconscious mind, is possible, even over great distances. According to a commonly accepted theory, telepathic phenomena are caused by waves that radiate from brain to brain. Other theories, more esoteric, maintain that such phenomena represent a direct communication between soul and soul.

In one form of telepathy—psychometry or clairvoyance in retrospect—the subject is able to perceive or relive occurrences that date back centuries or even thousands of years, by merely touching an object, a letter, a tool, or a piece of furniture. The medium believes that he has been transported back into a specific age or place at a specific time, as if he were a participant or an observer on the spot.

A recent book describing such an experiment with an American girl has caused a great sensation. Under hypnosis the girl claimed a prior birth in a specific city in Ireland, more than a hundred years ago. She described events, some of which seemed to be confirmed by research. But the case of Bridey Murphy is not the first of its kind. Two English women, Miss Moberly and Miss Jourdain, had a similar experience. The two ladies visited Paris in 1901. One day they took a walk in the gardens of Versailles, and strolled toward the castle of the Petit Trianon. Suddenly they found themselves part of and witnesses to an 18th-century scene. They met and talked to people from the 18th century and they also saw a wedding party at the castle of the Petit Trianon. Their first experience occurred on August 10, 1901, and on November 26 and 28, 1901, "each wrote an account for their own use, to discover what they had seen in common."[3] They returned twice to the place of their strange adventure, and in 1911, after adequate historical research, they described the events in a book. Their conclusion was that they had been set back to the tenth of August, 1792. This was a most important date in the history of the French Revolution, the day Louis XVI was deprived of the crown. On this day Marie Antoinette retired to her beloved Petit Trianon castle. In the evening of the same day the royal family was removed under escort, and later executed. Miss Moberly and Miss Jourdain, according to their own account, had never been particularly inter-

ested in French history. Yet they were transported in time and witnessed the last day in freedom of the hapless Marie Antoinette.

How explain such phenomena? First of all, it must be determined
whether one is dealing with a fraud. In the case of Miss Moberly
and Miss Jourdain fraud is excluded, in view of their proven integrity. This is not to imply that the story of Bridey Murphy is based
on fraud. But in her case other explanations are possible. First of all,
it can be simply a matter of a rich and vivid imagination. Such cases
are more common than is ordinarily known. Many of us indulge in
daydreams, and often it happens that with the passing of time persons with a strong and fertile imagination no longer distinguish dream
from reality. Some dreams, especially those dreamed under the influence of narcotics or hypnotic anesthesia, might readily assume the
shape and substance of distant realities in the mind of the subject.
Such illusions could also emerge from the semiconscious or subconscious memory of the medium. In other words, what was once heard
or read may emerge in the state of trance and be articulated with an
amazing clarity. I do not mean to imply by this that the Bridey
Murphy case has anything to do with narcotics.

In the case of the adventure of the Misses Moberly and Jourdain
it is known that prior to their experience they were not exceptionally
familiar with French history. Yet it seems that the figure of Marie
Antoinette once had made a deep impression upon Miss Moberly
when she was a young girl. This was because her brother had written
a long poem on the tragic destiny of the French queen. Theoretically,
we cannot exclude the supposition that although Miss Moberly did
not remember the details of her emotional experience thirty years
back, it arose in her consciousness in Paris on the very spot of the
queen's tragedy. The fact that Miss Jourdain had almost the same
"vision" can be explained as a phenomenon of telepathic transmission
from Miss Moberly.

Thus we arrive at the third explanation possible in such cases—
telepathy. Telepathic transmission can take place between the semiconscious or subconscious of one person and another, as sender and
receiver respectively. In the case of the search for Bridey Murphy,
then, it is not excluded that the medium receives, in her hypnotic

trance, the entire story from the semiconscious or subconscious store of memory of another person. It is not necessary, as has been said, that the transmitting (sending) person should know that he has a telepathic effect on the receiver.

Furthermore, it is not excluded that the story is suggested consciously to the medium while she is in hypnotic trance. This would be the most common explanation. But even in such a case the transmission goes via telepathy, not from the semiconscious or subconscious of the sender, but consciously, through hypnotic impression.

Finally, one cannot exclude in such cases the possibility of diabolical manifestation, although we do not venture to say that any of the aforementioned cases fall into this category.

Clairvoyance, second sight, and divination, are occult phenomena and are to be distinguished from prophecy. Prophets are men who, under the direction of God, predict for a specific purpose certain events in order to point out a danger or to foster faith and hope. The prophecies are all of a religious nature and their contents are directly or indirectly concerned with the salvation, the redemption, of man. Occult divination, clairvoyance, and second sight, however, are not necessarily the work of the devil. Indeed, they can be explained by telepathy, particularly when the clairvoyant does not specify forthcoming events in detail. This strange phenomenon has existed for centuries. It still exists in Scotland and in Westphalia, Germany, to a greater extent than in the rest of the Western world. These divinators actually suffer under this burdensome gift of nature, for frequently the events they foretell are unpleasant—death, fire, and war. Their cases can be explained by telepathy and hyperesthesia, but the answer is not completely satisfactory. The Church severely forbids the practice of divination in any form, whether one resorts to a crystal ball, a deck of playing cards, or any other device.

Once two Protestant ministers visited St. John Vianney, the pastor of Ars, and discussed with him some events that they could not explain to themselves or to their faithful. Of course the two ministers did not believe in Christ's real presence in the Eucharist. During the discussion the Curé d'Ars suddenly asked them: "Do you believe that a piece of bread can detach itself and, of its own accord, place itself upon the tongue of a person approaching to receive it?" "No," answered the ministers. Then the Curé d'Ars went on and asked them to listen carefully to what he was going to tell them: "I do not say that it happened *somewhere or other*, but I say that it happened to me. When the man presented himself to receive the Holy Communion, the sacred Host detached itself from my fingers while I was a good distance from him and went and placed itself upon the tongue of that man."

A similar incident is reported of Abbé Olier, the founder of St. Sulpice, in 1638, and of St. Catherine of Siena. Her confessor, Father Bartholomew Dominic, stated that the sacred Host seemed to fly into her mouth. There is also the story of St. Juliana Falconieri, who died in June, 1341. As a consequence of self-inflicted hardships, she suffered from a severe stomach disorder. She could not take any food, nor could she walk to the communion rail. One day she asked to be placed as near as possible to the altar during distribution of Holy Communion, but she herself did not dare to receive the Host. As she neared the altar rail the Host disappeared from the hands of the priest and Juliana's face lighted up with joy. After her death, "there was found upon the left side of the bosom the mark like the stamp of a seal reproducing the form of the sacred Host" (Roman Breviary, June 19).

The story told in the introduction of this book, to which similar occurrences can be added, seems to belong in the same category. The facts of telekinesis are undeniable. In the previous chapter was described that case of a diabolical possession when the body of the possessed was lifted into the air and remained thus for more than a half-hour. Are these phenomena equivalent to those in which the Host "flies through the air" to the privileged saint? There are reports of men and women, whose integrity is above suspicion, which tell of heavy tables and other pieces of furniture moving and lifting themselves up in a completely illuminated room and in the presence of ten, fifteen, or twenty persons. There are, of course, instances that are fraudulent—but not in the lives of saints. In his *Las Fraudes Espiritistas y Los Fenomenos Metaphisicos* (1931), C. N. de Heredia, S.J., describes cases in which the medium was in contact with the furniture, but he also reports others where no fraud was employed. And Padre Heredia himself was an expert prestidigitator. Thurston describes the accordion of Daniel Home. Daniel Home was an English medium, who for twenty-two years, 1855 to 1877, had exhibited an accordion that played with marvelous mastery—and *without being touched*—anything that was desired by people who participated in the seances. Home produced other "occult" phenomena. It is alleged that he "floated out of one window on the third floor . . . and in again at the furthermost window of an adjoining room."[4] Is it the devil's work or a purely natural phenomenon?

As for the reported telekinetic phenomena in the lives of saints, there seems to be no doubt about the veracity of such reports: thus we are faced with a genuine miracle. It should be added, however, that there have been many false mystics during the centuries, like Magdalena de la Cruz (1487–1560), whom for decades the Spaniards considered a living saint. Later it proved to be a deception. In the 19th century there was much discussion of the case of the miraculous communion of Palma d'Oria. When Pope Pius IX read the papers submitted to him, he cried out that these were sheer trickery.

In the case of diabolical possession, a telekinetic phenomenon could clearly be the work of the demon. But in the case of Home and others, to date no clear answer has yet been forthcoming. Heredia considers these seeming abnormalities to be purely natural, i.e., the violent movements of the furniture, and like prodigies, are produced by a purely natural force, exercised and controlled by the subconscious of the medium. This is close to the opinion of Professor Charles Richet, who attributes these activities to plasm (teleplasm) invisibly emanating from the medium. The spiritists, notably Sir Oliver Lodge, explain it by the presence of spirits. The Church has expressed no official opinion.

In levitation, another form of telekinesis, objects or persons defy the laws of gravitation, lifting themselves up and remaining in mid-air without external help. Again we must distinguish between levitation recorded in the lives of saints and alleged levitation produced deliberately. There is also the levitation resulting from diabolical influence, as reported in our chapter on satanic forces. The most famous cases, witnessed by people of undoubted integrity, were the levitation cases already mentioned in connection with Daniel Home in 1868. Thurston quotes the description of *The Spiritualistic Magazine*: "An invisible power then supported Mr. Home all but horizontally in space and thrust his body into space through the open window, head foremost, bringing him back again feet foremost into the room, shunted not unlike a shutter into the basement below."[5] Without going into technical detail and discussion, we share Thurston's opinion, which he summed up as follows:

"Assuming, then, that we have reasonable ground for crediting the fact of levitation, there remains the question of its possible explanation. Theologians for the most part offer the rough and ready solution that in the case of holy people it is a manifestation of divine power, effective perhaps through the ministry of angels; but that in such cases as those of Simon Magus, sorcerers, and spiritualistic mediums, it is the work of the devil. Without venturing to reject this explanation outright, I find certain difficulties, too complex to summarize here, which suggest that it would be wise to suspend our judgment. I may confess that as regards the levitation of material objects (e.g., heavy dining-room tables) without contact, the spiritualistic evidence seems to me quite convincing, and if a table can be suspended in the air, it is hard to see why a man cannot. Sir Oliver Lodge adumbrated a spiritistic theory to explain these phenomena, Professor Charles Richet a materialistic one. They attribute strange activities to the ether, to teleplasm, to cryptaesthesia, etc.; but it seems to me that in the present state of our knowledge we cannot even decide whether the effects observed do or do not transcend the possible range of what may be called the psychophysical forces of nature."[6]

Levitation took place in the life of many saints and mystics. One of the greatest saints of the Church, St. Teresa of Avila, described her own levitation in this way:

"I repeat it; you feel and see yourself carried away you know not whither. For though we feel how delicious it is, yet the weakness of our nature makes us afraid at first . . . so trying is it that I would very often resist and exert all my strength, particularly at those times when the rapture was coming on me in public. I did so, too, very often when I was alone, because I was afraid of delusions. Occasionally I was able, by great efforts, to make a slight resistance, but afterwards I was worn out, like a person who had been contending with a strong giant; at other times it was impossible to resist at all; my soul was carried away, and almost always my head with it—I had no power over it—and now and then the whole body as well, so that it was lifted up from the ground.

"This (the being lifted up into the air) has not happened to me often; once, however, it took place when we were all together in choir, and I, on my knees, on the point of communicating. It was a very sore distress to me; for I thought it a most extraordinary thing and was afraid it would occasion much talk; so I commanded the nuns—for it happened after I was made Prioress—never to speak of it. But at other times, the moment I felt that our Lord was about to do the same thing again, and once in particular during a sermon—it was the feast of our house, some great ladies being present—I threw myself on the ground; then the nuns came around to hold me; but still the rapture was observed.

"I made many supplications to our Lord, that He would be pleased to give me no more of those graces which were outwardly visible; for it was a grievous affliction to me that people should make so much of me, and because His Majesty could honor me with His favours without their becoming known. It seems that, of His goodness, He had been pleased to hear my prayer, for I have never been enraptured since. It is true that it was not long ago."[7]

Levitation (or apparent levitation) has been experienced by many other saints, in modern times, too, such as St. Peter Claver (1654), St. André Hubert Fournet (1821), St. Joseph Cottolengo (1824), St. John Bosco (1856), and St. Gemma Galgani (1878–1903)—to mention but a few.

Still other unbeatified mystics have received the grace of levitation. We mention here only a Syrian Carmelite nun (died 1878) who (according to her biographer) was lifted to the top of a tree, and Suor Maria della Passione (died 1912), who one day when very sick was carried by an invisible force up the stairs that led to her cell, without once touching the floor. This happened after she took Communion. Padre Pio, the Italian Capuchin whose case we describe in the Appendix, and who at this writing lives in Italy, is said to have been levitated several times. There are of course cases of fraud and suggestion. We deal here, however, with cases that have considerable evidence.

In the life of Daniel Home, we find several instances of bodily elongation (a fact also reported of some of the saints). According to witnesses, Home grew from six to eight inches—with his feet firmly planted on the ground. Among the saints there are occasions when only their limbs were elongated. In each case fraud seems to be out of the question. In 1880, Marie-Julie Jahenny, a French stigmatic, produced a shrinking of her body and shortening of her limbs. According to Thurston, "Her whole frame shrank together into a sort of ball." It is important to note that all such phenomena occurred in a state of trance. There is, however, insufficient evidence to venture further explanation.

CHAPTER 5

Mystics and Schizophrenics

One summer day in 1900 the pastor of a parish outside Paris told a doctor that he had witnessed an apparently miraculous cure, and asked the doctor for his advice. The putative miracle concerned a woman nearly forty years old, the mother of three children. The husband, a minor civil servant, had been transferred from another city, and his family had followed him. Their troubles had started upon their arrival in the new town in April of the same year. Only a few days after they were settled the woman, Mrs. F. E., lost her speech as well as her eyesight, and was forced to stay in bed because of a continuous high fever. This went on until June 13, when her condition became so critical that Extreme Unction was administered to her. From that day on her fever rose and oscillated between 105 and 108.° On July 2 the sick woman expressed the desire to receive Holy Communion, but when it was brought to her she was able to swallow only a minute particle of the Host because of her incessant vomiting.

After Communion, as she was praying, her husband had a "strange impression." It seemed to him that something had happened in the room: "As if something were present there," a strange feeling of "fullness," as he explained later. He asked the priest, who was still in the room, whether he too had experienced a similar sensation. The priest said that he had not, but that he had noticed that while the husband described this sense of "fullness," a smile had appeared upon the face of the sick wife. Accompanying the priest to the door, the husband told him that he was sure his wife had been cured. In fact, no sooner had the priest arrived home than the husband came to the rectory to report that his wife had completely recovered. The priest returned immediately to the sick room and ascertained that all the signs of the illness had disappeared. The woman talked, and her temperature was normal. Moreover, on the following day Mrs. F. E. resumed her normal routine.

Immediately thereafter she was subjected to a detailed medical and psychiatric examination. The examination disclosed that earlier, upon losing a child during birth, she had become ill and manifested the same symptoms. During the period of the examination, which continued for about a year, Mrs. F. E. had ecstasies and sudden effusions of blood on her limbs. Talks with her disclosed that she considered religion only as an occasion for suffering and that one of her innermost desires was "to save priests." The great French psychiatrist, Jean Lhermitte, after a careful examination, came to this conclusion: "All the phenomena are characteristics of hysteria, the sudden blindness and its disappearance, the excesses of meningitis accompanied by vomiting, etc., attacks of lethargy, all have been effects of what Charcot has called 'the great simulator—hysteria.' Like the majority of mythomaniacs the hysteric is impelled by an imperative urge to attract attention to herself and causes the strangest phenomena."[1]

It is obvious that without the intervention of energetic and competent doctors, credulous people—many of them in good faith—would have believed that a miracle had occurred. Medical examination, however, disclosed that it was a case of hysteria. It might be asked, then, whether the borderline between the manifestations of hysteria and other mental illnesses is so tenuous that they could be confused with the effects produced by miracles. The answer is Yes.

Here we shall cite another important case, that of a middle-aged nun, Sister O., who always went to confession to the same priest. For a number of years she had been confessing the same sin, which in reality was nothing but a temptation against chastity. One day the priest, never imagining the effect his words would have upon the nun, told her, half in anger, half in jest: "My dear daughter, you are obsessed." From this moment on, Sister O. literally became obsessed with the idea of obsession, and behaved as though she were possessed by the devil. The priest, erroneously believing it to be a case of diabolism, began a series of exorcisms without asking permission of the bishop. The poor nun was submitted to 300 exorcisms within the space of a year. The more exorcisms attempted, the more "obsessed" she became. Jean Lhermitte, together with one of the French Carmelites, also a psychiatrist, examined Sister O. During the medical examination they asked her to read a text where the name of the devil was mentioned. Instead, the pseudo-obsessed nun threw them an angry look, ripped off her veil, and began to dance wildly. And as she danced she poured a stream of obscene insults on the doctor and the priest. In short, her behavior was in complete accord with the description of mental automatism contained in medical tracts. After the second visit the two doctors decided to resort to shock treatment. Thus, results that were not achieved after one year of exorcism were obtained after a month of careful psychiatric treatment. Of the demon there was no trace or shadow.

Karl Stern, in *The Third Revolution, Psychiatry and Religion*,[2] writes that his students frequently asked him to explain the difference between a schizophrenic patient and a mystic like St. Teresa of Avila, since one of the symptoms of the schizophrenic—hallucinations—resembles certain symptoms accompanying the visions of a saint. According to Stern, however, "One can say that two psychic phenomena can belong in the same category and yet one be normal and the other pathological. They are phenomenologically the same, but within their respective contexts they have two entirely opposite values."

Mozart is an excellent example of such phenomena. He actually heard his music before composing it.[3] According to medical science, therefore, Mozart must have been an "hallucinator," i.e., a sick man. Phenomenologically there was something abnormal in him because "to be hallucinated is not the norm." Nevertheless, this phenomenologically abnormal person was not pathological. Karl Stern has designated it "supra-normal, above the normal." Both Mozart and Teresa of Avila were "healthy," for they did not insist that their "supra-normal" experience be an experience shared by everyone.

There is, again according to Karl Stern, a close phenomenological relation between paranoia and faith. The faithful who claim to possess truth look foolish in the eyes of the world. But they have developed a logical and coherent system of thought on the basis of their faith. The believing person sees "things behind things" as does the paranoiac but, as Stern writes, "While the climate of paranoia is distrust and its fruit is hatred the climate of faith is confidence and its fruit is love. Paranoia is the mirror image of faith in an ugly distortion."

This answers the question of how and where to draw the borderline on the one hand between faith, miracles, true diabolical obsession, and on the other hand between paranoia, hysteria, schizophrenia, etc.

With regard to diabolical possession we shall again cite Jean Lhermitte. In the opinion of this French psychiatrist: "There exist genuine psychopathic states whose chief symptom is the notion that the moral or physical personality, or perhaps the entire personality, is possessed by the devil. These states may be divided into two quite distinct types: the first is marked by the brutal, catastrophic occurrence of possession, which takes place during trances or severe crises, when the consciousness is in a state of more or less complete dissolution; the second is more complex, and consists of a strictly predetermined psychosis, whose development can be foreseen, and of which a very grave prognosis can be made."[4]

If pathological obsession can be mistaken for diabolical possession the question arises, whether the physical phenomena of mysticism can be the result of a pathological state, and, finally, whether any kind of illness or disease can be cured through psychic process. The answer is Yes, but it is the task of medical science to determine treatment of the case. If the psychiatrist in question does not believe in God, or at least leaves no margin for the unknown, he will tend to explain everything from a materialistic point of view. To such a psychiatrist, using Karl Stern's line of thought, Abraham's willingness to sacrifice his son Isaac would be as insane a gesture as that of St. Francis of Assisi, who "flung his clothes in his father's face," or that of St. Benedict Joseph Labre who wandered all over Europe unkempt, unclean, and covered with vermin. The rationalist would not concede that "God loves man with the madness of love, and he tries man's love to the point of madness."[5] The totally one-sided psychoanalyst would explain Bernadette's vision of the Blessed Virgin by analyzing her relationship to her mother, and he would conclude that "at that moment she had to produce a hallucinatory Great Mother."

Again, where draw the line? Karl Stern suggests that "The physician . . . no matter how firm his belief is, has to use the reductive method, the argument of 'nothing but.' By and large the distinction between morbid and healthy is not difficult. For example, where spiritual asceticism ends and compulsiveness (the scruple) begins is usually quite apparent in the picture of the total personality. What we have said about sanctity holds true here also; quite often the distinction between what is healthy and what is morbid in the spiritual life comes down to the simple rule—by their fruits you shall know them."

In our discussion of the principles underlying the definition of miracles it was stated that the miracle is a manifestation of God when He wishes to enlighten, to warn and help men, and, through such an event, to elevate and unite man with Himself. The true miracle is religious in nature and its significance is immediately understandable, whereas the false "miracle" is devoid of meaning. It is lost in chaos. Grotesque, vulgar, useless, pointless manifestations cannot be regarded as miracles. Furthermore, it was said that the miracle occurs with relative infrequency and that it is reasonable and of moral character. It has a spiritual finality, it is conducive to individual or general welfare, and though instantaneous, it can develop progressively. Finally, the effect of the miracle must be enduring.

In discussing the diabolical, reference was made to the Roman Ritual in order to discern the signs of actual diabolism.

These principles and precepts measured against the latest results of scientific research will provide an answer, not complete but tentative. After citing the case of St. Angela de Foligno, Karl Stern observes that "what she went through before she got there is described in words which are shocking and scandalizing to any modern reader, regardless of his clinical experience or lack of it." Quoting the description of her mystical state, Karl Stern writes: "Subtract the world of GRACE from all this, and nothing but neurosis remains. . . . it is almost too tempting not to wheel the psychological microscope into focus. Yet what would we obtain by it? It is, as Jung once said, like attempting a description of Cologne Cathedral by examining its stones chemically."

Armed with such precautions we can now look into some of the famous cases of false mystics, and cases yet unsolved.

England produced one of the strangest of fake mysteries, a certain John Thom, whom Father Thurston called "a pseudo-messiah and stigmatic."[6] Thom, who was not a Catholic, was born in 1799 and died as a farm laborer in 1838. He had always behaved "strangely" and finally he was committed to a mental hospital, where he called himself "Courteney, Knight of Malta, King of Jerusalem." In a manifesto he once declared himself to be a Messiah. In 1833 he started a newspaper, The Lion, written entirely by himself, in which he denounced Catholics and Protestants alike. Although it was known that he had been in an asylum, many people believed in him and became his followers.

Once, while working as a farm hand in the neighborhood of Canterbury, he delivered a subversive speech against the Crown. A warrant was issued against him, and when the police came to arrest him, he shot one of them. In the subsequent pitched battle between the police and his followers, thirteen people were slain, including the pseudo-Messiah himself. It was said that he bore stigmatic wound marks, which most probably were artificial. According to Thurston, the man was insane; yet his acts and expressions were of extreme interest. Thom exercised a great influence over a large number of people in Kent, forty miles from London. His insanity was acknowledged by some but not by others of his followers. His case bears a striking resemblance to that of Zelea Cordeanu, founder of the Legion of St. Michael, which was the predecessor of the fascist Iron Guard. Both apparently were compulsive hysterics.

Mention has been made of the stigmata—that is, the wound marks of Christ on the cross—in connection with John Thom. The very problem of stigmata is a case in point in the relation between psychiatry and religion. St. Francis of Assisi bore the stigmata, and these were and are considered great miracles. Later, other mystics received the stigmata, and there are three known cases of living persons who have the wound marks of Christ. Although it is hard to determine which are true and which not, it is impossible that nature without the intervention of God could create stigmata. We are discussing now only genuine stigmata, not fraudulent markings, which are easily detectable and generally the result of a self-inflicted wound.

Historical and medical archives record between three hundred and thirty and three hundred and fifty cases of stigmatists, of whom only fifty involve males. Eighty of these persons have been canonized. According to the latest research, the first to be canonized was St. Francis of Assisi, who received the stigmata in a vision on Mt. Alvernia in 1224, two years before his death. The Church has declared on several occasions that the wound marks of St. Francis are authentic and that their character is supernatural.

At this point a distinction should be made between stigmata that are deeply imbedded in the flesh of the person in question, as in the case of St. Francis of Assisi, whose hands and feet were pierced through and lesser wounds.

There are other, smaller wound marks and bleedings that may occur in highly excited, intensely passionate (neurotic) cases. It is known that sweating blood is not a miraculous phenomenon. The red color of the sweat is due to cromogene microbes or chemical processes. Since 1933 reliable experience has proved that in certain psychopathological cases the patient may produce wound marks, faintly similar to the real stigmata. But no experiment has ever produced wound marks identical with the authentic stigmata of St. Francis of Assisi or of any of the great mystics.

Thurston has cited, among others, the case of Mother Beatrice Mary of Jesus, abbess of a convent of Poor Clares in the Spanish city of Granada. According to her biographer, Mother Beatrice Mary entered the convent in 1665. At the age of 33 she fell "into an extraordinary condition in which she exhibited all the external characteristics of a little child of 4 years old." This condition continued, with interruptions, for about ten days. She had ecstasies and fell into trances that sometimes lasted an entire day. It was learned that earlier in her life, "she also suffered at frequent intervals from paralytic seizures." Moreover, her hyperesthesia was so strong that although she was allowed because of her ill health to eat meat during Lent she fell into convulsions when she smelled the food. Thurston described it as a typical case of conversion hysteria.

But this was not all. Although she desired the wound marks of Christ, Beatrice prayed that no such grace should descend upon her because that would attract attention. Nevertheless, on May 30, 1664, "after her crucifixion agony of three hours," she fell into a state of unconsciousness. Upon undressing her, a "crescent-shaped wound on her left breast" was discovered. Her fasts had lasted longer than any human being could normally endure. One lasted for 51 days. Her biographer also discusses levitation in connection with her but the description is so vague that it can be safely disregarded.

After comparing Mother Beatrice's case to others (mostly hysterics), Thurston concluded: "There is, it seems to me much still to be learned about morbid psychology before we can safely talk of the supernatural in cases where a disassociation of consciousness is either indicated or apprehended" . . . "The fact that there were no stigmatized before St. Francis of Assisi is a very important point for the researcher . . . What I infer is that the example of St. Francis created what I have called the 'crucifixion complex.' Once it had been brought home to contemplatives that it was possible to be physically conformed to the sufferings of Christ . . . then the idea of this form of union with their Divine Master took shape in the minds of many. It became in fact a pious obsession; so much so that in a few exceptionally sensitive individuals the idea conceived in the mind was realized in the flesh."[7]

The pseudo-stigmata of hysterical origin "vary . . . in degree according to the suggestibility of the particular subject. . . . It is noteworthy that in a good many cases the development never goes any further than a certain deep reddening of the skin or the formation of something resembling a blood blister."[8]

After 1918 it was proved that hysteria is not an exclusively feminine disorder, yet women are still more subject to it than men. This is important because of the higher incidence of women stigmatics in history. Thurston goes so far as to say that "there is hardly a single case in which there is not evidence of the previous existence of a complication of nervous disorder before the stigmata developed." Thurston lists many of the doubts in connection with "the alleged supernatural character of the stigmatization phenomenon." Many of these women were deeply religious, though afflicted by hysteria. Thus one can only reiterate his judgment: "There is, it seems to me, much still to be learned about morbid psychology before we can safely talk of the supernatural in (these) cases."[9]

Among the more recent "mystics," one of the most famous (and as yet not completely solved), was Anne Catherine Emmerich, born in 1774 in Westphalia, Germany. Her parents were poor, hard-working peasants. At the age of seven she was able to narrate Bible stories in so vivid a manner that when her father asked her where she had learned them, his daughter declared, "I saw them." As a child she already practiced self-mortification, prayed day and night, and expressed a wish to enter a convent when she was 15. But the poverty of her parents prevented the realization of this wish before she was 28, at which time she became an Augustinian nun. When the convent was suppressed, as a result of the secularization, she fell sick and remained bedridden all her life. Anne Catherine continued to have visions that became known all over Germany, and wound marks appeared on her limbs. Throughout her life Anne Catherine remained a pious woman and had many extraordinary visions.

Her case became even more famous as a result of her meeting with the romantic German poet, Clement Brentano. After their first meeting the poet never left her bedside, where he made notes of her visions, later publishing them. In her visions Anne Catherine recounted stories from the Old and the New Testament and the history of the Church to the poet. Her descriptions of certain Biblical scenes, for instance, the story of Mary Magdalene and many others that are of the greatest beauty and unique insight, are recorded by Brentano. In 1823 she predicted her own death. Her suffering increased, her visions became ever more terrifying and full of horrors. She died on February 9, 1824. According to her account, her guardian angel had appeared to her and while her body had remained in bed the angel had led her around the world. On the day she received the stigmata (December 29, 1812), Christ appeared to her almost in the same way as He had appeared to St. Francis. The wounds were bruises from which blood flowed. Thurston has pointed out that the cross wound on her breast had a Y-shape, exactly the same shape as the crucifix which had such a great influence upon her in her childhood, and which she venerated in a most extraordinary way.

Another stigmatized woman, Gemma Galgani (1878–1903), was recently canonized. Throughout her life she had extraordinary ecstasies and seemed to be the source of miraculous events, which will be described in our chapter on 19th century saints. Gemma Galgani received the stigmata on June 8, 1899. According to her biographer, on the day following Communion, "the Lord let her feel that he prepared a unique grace for her for the same evening. She did not know it yet, but she ran to advise her confessor and asked him for general absolution. . . ."[10] That evening she felt great pains on both sides and she thought that she was going to die. She concentrated on her prayers and fell into an ecstasy. She had a vision of the Blessed Virgin.

Gemma received a vision of the Blessed Virgin, who assured her that all her sins were forgiven and then enveloped her in her mantle; and in this state Gemma witnessed the Passion of Christ, from whose wounds not blood but flames streaked toward her, licking at her hands and feet. She felt such a mixture of pain and joy that she thought she was going to die. Indeed, in her autobiography she wrote that she would have died if the Blessed Virgin had not helped her. Still enveloped in Mary's mantle, Gemma rested against her, passing several hours in this state. Then the vision kissed her and disappeared. After the ecstasy Gemma found herself kneeling on the floor, her entire body wracked with pain. She tried to lift herself up without success. Her wounds were bleeding. She wanted to hide them but it was impossible. Other visions had also come to her. On the basis of her canonization, therefore, her mystical experience should be accepted as authentic. Gemma Galgani's autobiography runs to several hundred pages. Some of these pages bear mysterious signs

St. Nicholas of Bari with the three children whom he raised from the dead. Painting in the Church in St. Goar, Germany. Artist unknown.

St. Martin of Tours sharing his cape with a beggar. B relief by the Master Naumburg in the Church of Bassenheim, Germany.

Left: St. Nicholas of Bari saving a sinking boat. Painting by Gentile da Fabriano in the Vatican.

The vision of St. Augustine. Painting by Botticelli in the Uffizi Gallery, Florence, Italy.

(Alinari, Rome)

St. Francis of Assisi appears in a vision to the Franciscan monks. Painting by Giotto in the Gallery of Ancient and Modern Art (Galleria Antica e Moderna), Florence, Italy.

St. Anthony of Padua healing the sick. Painting by Francesco Pesellino in the Gallery of Ancient and Modern Art, Florence, Italy.

St. Elizabeth of Hungary. Stained window at the Elizabeth Church in Marburg, Germany.

Left: St. Catherine of Siena. Fresco by Andrea Vanni in the St. Dominic Church, Siena, Italy.

The Blessed Virgin appears to St. Bernard. Painting by Fra Bartolommeo at the Accademia, Florence, Italy.

St. Margaret of Cortona. Painting by Giovanni Barbieri della Quercia in the Vatican.

as if somebody sought to deface or cancel out certain lines. The signs cannot be removed and a chemical analysis of them failed to solve the mystery of their origin. Several theologians are inclined to attribute these signs to diabolical intervention.

The stigmata of Gemma Galgani may be considered genuine, but what is one to say about two living stigmatics—the Bavarian Theresa Neumann and the Italian Capuchin priest, Padre Pio?

It is worth while to cite first the strange case of a Brooklyn woman known as a clairvoyant, who for years ate no food whatsoever. Thurston deals at length with her case. Mollie Fancher was born in 1848 in Brooklyn, and lived there and in Manhattan alternately. She died in 1894. It is not certain whether she had contracted tuberculosis in her childhood; but what is certain is that as a result of two accidents, one in 1865 and the other in 1866, she became a complete invalid and did not leave her bedroom for thirty years. First her legs became atrophied, then blindness struck her, and thenceforth for many years she received no food. It is said that Mollie could read the contents of sealed letters. She knew what was written in a book merely by putting her hands over its pages. And by merely touching a piece of material she could tell its color. She almost never slept. Significantly, she had no connection whatsoever with spiritualists, nor any interest in such practices. Her case was, and is still, subject to the closest research because of its resemblance to that of Theresa Neumann of Konnersreuth, Bavaria, and another German "mystic" of the last century, Anne Catherine Emmerich (both already mentioned).

No full medical explanation has yet been offered of the case of Mollie Fancher, though at the time of these curious happenings she was visited by many persons who examined her thoroughly. Hers appears to have been a complicated case of hysteria.

Hundreds of articles and many books have been written about Theresa Neumann. Although the facts of her case are well known, a brief summary may be in order here. Theresa Neumann was born in 1898, in the small Bavarian village of Konnersreuth. Her parents were typical hard-working, God-fearing Bavarians. Her father was a tailor, but he also possessed some land which he cultivated with the help of his family. Theresa grew up in the deeply Catholic atmosphere so characteristic of Bavaria, where in the smaller villages piety is not completely devoid of remnants of superstition. Theresa was a strong, healthy girl and quite attractive. When she reached the age when peasant girls were expected to marry she told her would-be suitors that she planned to become a nun. At the request of her father, and also because of the outbreak of World War I, she postponed the realization of her plan.

Nothing extraordinary ever happened to Theresa Neumann until March 10, 1918. On this day, fire broke out in the village and, like everyone else, Theresa helped to put out the fire by joining the water-bucket brigade. On one trip she stumbled and dropped her bucket, complaining at the same time of pains in her back. This was the day when her "troubles" started, from which she has never recovered. She complained of other maladies, too, including failing eyesight. Finally, six weeks later, the family sent her to a hospital. Here she concealed the fact that she had convulsions almost every night, and after several weeks in the hospital she was released. At home Theresa's condition deteriorated constantly. Since she could barely walk, she could not go to church, so she asked for Extreme Unction. And in December, 1919, she began to cough up blood. Everyone in the village expected Theresa Neumann to die. Doctors were unable to diagnose her case. She could not eat or drink, and she felt a constant pain in her back. But she bore her suffering in silence and with dignity.

On April 29, 1923, when she read the news of the beatification of St. Thérèse of the Child Jesus (Thérèse of Lisieux), she felt suddenly well. Her family thought that she was completely cured, and, further, that this "miraculous" cure should be submitted as evidence in the canonization process of St. Thérèse. Theresa Neumann had told her family that "a light appeared above her bed" and that an inner voice had told her to fear nothing, and that only through suffering could she realize her desires. Far more souls have been saved through suffering than by the finest sermons, this inner voice had said. The parish priest of Konnersreuth recognized this last sentence as an exact repetition of a sentence from a letter written by St. Thérèse of Lisieux. According to those who knew her well, Theresa

Neumann had never read those letters. Now she could walk and seemed to be in a normal state of health again. On September 30, 1925, she had a second vision, and on November 7, a third one. The most important phenomenon connected with her, however, is that since April 25, 1923, she has refused to take any solid foods. For some time she did receive liquid food but then she declared that she no longer felt the need to eat. Theresa Neumann has allegedly lived without eating any food for more than 33 years. During the Lenten season of 1926 Theresa again became sick: she contracted influenza and had an abcess in the right ear; in addition, her eyelids dripped blood. On the night between March 4 and 5—i.e., Thursday to Friday—of that year, she claimed to have had another vision, in which she saw Christ with the Apostles on the Mount of Olives. From this time on her alleged visions recurred, and in these visions she re-lived the Passion of Christ while the stigmata appeared on her hands and feet and on her sides. Many doctors and ecclesiastical authorities have visited her and investigated the case.

According to her own account, ". . . it is just as if everything I see and contemplate was taking place before me, right in front of me for the first time. . . . The first thing that I always see is Christ on the Mount of Olives." Further, she claims that she sees the scourging of Christ, His crowning with thorns, the jeering of the soldiers, the scene when they spit in His face, the Way of the Cross and the meeting between Jesus and His Mother: in short, all the important scenes related in the Gospels, including the crucifixion on Mount Calvary. The Church, however, treats the case of Theresa Neumann with extreme reserve. No judgment has yet been passed upon the authenticity of the stigmata or the visions.

Other extraordinary, so-called occult phenomena surround the case of Theresa Neumann. In her trances she seems to possess the gift of tongues. None of these phenomena, including that of being without food, has anything new about it. We have already mentioned the case of Mollie Fancher in Brooklyn in the last century. Many people also have been disconcerted by Theresa's claim that she can distinguish the saved from the damned. On one occasion she was asked what had happened to an excommunicated French priest who had died without absolution. She answered that the priest was saved. On another occasion someone submitted an unidentified relic to her, asking her to name the saint to whom it belonged. She promptly declared that it was the relic of "St. Marcel, laybrother." No such saint, however, is listed in the annals of the Church.

Jean Lhermitte, the French psychiatrist, writes as follows:

"The truth is that the life of these unfortunate people is very often extremely painful. They inflict upon themselves the most horrible tortures out of a morbid and extraordinary desire to identify themselves with the suffering Christ. But we cannot claim any right to deny the sincerity of their love. The fact that they are sick and affected by neurosis does not give us any right or pretext to forget that they are filled with love. We repeat, and repeat again, that there is nothing fraudulent in their state. They are not playing a comedy. They are not doing anything freely in full consciousness. The duty of the doctors is to liberate the sick, if necessary, even with the most drastic means, to liberate them from their psychoneurosis, and to treat these unhappy people with understanding and untiring charity."[11]

Prof. Lhermitte lists Theresa Neumann among the sick.

Here it is desirable to repeat the explanation that has been offered of the phenomenon of stigmatization. Most researchers declare that it usually occurs in a hysterical state when certain images in the mind of the patient can actually create functional disturbances and even lesions, which can in turn produce the phenomenon of bleeding.

"In reality corporal stigmatization in the life of any person has validity only in connection with the whole spiritual climate of the person; the phenomenon of stigmata must be judged exclusively from the point of view of the results and fruits of the life of a mystic and this is revealed only through a life of perfection seen after his death."[12]

What, Prof. Lhermitte has asked, would St. Theresa of Avila and St. John of the Cross, two of the greatest genuine mystics, have thought about ecstasies caused by a mere trance and sustained, sometimes, by an obvious eroticism? This is, indeed, an interesting question.

There are, of coures, "mystics" in modern times who could be characterized as totally morbid, hysterical, neurotics, that is, in search of pseudomystical experience. A famous case was that of the French pseudomystic, Rose Tamisier, which acquired a certain notoriety because her alleged "mystical" experience with St. Saturnin occurred before the apparition in Lourdes in 1850. Unfortunately, the true miracles in Lourdes were associated with the fake miracle of St. Saturnin by those who categorically denied the existence of all miracles, true or false. Rose Tamisier was born in a peasant household in 1818, the eldest of five children. She claimed to have had visions of the Blessed Virgin as early as the age of nine.

On November 10, 1850, together with a friend Josephine, Rose walked up to the shrine located on a hill of their native village and prayed in the little chapel there. Above the main altar of the chapel was a picture depicting the descent of Christ from the cross and to the left of this picture was a statue of St. Saturnin, patron of the village. As they were praying, Rose felt a compulsion to kiss the wound on the picture, and when she did so she felt that blood was literally dripping from the wound. From this moment on Rose went into a state of intense exaltation. It was claimed that she received Communion in a secret, mystical way—that is, that the Host went through the air to her. But it was also charged that Hosts were missing from the locked tabernacle on the altar of the church. More and more people, however, began to believe in Rose's "supernatural" experience, and the doubters and skeptics were furiously criticized by the village priest. The efforts of higher ecclesiastical authorities to ascertain the truth were hampered by the hysterical behavior of the villagers.

At length the "miracles" of Rose Tamisier came to a sudden end. She fell into the trap laid for her by two skeptical priests. One of these priests wrote her a letter in which he described supernatural phenomena that had really never occurred, among them being the reception of the Host through the air because of her intercession. She promptly answered him that God had indeed revealed to her the supernatural phenomena described in the letter. It was evident now that she was lying. The Archbishop of Avignon began his inquiry immediately after the first "bleeding" of the picture and, at the beginning of 1851, an ecclesiastical commission denied that any miracles had taken place. She was arrested for "offense against religion and for theft"—since she had stolen the Hosts for her "mystical communion." Rose spent twenty-four months in prison and refused to make any retraction. Even stranger is the fact that she refused to go to confession. There is not the slightest doubt that she was afflicted with a compulsive neurosis to lie, to appear important, and to seek notoriety.

False mystics and fake visionaries, unfortunately, are common and perennial phenomena around holy places and shrines.

Once a young woman presented herself at the Medical Bureau of Lourdes and, with a voice full of joy, announced that she had been totally cured. She claimed that she had an incurable fistula in her rectum and as a witness she had brought a nurse. The head of the Medical Bureau calmly asked the nurse how she could attest to the instantaneous cure of the fistula. Had she immersed the patient, for example, head downward into the basin? This would be the only way to see the sudden healing—if the patient escaped drowning. Whereupon both women retired, ashamed of themselves and their hoax that had failed. Another case involved a young man who, pretending to have been a deaf-mute since birth, also announced to the medical board that he had just been cured. Careful investigation, however, disclosed that he had regained his speech two years before in an institute for the deaf and dumb.

Obviously the reason for the fraud in the first case was an exhibitionist hysteria. The second case represented an attempt to exploit a false miracle for profit. The fake deaf-mute had had thousands of postcards printed with the inscription "Greetings from a cured person of Lourdes" which he offered for sale.

On July 2, 1954, a forty-year-old middle-class woman appeared before a church in Reggio Emilia, Italy. She attracted a crowd by claiming that the Blessed Virgin had favored her with a vision. And she told the crowd that the Virgin would reappear three months later. Although the ecclesiastical authorities had severely forbidden such demonstrations around the church and had refused any ecclesiastical assistance or encouragement, the woman came back seven times. She appeared at this church as recently as November, 1955, claiming again to have had visions. Ecclesiastical authorities discouraged the people from believing in these alleged visions; medical science is extremely skeptical about the mental condition of the *visionnaire*. Similar cases could be listed endlessly. But our aim has been to cite some of the more famous ones and to compare them with cases of authentic miracles in order to show how careful and conscientious is the approach of the Church in such matters.

The case of Padre Pio is totally different. Padre Pio is an Italian Capuchin monk, 69 years old: a normal, hard-working priest full of common sense and endowed with a gracious sense of humor. For the last thirty-seven years he has been living in the monastery of San Giovanni Rotondo, near Foggia, on the Adriatic coast of Italy. On September 20, 1918, the thirty-two-year-old Capuchin was immersed in prayer in the church, together with his brethren, when suddenly he collapsed, after which five wound marks appeared on his body. Two wound marks were on his palms, two on his feet, and one on his side. The wound marks, or stigmata, have never disappeared and on certain occasions they bleed copiously. The bleeding occurs when Padre Pio celebrates Mass. It is true, as an impartial observer has remarked, that it is almost impossible to describe a Mass celebrated by Padre Pio. The Mass begins at 5 A.M. and lasts more than an hour and a half.

During the summer of 1955 a young American priest decided to attend this famous Mass, and went with a friend, an Italian doctor, to the church for this purpose. There the doctor told him to wait in the corridor connecting the sacristy with the monastery, so that he could see Padre Pio as he walked to the sacristy. The American posted himself as suggested, but after about five minutes' wait he decided to forego his curiosity about the saintly Capuchin, who, anyhow, was besieged on all sides by all sorts of miracle-seekers. He withdrew into the sacristy, firmly determined not to approach Padre Pio. The Capuchin arrived and started to arrange the sacred vestments necessary for the Mass with the assistance of the Italian doctor. While assisting Padre Pio the doctor constantly motioned to the young priest to come closer, and he whispered the suggestion that he kiss the wound marks on Padre Pio's hand. The American did not follow these suggestions, having decided against kissing Padre Pio's hand since he was not convinced of the supernatural origin of the wound marks. Nor was he required to venerate any living human being as a saint.

Suddenly, after several further attempts by the doctor, Padre Pio calmly said: "Leave him in peace." At this moment the young priest approached, and Padre Pio, with a smile on his face but without a word, gently embraced him. Interpreting this as the gesture of an older and saintly brother priest, the American felt it was entirely proper to kiss the hand, but not the wound marks, of Padre Pio. As the American said to us later, it seemed as though the old Capuchin wanted to express at one and the same time his disapproval of veneration but his approval of true brotherhood in Christ. Now the young priest, still skeptical, could observe Padre Pio's Mass calmly and objectively.

The Capuchin begins in deep recollection. His gestures, his steps from the first moment when he pronounces the *Introibo* show that he is fully aware of the mystery that he is about to perform. Yet there is nothing extraordinary in his behavior. His celebration, however, after the Offertory, becomes different from any other Mass witnessed by any congregation. His gestures become increasingly slow, his steps, his every move, give the impression that he is working against an almost material, though invisible, hindrance. He works himself up, in the strictest sense of the word, to the Canon of the Mass. The Elevation lasts about fifteen minutes. The congregation senses that something extraordinary is going on. Padre Pio's eyes are fixed on an invisible point. When he elevates the Host and the Chalice, one can clearly discern that the blood is fresh. His hands are wrapped in absorbent cloth in order to protect the altar cloth and his sacred vestments. Half of the palm of each hand, however, is visible and it can be seen, even from a distance, that the wounds are bleeding profusely. After the Elevation his gestures and movements become slower and slower by degrees, never abruptly. At the end of the Mass he is once again completely himself.

It is hard for him to avoid the curiosity of the people. He chose the early hour for the celebration, convinced that this would deter many of the "tourists." Yet, as early as 5 A.M. there is always a crowd of people in the church and he is literally assailed by them. The young American priest observed that at least thirty persons volunteered to serve Padre Pio at his Mass, and that some left the church after the Elevation. But when later the young priest asked for an altar boy to serve his own Mass, nobody volunteered. Thus it is clear that for many people Padre Pio represents nothing but an interesting spectacle.

Is, then, Padre Pio a genuine mystic? Will the Church canonize him after his death? These questions would be superfluous and even sacrilegious had the same questions not already been answered in the affirmative by absolutely incompetent, unauthorized sensation-seekers, or credulously naïve fanatics. The correct and only answer is that nobody knows.

The case of Padre Pio has been discussed here primarily because of the appearance of the stigmata and not in order to speculate whether or not he is a saint or will be canonized as one. We do not deny, however, that he might be. The stigmata are genuine wound marks, but, as has been seen, stigmata can be produced by other than supernatural means. His case merits deeper consideration, for one very important reason: a medical examination of Padre Pio disclosed no sign or symptom whatsoever of hysteria. In the life of Theresa Neumann, it will be remembered, there is an important event that marks the onset of her "mystical experience"—namely, her collapse during the great fire that swept her village, and the sudden pain in her back which almost undoubtedly was of hysterical, neurotic origin.

In Padre Pio's life all this is conspicuously absent. He is completely normal. He walks about taking care of people on his routine pastoral duties; he eats and jokes. In the monastery he enjoys no special privileges. There is nothing morbid about his personality and there is nothing morbid in the fruits of his activity. People from all over the world send him money for which he has never asked. And if there is a genuine miracle (in the highest earthly sense of the word) in the life of Padre Pio, it is his success in building huge hospitals, in the neighborhood of the monastery, literally out of nothing. Can the stigmata of Padre Pio perhaps be explained by the same medical theory described by Thurston, even though the absence of any pathological element is strikingly evident? Yes, we think so.

Now, concerning his stigmata, there is a decision of the Sacred Congregation of the Holy Office, issued July 5, 1923, which states that the Holy Office, after due investigation, is of the opinion that the occurrences associated with the name of the devout Capuchin, Padre Pio da Pietralcina of San Giovanni Rotondo, have not been proved to be supernatural in origin. Further, the faithful were exhorted to maintain an attitude in accordance with the above declaration.

Since the Holy Office makes very few declarations, this one assumes great importance. The case of Padre Pio is not of hysterical origin because he has never fainted, nor has he had convulsions, horrible dreams, or nervous disorders. The question arises, then: How explain it? Medical science suggests another answer—the possibility of "suggestion neurosis," which could produce similar phenomena in persons who are otherwise balanced and who are not subject to any manifestations of hysteria.[13] Phenomena other than wound marks have occured in the life of Padre Pio. About his sanctity there is no question. He sometimes spends as many as eighteen hours in the confessional. He has the gift of clairvoyance and tells people who are total strangers to him about their lives. There are well-substantiated stories about miraculous cures through his instrumentality.

There are also persistent rumors that the Capuchin has the gift of bilocation. It is said, that is, that while remaining in his monastery of San Giovanni Rotondo he has been seen, and or has even spoken, in places hundreds of miles distant from the monastery. One of these rumors claims that he participated in the canonization ceremonies of St. Thérèse of the Child Jesus (Lisieux), although at that time he was actually in the monastery, where he celebrated his Mass and talked to people. As a matter of fact, Padre Pio has not left the immediate vicinity of San Giovanni Rotondo for more than thirty-seven years.

Some of the reported bilocation cases are very hard to authenticate. An Italian radio commentator who knew Padre Pio well tells the following story about himself. Once, just before beginning his broadcast, he suddenly experienced a headache so strong that it paralyzed him, making it impossible for him even to see. A few seconds later he saw Padre Pio entering his studio. The priest put his hand upon the commentator's head, whereupon the pain immediately disappeared. The commentator was convinced that the vision was nothing but hallucination. A few days later he visited Padre Pio and before he had an occasion to relate his experience, Padre Pio put his hand upon the commentator's head and said, smiling, "Oh, oh, these hallucinations. . . ." A Milanese electrician reported that while he was repairing an electric motor fed by high tension current, a short circuit resulted that destroyed the engine but did no harm to the electrician—this despite the fact that he had been holding two high-tension cables in his hands. Some months later he visited Padre Pio whom he knew, and the Padre whispered into his ear: "Be careful, be careful, with those cables."

Padre Pio is allegedly responsible for the miraculous restoration of sight to blind persons, and for instantaneously curing a child who was injured well-nigh fatally after falling from a second-story window. Many sick people have declared that they have seen Padre Pio come into their room and help them. Pilgrims who left the monastery, knowing that the Padre was still there talking to others, have claimed to see him walking on the beach several miles distant from the church.

That Padre Pio is a clairvoyant is a fact not to be questioned. Hundreds of people who go to him for confession have had the experience of being told their sins by Padre Pio before they began relating them. If a so-called penitent is not sincere, Padre Pio senses it immediately and tells him, very frankly, to go away and return after a month or even after a year, but totally penitent and contrite.

The church has made no official statement concerning these cures or any other phenomena (bilocation, clairvoyance, etc.) that have recently occurred in connection with Padre Pio.

The most tangible "miracle" is the great hospital built by Padre Pio about a hundred yards distant from the monastery. It cost more than a billion lire (about two million dollars), which is a considerable sum if it be borne in mind that most of the donations came from the little people in Italy and all over the world. Two hundred million lire were provided by UNNRA. This great hospital is the most modern in Europe.

As has been said, the case of Padre Pio deserves special study because even though the wound marks might be explained by suggestion neurosis, the life and works of this saintly Capuchin monk are anything but abnormal. During the last thirty-seven years, when the stigmata started, there has not been one incident in his life which could have been criticized by ecclesiastical or other authorities. He remains a humble priest, a servant of God and man. The sensationalism created around him is not his fault. He cannot prevent the publication of articles alluding to his eventual canonization, nor can he prevent people from looking at him with morbid curiosity. He does not invite anybody. His primary concern is the monastery and the care and cure of souls in its immediate vicinity.

The most recent case (1956) of alleged stimgatization involves a twenty-one-year-old Italian, Francis Santoni, a native of the island of Sardinia. He is known because of his great physical strength and unusual height, being well above 6 feet tall. But he is gentle and good-natured, and considered a benevolent "giant." Francis is illiterate, but of course he did receive some religious instruction as a child. In any case, he sweats blood from several parts of his body; blood appears on his forehead, and sometimes on his hands and feet. The phenomenon occurs when he is in a state of trance, and when the trance is over the bleeding stops and the blood disappears. During his trances Santoni is insensitive to pain, and does not react to the pricking of hot needles. The bleeding phenomena began late in 1955, and at this writing occurs repeatedly. At first sight it seems to be strictly a medical case.

CHAPTER 6

The Miracles of the Old Testament

The Old Testament is the history of the Christian religion. God manifested Himself from the very first day after the creation of man. He had a purpose with the human race, even after the Fall. God wanted to save man because He had created him out of love. But after the Fall, and because of it, human history inevitably became confused; violence and suffering became leading factors; mankind turned away from God, tended to believe only in itself, in its own pride and strength. Without the help of God, however, mankind would have been unable to formulate in an articulate way the greatest questions and obtain answers to them in each age: Who is God and what are His aims with us? God rescues mankind from confusion through salvation: first by the creation of chosen people to whom He revealed His Own Divinity, His precepts and prophetical messages. Through this chosen people He promised that mankind, doomed by the Fall, would be redeemed.

As Paul Claudel, the distinguished French poet, has written: "The Old Testament is not so much a continuous as a continuing history." It is the history, the doctrine and the rule of life, of the covenant concluded between God and His people. The condition of the covenant was the liberation from slavery in Egypt; its guarantees were the wondrous works—many of them true miracles—wrought by God in Egypt, in the Red Sea, and in the desert. The covenant itself was concluded amid the prodigious events that took place on Mount Sinai—the chief miracles of the Old Testament. God's purpose in these miracles was to let Himself be *known to His chosen people* in order to preserve them from evil and unite them around Himself.

"This history is ours," says Albert Gelin, "since, as St. Paul says, we are Abraham's descendants; and its great themes, its great constants, must be returned again and again. Then we can begin the unique actuality of the Old Testament."[1]

The Old Testament tells about the promise made to Abraham, whereby his descendants were to become the chosen people, created by God, "set apart from all others on the basis of a religion." Under Joshua this people finally achieved territorial and political unity to protect and symbolize its religious unity. The reign of David is the fullest flowering of this unity. Before the prophets appear, one great crisis after the other befalls this people, and the prophets raise their voices against the sins prevailing among the Jews. The political unity of the chosen people is destroyed, but its monotheism remains, i.e., its belief in the true universal God. After the exile the Temple is rebuilt, but other influences gain currency and attempt to contaminate the true religion with Greek ideas. In 63 b.c. the Romans become the rulers of Israel, and under Augustus, the special mission of the chosen people is ended.

In this sacred history are expressed those ideas that God defended by the giving of Himself, by chastising the people, and by constantly speaking through the prophets about the coming of the Redeemer. These fundamental ideas were the revelation of God, who is one and altogether spiritual and tolerates no idolatry; a God who is God and not a man; not an abstract God but a living God who is transcendent and always near. The Old Testament unfolds the plans of God. It is He who promised Abraham before the nation was created that "In thee shall all nations be blessed." In the Covenant God fulfills the promise. It is an act of love, a contract of marriage. It is not a simple trademen's pact on the basis of which one party gives something in exchange for something from the second party. The Covenant means that God will protect Israel if Israel obeys, and the pledge is the Ten Commandments. But the Covenant is not an end in itself, it leads towards the Messiah, i.e., to salvation: not only the salvation of a people, but the salvation of each and every individual.

If miracles are essential to the body of the New Testament they are even more so with regard to the Old Testament. One should never forget when reading the Old Testament that its miraculous element —the genuine manifestations of God—serve to protect the people elected to be the Vessel of Salvation from the continuous influences of hostile, pagan neighbors. And further it should be kept in mind that accepting the Bible as sacred, inspired Scripture, *one is always on holy ground.* The Old Testament is not only the history of the Jewish people, it is the history of the progenitors of the Christian religion. Thus it deals from beginning to end with the supernatural— God's way of manifesting Himself before He is sufficiently known.

The Scriptures and particularly the Old Testament should not be approached with the matter-of-fact attitude of a child who does not ask any questions about radio, television, or atomic energy, for he takes for granted all these achievements of science and technology. Those who discovered the laws underlying our scientific and technological achievements fought for a long, long time with resistant materials. The scientific revelation did not come easily or at once to man. And during the process there were many marvels to behold. The same is true in an infinitely higher sense of the Old Testament, which leads us on the road where true religion, the true link between God and man, has been established and revealed step by step. God had to prove His existence to a people that did not know Him, to a people whom He had chosen. But the price of this distinction was high, the burden of such formation heavy. (The Old Testament's Israel was the one "nonconformist" group in the entire known world!) God had to be constantly *with* his people in the literal sense of the word. Hence the great number of miracles in the Old Testament. One feels he is in a forest of marvels while reading the Old Testament.

As we have already explained, we are certainly bound to believe in the existence of miracles as a whole, but it would not be heretical to hold that some particular marvel narrated in the Old or New Testament is not actually a true miracle. The Church leaves adequate room for speculation concerning the miraculous character of specific events. The recent explicit approval by Pope Pius XII of the doctrine that there are varieties of literary form in the Bible emphasizes this freedom. Thus, it is arguable that the common, literal interpretation of the story of Jonas and the sea monster is not necessarily the correct one. Again, something might be said for the view that the Book of Tobias, with its strange miracles, is not really intended to be regarded as history.

The intentions of God are clear from the very first moment of sacred history. He rewards the virtuous and makes promises to Abraham—all through miraculous events. God took Henoch into heaven when he was 365 years old because he had led a very virtuous life informed by faith: "By faith Henoch was taken up lest he should see death" (Heb. 11:5). St. Paul is stressing the importance of faith in figures like Henoch, who believed implicitly in the testimony of God. "And all the days of Henoch were three hundred and sixty-five years. And he walked with God, and was seen no more: because God took him" (Gen. 5:23–24).

The destruction of Sodom and Gomorrha (in Gen. 19) was of divine origin because it came as a punishment, even though it might be explained by natural causes. Because the Sodomites had failed in the test proposed by God, the city was destroyed. According to Biblical research, "the cause of the disaster was probably the escape through earthquake action of compressed gases and petroleum from the subterranean deposits in the neighborhood of the doomed cities. Spontaneous combustion was apt to occur in such circumstances and domestic fires would quickly ignite the escaping gases and oil. Such a fire would cause immense, heavy floods of smoke. Thus the destruction of the cities was due to these natural forces. God can obviously make use of the agencies He has created."[2]

The selection of Jacob was also accompanied by signs and miraculous events. The vision in which Jacob saw a ladder in his sleep, "standing upon the earth, and the top thereof touching heaven, the angels also of God ascending and descending by it" (Gen. 28:12–13), is a physical vision whose specific purpose is to renew God's promise to Abraham of His intentions and His help: "And in thee and thy seed all the tribes of the earth shall be blessed."

Even more solemn is the second vision of Jacob, in which he wrestles with an angel (Gen. 32). Here, even more explicitly, God reveals His intentions and plans for him. Jacob did not realize that he was wrestling with an angel, but he had confidence in God, and God tested his confidence and strength by confronting him with a superhuman task. After the struggle God says to him: "Thy name shall not be called Jacob, but Israel: for if thou hast been strong against God, how much more shalt thou prevail against men?" (Gen. 32:28). In other words, Jacob's strength was from God. Now he understood that God would never abandon him and his seed to his enemies.

God manifested Himself directly and several times and in the most varied forms during the exodus from Egypt, until the offering for the Tabernacle. These miracles are at once important and interesting: important because, as has been said, they are articles of faith standing at the foundation of the Mosaic religion; and interesting, because they are manifold and give us an opportunity to determine which ones rose from natural causes and which were really miraculous.

God ordered Moses and Aaron to go to the Pharaoh and speak in the name of God, requesting freedom for the children of Israel. The Pharaoh wanted "signs and wonders" to prove that Moses and Aaron really were sent by God. Moses and Aaron turned the staff into a serpent and the waters of Egypt into blood. Since, however, the magicians could do as much, Pharaoh was not impressed; his heart was hardened, and he refused to allow the children of Israel to leave his land. Then other "signs and wonders" followed: the cattle were stricken with murrain, men and beasts got ulcers, and millions of frogs, clouds of mosquitoes and flies besieged Egypt. All this was wrought by God through Aaron and Moses. Still Pharaoh's heart did not soften. Then hail storms destroyed the crops, locusts devoured whatever remained, and finally darkness enveloped the entire country.

Biblical research rightly holds that "these nine plagues are not infrequent disasters which afflict the land of Egypt."[3] The crossing of the Jordan (Jos. 3:4) could be explained by an unexpected and sudden earthquake or landslide, since earthquakes are not rare in that region. In this event, was the crossing a miracle? Again, when the Israelites went to Jericho, the walls crumbled and fell down. Most recent archeological research has proved that one of the walls of the city actually did collapse, and some savants were ready to suggest that the cause was earthquake. If all these phenomena can be ascribed to natural causes, even by Catholic theologians, what, then, is miraculous about them?

The divine intervention in these instances was not the fact of the disaster itself, but the fact that these disasters befell the land and suddenly subsided at the apparent command of Moses. But there were other occurrences during the plagues which cannot be explained by natural causes and so should confirm our belief in divine intervention. For example, the children of Israel were immune to the effect of the flies; and it was only the first-born among the Egyptians who died. These two terrifying signs of God will dissipate any doubt of the miraculous character of the plagues. And when the Israelites finally left the land of Egypt, God multiplied miracles for them: "He led them out by the way of the desert," and "the Lord went before them to shew the way by day in a pillar of cloud and by night in a pillar of fire, that he might be the guide of their journey."

The passing of the Red Sea (Exod. 14) is another sign of God's love for the children of Israel, and serves as well as proof that God keeps His promises. "When Moses had stretched forth his hand over the sea, the Lord took it away by a strong and burning wind blowing all the night, and turned it into dry ground: and the water was divided. And the children of Israel went in through the midst of the sea dried up: for the water was as the wall on their right hand and on their left." The Egyptians who pursued them with all their chariots and horsemen were drowned when the sea returned "at the first break of the day to the former place."

The Old Testament is one continuous proof of the unceasing benevolence and self-manifestation by which God purposed to keep the Israelites faithful to the one true God. And yet, despite the miraculous exodus from Egypt and the great sign given them by the opening of the Red Sea, the people again murmured their dissatisfaction with God. In the next miracle, the next manifestation of God's existence and providence, God saw to it that the nation was well fed. "In the evening, quails [came] up toward the camp," and in the morning, "a dew lay round about the camp." This was certainly divine intervention, for quails come in the springtime from the interior of Africa to the Sinaitic Peninsula. Their appearance for the Israelites (in June) was thus much later than "the ordinary period of migration." God again used an ordinary natural phenomenon—but at His will, for so late an appearance cannot be explained by the statistical laws of probability, and, moreover, the quails were so numerous that forty thousand Israelites were provided with meat for one month.

The appearance of manna is a different kind of miracle. First of all, the Israelites were fed with manna all the time.

"This continuous and miraculous provision of food (manna) was a signal prodigy worked by Yahweh on behalf of his people. The bread from heaven was thus the most fitting type of the true bread from heaven, the Sacrament of the Eucharist, or spiritual food during our journey to the promised land. The manna, however, was not entirely praeter natural. A substance found beneath the tamarisk trees in Sinai in late May, June, and July is called manna by the natives. In an expedition to Sinai in 1927 two professors of the Hebrew University of Jerusalem discovered that it was produced not by the tamarisk tree itself but by two species of cochineal which feed on its leaves. The viscous substance falls to the ground during the night and appears in the morning in the form of little balls never bigger than a hazel nut and usually of yellow-brown color, and transparent. It must be collected early since ants appear after eight thirty A.M. and devour or carry away what they find. Once hardened it neither melts under the heat of the sun or becomes in any way corrupt. As its content is mainly sugar, it is very nourishing. The present annual output in Sinai is about 6 cwt., but the ancient yield was greater since there were more tamarisks. The Biblical narrative . . . agrees with this description. The manna is food from heaven for coming from above and also miraculously multiplied since the natural supply was altogether insufficient."[4]

The miraculous element, as we have seen, was not the existence of the manna but its multiplication.

Later in the Bible it is mentioned that suddenly the manna became tainted, although heretofore it had miraculously provided them with nourishment. "Neither had he more that had gathered more: nor did he find less that had provided less: but everyone had gathered, ac-

cording to what they were able to eat." The Jews had disobeyed
Moses when he ordered that no one should leave the camp until
morning. Thus, the manna that they gathered one day "began to be
full of worms, and it putrified, and Moses was angry at them" (Exod.
16).

The corruption of the manna was a miracle by which the people
were warned to obey God and trust in Him. It was miraculous, too,
that the Jews were fed by manna all the year round, although its
natural appearance is only during the months of May, June, and July,
and that on the sixth day they gathered twice as much as usual, it
was written that the seventh day should be completely dedicated to
the Lord.

A further miracle occurred when Moses smote the rock Horeb
and water gushed forth, providing the thirsty multitude with sufficient drinking water in the desert. This cannot be attributed to any
natural cause. It was a genuine manifestation of God, who once again
wished to demonstrate His care and love for His people.

The most important, indeed, the basic, miracle in the Old Testament, is the encounter between God and Moses, God and the chosen
people on Mount Sinai. Through the covenant entered upon here,
Israel became God's chosen possession. The climax of the series of
mystical events, one that shook the people like an earthquake for the
tremendous responsibility that it put upon every individual, was the
appearance of God. God appeared to Adam (Gen. 3:8), to Abraham
(Gen. 12:7), to Isaac (Gen. 26:2,24), and now to Moses for the
second time (the first time being during the episode of the burning
bush). It is the accepted opinion now that God did not appear Himself, since He cannot be seen by man, but that angels came representing God and speaking for Him. It was so important to God that He
make Himself known to the people to whom He desired to entrust
the truth, that He promised: "The third day the Lord will come down
in the sight of all the people upon Mount Sinai" (Exod. 19:11).
And truly when the morning of the third day appeared: "Thunders
began to be heard, and lightning to flash, and a very thick cloud to
cover the mount, and the noise of the trumpet sounded exceeding
loud" (as God had promised to Moses). "And when Moses had

brought them forth to meet God in the place of the camp they stood at the bottom of the Mount. And all Mount Sinai was on a smoke: because the Lord was come down upon it in fire, and the smoke arose from it as out of a furnace: and all the mount was terrible. And the sound of the trumpet grew by degrees louder and louder, and was drawn out to a greater length: Moses spoke and God answered him" (Exod. 19:16–19).

On the basis of objective and exhaustive research, one may rule out the possibility that a volcanic eruption took place on this occasion. The people had assembled on the lower slope of the mountain; thus, if there had been any lava it would have flowed downwards, frightening the people. And surely it would have been mentioned in the text. The smoke, according to Biblical research, is "a figurative equivalent of dark storm clouds."[5] Furthermore, the text clearly distinguishes between lightning and thunder before the appearance of God and the fire. The sound of trumpets was neither thunder nor was a fanfare provided by the Jews. Briefly, God wanted to "appear" on this supreme and most solemn occasion under such memorable circumstances that the people with whom He intended to ally Himself should shatteringly perceive the majesty and miracle of the occasion. While the miraculous manifestations of God during the ages differ visibly, according to the characteristics and the exigencies of each particular age, the purpose is always to achieve a supreme spiritual good. God Who is infinite goodness and the greatest reality—I AM WHO AM—almost pursues Israel with His love, despite the sins of the people. His purpose is the same in manifesting Himself in the burning bush on Mount Sinai, in the miracles of Jesus Christ, or in a miraculous healing in modern times. And this purpose is to remind man (not, to be sure, in a threatening manner) that He is the only, the ultimate reality, and that He wants man's love in exchange for His own.

Israel as a nation began with the revelations on Mount Sinai under the leadership of Moses. This is the beginning of the true religion based on the past of the Israelites. It is written that while Moses was feeding his father-in-law's sheep in the neighborhood of Mount Horeb, "The Lord appeared to him in a flame of fire out of the midst

of a bush: and he saw that the bush was on fire and was not burnt."
God could not manifest Himself in a clearer, and at the same time in
a more miraculous way. He wrought the miracle and then identified
Himself: "I am the God of thy father, the God of Abraham, the God
of Isaac, and the God of Jacob."

This was a proof that He was not a strange god and that the religion He would bestow upon the people was not something entirely
new; rather, that it had its roots in the past of this very people. God
knew that He was dealing with a stubborn people and that He had
to act according to their natures. (According to the Church, grace
works differently in each human being according to the peculiarities
of the person's nature and temperament). God immediately pledged
the Covenant: "And I will give favor to these people . . . and when
you go forth, you shall not depart empty." And He crowned His first
appearance to Moses with the statement that is and remains the key
and basis of every belief in a personal God: "I am who am. . . . Thus
shalt thou say to the children of Israel: HE WHO IS hath sent me to
you." With this miraculous appearance HE WHO IS declared Himself in His totality. "I am who am" means *ever-existing*, uncreated.
The burning bush that is not consumed by the fire stands at the
beginning of the Judaeo-Christian revelation as the miracle—the
mystery of the eternity and the love of God—that is unending.

The miracles of the Old Testament served to steel the will of the
Israelites and to teach them to distinguish good from evil in order to
keep pure their faith in one God. This is once more evident in the
miracle of the brazen (bronze) serpent. God intervened and the
Caananite king Arad was overcome, but afterward the people became
weary and troubled and again murmured against God and Moses:
"Wherefore the Lord sent among the people fiery serpents, which
bit them and killed many of them" (Num. 21:6). The frightened
people changed their attitude immediately and asked Moses to be
relieved. "Moses therefore made a brazen serpent, and set it up for a
sign: which when they that were bitten looked upon, they were
healed" (Num. 21:9). It is a clear sign of God's power as well as a
test of faith, since only God could perform a miracle whereby a person bitten by a serpent should be healed by looking up at a bronze

serpent fixed on a cross-like structure. This miracle also adumbrates the glorification of Christ on the cross, and the power of the cross.

In the story of the Battle of Gabaon we find similar evidence of God's unceasing providence:

> "And the Lord troubled them at the sight of Israel: and He slew them with a great slaughter in Gabaon, and pursued them by the way of ascent to Beth-horon, and cut them off all the way to Azeca and Maceda. And when they were fleeing from the children of Israel, and were at the descent of Beth-horon, the Lord cast down upon them great stones from heaven as far as Azeca; and many more were killed with the hailstones than were slain by the swords of the children of Israel.
>
> "Then Josue spoke to the Lord, in the day that he delivered the Amorrhite in the sight of the children of Israel, and he said before them: 'Move not, O sun, toward Gabaon, nor thou, O moon, toward the valley of Ajalon.'
>
> "And the sun and the moon stood still, till the people revenged themselves on their enemies. Is not this written in the book of the just? So the sun stood still in the midst of heaven, and hasted not to go down the space of one day.
>
> "There was not before nor after so long a day, the Lord obeying the voice of man, and fighting for Israel" (Jos. 10:10–13).

In this case as with Josue's miracle quoted above, it is very important to note the description. Authoritative Biblical scholars have pointed out that at Gabaon "the sacred writer is here not chronicling an astronomical observation or teaching us astronomy, he is really recording an ancient tradition . . . in language . . . adapted to the comprehension of his contemporaries who believed that the sun moved daily across the heavens and that the prolongation of the day or light period implied a temporary cessation of that movement. He did not teach or affirm anything about astronomy, or the other natural sciences, but accommodated himself to the ideas and language of his time in these matters. He did not err, therefore, by expressing his religious teaching in terms of an ancient astronomical belief now known to be false. Nor does his language authorize us to conclude that there was a disturbance in the movements of the heavenly bodies, since it was not an astronomical description but an accommodation to the ideas of his contemporaries. He did not describe the mechanics of the miracle; we only know that God said let there be light. And there was light, when according to nature there would have been darkness."[6]

The life of the prophet Elias is full of miraculous works. After Henoch, Elias is the only other holy man mentioned in the Old Testament who was taken up to heaven without first dying. This was a sign of extraordinary sanctity and particular grace—indeed, the exceptional grace of God, but Elias understood that he had been chosen, that he had to be humble and accept God's will. Elias lived at a time when a great religious crisis had fallen upon Israel. Human sacrifices were being performed, the monstrous pagan god Baal was venerated. When Yahweh gave him power to intervene, Elias challenged Baal, destroyed the altar of the monster god, and purified and reinstated the faith in the one and true God. Mount Carmel, where monotheism was reaffirmed, almost equals Mount Sinai in importance. It is obvious that the man who acted upon God's commands should be empowered with the gift of miracles; he should be able to prove that he was a prophet. Elias resurrected the dead son of a widow; and while he dwelt in a cave he was miraculously fed by ravens, who brought him bread and flesh in the morning and in the evening. After the destruction of Baal's altar, when Elias had to flee because he was pursued by Jezabel, he was miraculously fed by an angel in the desert. The food Elias received was enough for forty days; and, like the bronze serpent, it is an adumbration of things to come. The angelic nourishment of Elias was a symbol of the bread of life that Christ later instituted in the Blessed Sacrament.

God favored Elias once more with a vision, or better, with a message. First there was an earthquake and then a fire, but God was neither in the earthquake nor in the fire, for it is written, "And after the fire the whistling of a gentle air. And when Elias heard it he covered his face." God was speaking to him. This time, through this peaceful and calm vision, God wanted to temper Elias' great zeal. Finally, God took him without death up to heaven through the agency of His own inscrutable grace—inscrutable, because Moses the greatest did not receive this grace. After Elias and Henoch, the

Blessed Virgin was the only mortal to be assumed into heaven, according to revealed tradition confirmed in 1950 by the dogma of the Assumption pronounced in an *ex cathedra* statement by Pope Pius XII.

Two other miracles of the Old Testament can be cited as examples of precise and credible reporting. In IV Kings 20 we read that seven hundred fourteen years before Christ, the king of Judah, Ezechias, "was sick unto death." Upon the order of God, the prophet Isaias visited the dying king and told him that in three days he would be cured and healthy, and that he would live for fifteen more years. Ezechias, however, did not want to believe it; he was as skeptical as modern man. "And Ezechias had said to Isaias: what shall be the sign that the Lord will heal me?"

Isaias, however, believed the word of God and he offered an immediate sign to the skeptic. He asked Ezechias: "Wilt thou that the shadow go forward ten lines, or that it go back so many degrees?"

Ezechias, who was full of a critical spirit, pondered the question and replied: "It is an easy matter for the shadow to go forward ten lines: and I do not desire that this be done, but let it return back ten degrees."

"And Isaias the prophet called upon the Lord, and He brought the shadow ten degrees backwards to the lines, by which it had already gone down in the dial of Achaz." The attitude of Ezechias was, of course, naïve or unreasoningly critical because the acceleration of the shadow, which in itself was miraculous, was not a sufficiently convincing phenomenon for him.

In our second example (Dan. 3), Nabuchodonosor, the king of Babylon, set up a golden statue and commanded everyone to adore it. Three young Hebrews refused to do so, and as punishment they were cast into a fiery furnace.

"Then was Nabuchodonosor filled with fury. . . . And he commanded the strongest men that were in his army to bind the feet of Sidrach, Misach, and Abdenago, and to cast them into the furnace of burning fire . . . with their coats, and their caps, and their shoes, and their garments. . . . And the furnace was heated exceedingly. And the flame of the fire slew those men that had cast in Sidrach, Misach, and Abdenago.

But these three men, that is Sidrach, Misach, and Abdenago, fell down bound in the midst of the furnace of burning fire. And they walked in the midst of the flame, praising God and blessing the Lord. . . . The king's servants that had cast them in ceased not to heat the furnace with brimstone and tow, and pitch, and dry sticks. And the flame mounted up above the furnace nine and forty cubits; and it broke forth and burned such of the Chaldeans as it found near the furnace. But the angel of the Lord went down . . . into the furnace, and he drove the flame of the fire out of the furnace, and made the midst of the furnace like the blowing of the wind bringing dew, and the fire touched them not at all, nor troubled them nor did them any harm. . . . The fire had no power on their bodies, and not a hair of their head had been singed, nor their garments altered, nor the smell of the fire had passed on them."

It is remarkable with what detail the Old Testament author has described this miracle for his own and future generations. It was a testimony of the living God of Israel, revealing Himself as the one and true God in order to strengthen the faith of the chosen people whom He had entrusted with His mission.

The prophetic value of the Old Testament is immeasurable. The prophecies of the saints of the Christian world (with the exception of the Gospels) hardly approach, in volume and significance, the predictions of one Old Testament prophet. One of the greatest of them was Isaias, and we quote from his prophecies in order to reveal their special quality and to illustrate their fulfillment.

In one place Isaias wrote:

"Therefore the Lord Himself shall give you a sign. Behold, a virgin shall conceive, and bear a son, and his name shall be called Emmanuel" (Isa. 7:14).

This most important prophecy, as is well known, predicts the birth of the Messiah of the Holy Virgin.

In another place Isaias prophesied:

"For a child is born to us, and the government is upon his shoulder; and his name shall be called Wonderful, Counselor, God the Mighty, the Father of the world to come, the Prince of Peace. His empire shall be multiplied, and there shall be no end of peace; He shall sit upon the throne of David and upon his kingdom; to establish it and strengthen it with judgment and with justice, from henceforth and forever; the zeal of the Lord of Hosts will perform this" (Isa. 9:6–7).

This phophecy announced the birth of the Kingdom of Christ, the birth of a child, the Son of man who is God and Father of eternity. Isaias also prophesied the destruction of Babylon. This he did around 740 B.C. and Babylon was totally destroyed by Cirus the Great in 539 B.C.—that is, two hundred years later:

"Howl ye, for the day of the Lord is near: it shall come as a destruction from the Lord. Therefore shall all hands be faint, and every heart of man shall melt, and all shall be broken. . . . The day of the Lord shall come, a cruel day, and full of indignation, and of wrath and fury, to lay the land desolate. . . . For the stars of heaven . . . shall not display their light; the sun shall be darkened in its rising, and the moon shall not shine with her light. . . . Everyone that shall be found shall be slain; and everyone that shall come to their aid shall fall by the sword. Their infants shall be dashed in pieces before their eyes . . . and they shall have no pity upon the sucklings. . . . And that Babylon, the glorious among kingdoms, the famous pride of the Chaldeans, shall be even as the Lord destroyed Sodom and Gomorrha. It shall no more be inhabited forever, and it shall not be founded unto generation and generation: neither shall the Arabian pitch his tents there, nor shall shepherds rest there" (Isa. 13).

Isaias predicted not only the coming of Christ but even, in many details, His Passion. In Chapter 53 we read:

". . . He was wounded for our iniquities, he was bruised for our sins; the chastisement of our peace was upon Him, and by His bruises we are healed."

CHAPTER 7

The Miracles of the New Testament

The resurrection of Jesus Christ constitutes almost the exclusive basis and content of the preaching of the Apostles, who were "witnesses of the resurrection" (Acts 1:22). From the exhortations and sermons of St. Peter on the resurrection as reported in the Acts of the Apostles we derive the fundamental teaching of Christianity. In a sense the entire New Testament converges toward this supreme miracle, the miracle of the resurrection.

A good number, but by no means all, of the miracles of Christ are reported in the New Testament. St. John wrote that the miracles of Christ would fill all the books in the world (John 21:25). The recorded miracles of Christ, however, are not isolated signs, wonders, prodigious events. They all have one purpose—the same purpose that underlies the miracle of the resurrection—and it was clearly stated by the Evangelists and even more explicitly by Christ Himself. These miracles are supreme manifestations and testimonies of the Father; they are the miracles of the promised Messia, wrought so that the Jews, His contemporaries, and later all humanity, could believe in Him and accept Him as the Saviour.

The Old Testament describes how God saved His people, and how He contracted an alliance, the covenant, with them. In the Old Testament, God gave a mission to His people, He constantly instructed and chastised them, compelling the Jews to be the permanent bearers of the covenant, the servants of God, and the inheritors of all that was promised (Rom. 9:3). In the Old Testament, God prepared the Jews and mankind for the coming of the Messia. Only for this reason did He save his people. The signs of His care and of His intentions were the miracles of the Old Testament. The New Testament wrought salvation not only for one people but for all mankind, and the miracles performed by God through Christ and the Apostles were intended to confirm salvation and to invite humanity to seek it through sanctification.

St. Augustine says that the miracles are words of God destined to accomplish His work in the souls of men. The miracles of the New Testament prove in the clearest way that all Christian miracles are spiritual miracles having a spiritual purpose. Religion is the living link between God and the individual soul. It is a two-way communication characterized by personal actions on the part of God and on the part of the individual soul. We have already said that a miracle would be inconceivable and nonunderstandable without the existence of a personal and supernatural God. This also means that God cares individually for every single human being. The individual, personal action of God concerning each human being, i.e., each soul, would be impossible in a framework of universal determinism in which God, deprived of "personality," is unable to enter into a personal relationship with each individual.

Developing this thought further, we see that the history of mankind and civilization is identical with the history of man's conquest of nature. Man, with the help of science and technology, has succeeded in discovering and utilizing certain laws of matter, of nature. Owing to these discoveries man has been able to explore and achieve results which nature by itself could never have made possible. Obviously, material achievements such as buildings, roads, railways, ships, planes, power stations, are the result of man's creative use of the laws of nature (physics). If man could master these laws and learn to use them to his advantage, how is it possible to maintain that God, who created nature, should not know the laws of this nature or to doubt that He is able to use them in whatever way He sees fit? For those who believe that God exists and recognize Him as Supreme Being, Supreme Goodness, and Supreme Intelligence, the miracle is a self-evident possibility.

Rationalists, particularly during the 18th century, tried to maintain that the physical laws of the universe had been once and for all imposed by God upon nature and we must respect them, so much so that any interference on His part is impossible. Since this was an accepted opinion, the Deists hoped to prove that the miracles of the Gospel actually were natural events. The raising of the dead is "a cure from lethargic slumber"; the resurrection of Christ was a vision of imaginative dreamers. Since the Resurrection is the center and the key to all Christianity, testimony relating to the authenticity of the Resurrection was extremely important.

Daniel-Rops in his *Jesus and His Times*[1] states that although the miracles of the Old Testament were "obviously interventions of the Divine Power," there is a striking difference between the miracles of the Old and the New Testament.

The question is, For what reason and in what manner did God perform the miracles in both cases? In the Old Testament God wished to manifest His glory and aid His servants. This called for spectacular methods: earthquake, storms, epidemics, plagues, tremendous thunder, flash of lightning. But the miracles of Christ are different; they have no parallel in the natural order. "Changing water into wine or multiplying seven loaves to feed thousands of people has nothing in common with any natural phenomenon. The miracles of Jesus thus appeared as direct manifestations of the creative power of God, and those who declined to recognize God in Him must have been enraged by them."[2] As Daniel-Rops expresses it, all miracles are "signs of contradiction," for His appearance in the world brought a permanent contradiction between the one truth eternally revealed and incarnated in Him and the world from whose fallen inhabitants He desires a self-knowledge that they are most loath to acknowledge —that is, the nothingness of themselves. "We shall know too well what is meant by hardness of heart. Everything which Jesus taught was against the natural inclination of man to follow his passions."

Thus the miracles were "signs of contradiction" also because it is undeniable that these were authentic miracles and came from God. To accept the miracles meant then and now that one accepted the universal truth of total self-denial as expressed by Christ. Daniel-Rops reminds us of the discerning observation of St. Augustine:

"What is now called the Christian religion has not ceased to exist since the creation of mankind and up to the time that Christ Himself came in the flesh." For the Christian, the teaching of Jesus is not a philosophical system issuing from the brain of a man of genius, but a revelation by God not merely of one truth but of the eternal truth. Any person who accepted or accepts the miracles of Christ has to accept His teaching—i.e., the one eternal truth.

It should be borne in mind that the miracles of Christ form an integral part of the story of the Evangelists, both in the Gospels and in the Acts of the Apostles. In other words, the miracles are essential to the New Testament and not imaginative decorations or literary "embellishments." Hastings' *Dictionary of the Bible*[3] states: "We cannot construct a consistent picture of the life of Jesus Christ from the Gospels if we do not take account of His miraculous powers. . . . We cannot contrive any theory by which we may entirely eliminate the miraculous, and yet save the historicity, in any intelligible sense, of the wonderful narratives."

The Evangelists used various expressions to describe miracles. Sometimes they are described as miraculous events, and on other occasions as extraordinary events, forces, signs, and works. Hastings enumerates 41 miracles wrought by Christ. One of the most authoritative scholars of the life of Christ, Louis de Grandmaison, has counted 24 miracles in the Gospel according to St. Matthew, 22 in St. Mark, 24 in St. Luke, and nine in St. John.

It is interesting to note that none of the Gospels claimed to be complete transcripts of the events in the life of Jesus. Often they describe the same miracle from a different angle. This confirms the fact that there was no collusion among them, that each reported honestly on the basis of information available to him.

Of singular importance is the fact that Jesus employed various ways of producing miracles, particularly the acts of healing. Often He pronounced only a word or made one gesture, and the miraculous effect was wrought. More often He put His hands upon the sick or even upon the diseased part of the body, and there were instances when He lifted His eyes heavenward and prayed. These were but outward signs without any influence whatsoever on the miraculous effect. They show, however, that there was no ostentation, no magic ceremony, surrounding the miracles, but rather the greatest simplicity.

There are several proofs of the authenticity of the miracles of the New Testament. Some of the most important miracles, like the multiplication of bread, and the resurrection of the daughter of Jairus, are described in two or three Gospels. It is interesting to note the difference between the miracles described in the Apocrypha and in the New Testament. The Apocrypha present the miracles in such a wise that it is evident that the authors were primarily interested in their extraordinary content. The miracles of the New Testament, on the other hand, are integral parts of the text. They do not protrude ostentatiously, they are not on parade. Their aim is manifest. They are not prodigious events wrought to amaze the populace; their purpose is to reveal the mission of Christ, and first and foremost among the Apostles themselves. And they are related with a naturalness of manner peculiar to the personality of Christ.

Another characteristic of the miracles of Christ, as related in the Gospels, is that sometimes He Himself performs the miracle by giving a simple order, and at other times He prays to the Heavenly Father, whom He then thanks for granting His prayer. The explanation of this double attitude lies in the dual nature of Christ. When He said to the leper: "I will; be thou made clean" (Matt. 8:3), it was His divine nature that acted immediately. At other times He refers to the spirit of God: "But if I by the spirit of God cast out devils, then is the Kingdom of God come upon you."

Of especial interest is the procedure of the resurrection of Lazarus. When Jesus heard about the death of Lazarus and decided to raise him from the dead He could have done so from a distance. Nevertheless, He went to the tomb and first prayed. "Jesus lifting up his eyes said: Father, I give thee thanks that thou hast heard me. And I knew that thou hearest me always; but because of the people who stand about have I said it, that they may believe that thou hast sent me" (John 11:41–42).

This indicates most clearly that He was able to perform the miracle without going to the tomb. But this was an opportunity to prove His mission, that He was the Messias sent by the Father. Nevertheless, the miracle happened instantaneously, i.e., at the very moment that Christ spoke the words, "Lazarus, come forth" (John 11:43). The miracle was performed by the divine Word that has the power to animate and raise the dead.

The miracles of Christ are his dowry as Messias, the very signs that were predicted by the prophets. He identified himself with John the Baptist when He told the emissaries of "the voice in the desert," that they should help him and make the blind to see and the deaf to hear. On the other hand, since the miracles were the signs of His identification with Heaven—divine facts to create confidence—they were limited in the divine plan. For example, at the wedding of Cana, He said to his mother: "My time has not yet come," and requested the persons whom He healed not to divulge yet what He had done. The limitation in the divine plan conceivably might have been due to the fact that Christ, knowing well the history and the reactions of the people in whose midst He was born, felt that a premature divulging of His messianic mission might give rise to a wave of nationalism.

In this connection we should recall that Christ clearly rejected the idea of becoming a wonder-worker. The most important illustration is His rejection of Satan's temptation to become one:

> "And the tempter coming said to him: If thou be the Son of God, command that these stones be made bread. . . . Then the devil took him up into the holy city and set him upon the pinnacle of the temple, and said to him: If thou be the Son of God, cast thyself down . . ." (Matt. 4:3–7).

Unlike a wonder-worker or *magus*, Christ performed miracles either as a final attempt to convince the incredulous, or as an act of grace, like that of the wedding feast of Cana. But often the miracles affected the malicious and the prejudiced in a contrary way and actually hardened their resistance. This was analogous to the situation during the plagues of Egypt when the miracles performed by Moses did not soften but hardened the heart of the Pharaoh. For certain people in modern times the miracles of the Gospel prove to be actual obstacles to faith. And in the time of Jesus those who had decided not to believe Him looked upon His miracles as works of Satan. This is one of the most important teachings of the Gospel. Some of those who did not believe in Christ regarded the miracles as manifestations of the power of God, other people attributed them to the power of Satan. In vain did Christ try to convince them that miracles are primarily manifestations of God's infinite love: "The praeter natural works of Jesus were almost without exception beneficent deeds—to alleviate human misery or to further the interests of the Kingdom. They were not arbitrary interferences with the course of nature, a show of divine might without reference to the needs of the situation or the saving character of Christ's mission. On the contrary they were outpourings of God's favour, wholly of a piece with the mercy and loving kindness which received their supreme embodiment in the person of Jesus. For this reason He Himself seems almost to make light of His miraculous healings, or to desire at least to keep them secret. (Mk 7:36;8:26); there was a moment when the people would have acclaimed him as the mighty wonder-working Messias of their earthly expectations (John 6:14) and he openly rebuked them for seeing in his miracles more than the alleviation of material necessities (v 26). Our Lord's wonderful works were thus symbols of God's goodness, and only goodwill could rightly respond to them. Considered as mere evidence, they were not sufficient to produce belief; there was needed also the inward enlightenment of the mind and heart for which they were the occasion. For all the persuasive power of the miracles of Jesus, they would not of themselves have sufficed to make the refusal to accept him inexcusable, had they not been accompanied for the unbelievers by an interior grace of illumination (S. Thom., *Ex. pos. in Joan.*, 15, 5, 4, Parma edit., 10, 573)."[5]

Apologists emphasize that the supreme motive of credibility was not the miracle but the person of Christ who worked them. As a matter of fact, in any miraculous occurrence, whether a vision or any other sign, the first question to arise never concerns the miracle itself but rather the personality, the background of the person through whom the wondrous event has happened. The personality of Christ was full of majesty, goodness, and charm. His teaching touched the heart and mind, His presence radiated purity and serenity, and everything that He said or did was "proclaimed" with a divine assurance. Whatever He said had an immediate appeal to everyone because it bore the light. And while the supreme truth was understood by the intelligence, the hearts of His hearers opened too, and the people responded with love.

Every miracle in itself is perfect because it is the manifestation of God. Thus, when we say that the miracles of Christ were the most perfect miracles we refer only to perfection with regard to the fulfillment of their purpose, namely, to be the miracles ANNOUNCING the coming of the Messias. There is ample evidence in the New Testament that the disciples and many others accepted this testimony. "And his disciples believed in Him" (John 2:11) . . . "Now when he was at Jerusalem . . . many believed in his name, seeing [his] signs" (John 2:23) . . . The official whose son He cured "believed, and his whole house" (John 4:53). Nicodemus is more explicit: ". . . no man can do these signs which thou dost, unless God be with him" (John 3:2).

Jesus constantly refused, however, to perform miracles for the sake of the miracle. He refused the request of the Pharisees who asked Him to work a miracle in order to prove that He was the Messias, for this request was prompted by malicious curiosity and skepticism. He knew that the Pharisees would not believe even if He granted their request. Faith cannot be created by miracles; those who are not pure and humble of heart will never acknowledge a miracle. The works and signs of Christ clearly show the terrifying differences between the skeptic and the person whose heart is hardened. A pure skeptic is a potential believer, or a habitual believer like Thomas the Apostle. The skeptic, even without active faith, is always prepared to accept truth in his heart whereas the person whose heart is hardened is in chronic revolt against the superiority of God and is therefore touched by evil. That is why Christ refused to perform a miracle before the Pharisees. It would have been wasted exhibitionism; for since He knew their hearts and knew that grace did not yet work upon them, His miracle would not have been accepted by them as a sign of His divine mission. On the contrary, it would have been mocked, distorted and ridiculed.

There were many objections to Christ's miracles on the part of those who, though accepting Him as a prophet or a great teacher yet denied His miracles. According to Harnack, the well-known Protestant historian and theologian, miraculous or near-miraculous events were a daily phenomenon in those times when extraordinary happenings, short of natural explanation, were made understandable through Divine intervention. Harnack adds that people always attributed exceptional human qualities to some miraculous powers. Père de Grandmaison answers this reasoning by asking how it was possible (according to all witnesses, and not the Evangelists) that Christ's miracles caused such tremendous sensation and "scandal," if the miraculous was an everyday affair.

As for attributing miracles to great personalities, no one has attributed miraculous powers to St. John the Baptist, Plato, Aristotle, Cicero, Luther, Calvin, or Napoleon. At best Virgil was considered a *magus* during the Middle Ages. Indeed, attempts have been made to explain Christ's miracles as the work of a *magus*, a magician who performs amazing tricks before an audience.

"Careful study of the Gospels reveals an unspeakable beauty in the fabric of the miracles. We are in such harmony with the evangelical doctrine as to feel ourselves before something that is truly divine. The miracles of the Gospel altogether have historical veracity and apologetical veracity. The miracles of the Gospel are authentic and true miracles from the factual and historical point of view, and at the same time they express the apologetic truth."[4]

And, says St. Thérèse of Lisieux, "Jesus donates these miracles as only a God could give them, but first He wants humility of heart."

It is almost useless to classify the miracles of Christ—although we could press them into the categories set up in our chapter on Principles. The most obvious classification, used by many scholars, is that of material miracles and miracles involving the human body sometimes called cosmic miracles and miracles of healing.

The personality of Christ was the greatest source of credibility for the miracles. Not even Pilate found anything to reproach in Him, although this aloof and realistic representative of the Roman power was sufficiently equipped to distinguish the guilty from the innocent, and he had enough sense of abstract justice and expediency to eliminate anyone who came into conflict with the law.

That miracles are mysteries of love is nowhere demonstrated with greater clarity than in the life of Jesus. God loved the world so much that He gave His Son for its salvation. If a sacrifice does not generate joy, if it is made with bitterness or with a heavy heart—in short, if it is not embraced in a spirit of love, it has no value. To a Christian the mystery of the salvation is the greatest miracle of love. The very purpose of the miracles of Jesus, according to the Evangelists and Jesus Himself, was to win the love and faith of the Jews, and all humanity in them, until the end of the world.

The miracle of miracles is Christ's resurrection. But His miracles begin with His birth, which was in itself doubly miraculous. As predicted by the prophets and announced by the Archangel Gabriel, he was born of a virgin. The phenomenon of the star of Bethlehem, which announced the arrival of the Messias, was not a comet but a genuine miracle.

No human mind can conceive and explain how it was possible for Christ to have two natures, a divine and a human one. His human nature possessed a human body like that of any one else and a human soul that was not like the spirit of the angels but like the soul of any other human being. But this did not interfere with the fact that He was God at the same time—and God is pure, the purest spirit. This is the miracle of the Incarnation.

The miracle of the Incarnation involves Mary of Nazareth, who was chosen to be the vessel of this miracle. In defining the doctrine of the Immaculate Conception, Pope Pius IX in his Bull *Ineffabilis Deus* (1854) wrote:

"God foresaw from all eternity the unhappy ruin of the whole human race of man through the sin of Adam . . . and determined, by a mystery hidden from all ages, to accomplish the first work of His goodness in a secret dispensation by the Incarnation of the Word. . . . God chose and ordained from the beginning and before all ages, a mother for his only-begotten Son, that by taking flesh from her, he might be born in the blessed fullness of time."

The divine motherhood of Mary is stressed in a second miracle, that of her bodily assumption into Heaven. The New Testament is silent about her assumption, but the Church considers that Revelation comes not only through the Bible but through sacred tradition. Theologians are currently discussing whether the Blessed Virgin was taken, body and soul, into Heaven after her death, or whether she actually died at all. According to Christian tradition the alleged scene of her "death" was the Church of Dormition, or "the falling asleep of the Virgin Mary." There are only two other analogous passings from this world, that of Henoch and of Elias. Nevertheless, the assumption of the Blessed Virgin is a different kind of miracle. The assumption became a dogma, i.e., an article of faith, with publication of the Apostolic Constitution *Munificentissimus Deus* on November 1, 1950, but it has been accepted in the Church at least since the sixth century. In the order of salvation the assumption of the Blessed Virgin is understandable to any Catholic; the definition of this Catholic belief as an article of faith, declared by Pope Pius XII, in the midst of the atomic age, is an important affirmation of the Church in behalf of the reality of fundamental supernatural principles.

The appearance of the star of Bethlehem, as has been said, is also miraculous.

"Where is he that is born king of the Jews? For we have seen his star in the east and are come to adore him. . . . Then Herod, privately calling the wise men, learned diligently of them the time of the star which appeared to them. . . . [And the wise men] went their way. And behold, the star which they had seen in the east went before them, until it came and stood over where the child was" (Matt. 2:2–11).

First of all, the authenticity of the narrative is beyond question, for the wise men were certainly members of an Oriental priestly class whose empirical knowledge of astronomy is an accepted fact. There is therefore no doubt that they saw an unknown star.

There have been many interesting speculations about the origin of this star of Bethlehem. The first to formulate an hypothesis was the great 17th-century Catholic astronomer Kepler; later Tycho-Brahe, in 1672, produced another. Other astronomers tried to identify it with Halley's Comet. All these hypotheses sought to explain its appearance as a conjunction between planets which could create a similar phenomenon, but their conclusions were not tenable. According to modern astronomers no natural celestial phenomenon can be identified in a scientific way with the star of Bethlehem. This is confirmed by the experience of the Orientals in the field of astronomy. A thousand years before the Christian era Chaldean priests had observed with such precision the motions of the moon and the planets that they were able to predict their future position. And in their language the star of Bethlehem was a star and not a comet.

The solution cannot be other than that suggested by the early Christian authors. The star of the wise men was a meteor lighted up by the light of God and sent on its mission. It followed a path traced not by the laws of astronomy but by the will of God, who is able to intervene in nature.

The miracles of Christ are an integral part of his teaching, organically connected with His mission. The miracles proved that Christ always pronounced the truth—hence the faith of his disciples, the enthusiasm of the crowds, and the increasing envy of the rulers, who did not dare to deny the reality of these facts. They would have preferred to see diabolical marvels and snares in order to capture Christ and His disciples.

It is significant that the first miracle performed by Christ is the changing of water into wine at the wedding of Cana. "And the wine failing, the mother of Jesus saith to him, They have no wine" (John 2:3). It is significant for several reasons, for as has been said, the first answer of Christ is: "What is that to me and to thee? My hour is not yet come."

The words of Christ indicate that He felt that there was no reason at that moment to prove His true identity. But later in the course of the wedding festivities, His mother said to the waiters: "Whatsoever he shall say to you, do ye." It would be difficult to express in a more delicate and yet explicit manner His mother's absolute confidence in Him, that whatever He does will be right. She did not want a prodigious feat to be performed, she did not hint at the lack of wine in order to press Him for a miracle of ostentation. She simply observed that there was no more wine at so festive an occasion. It was an impulse to be of help that prompted her to this act of love. In the meantime Jesus made his decision. First he said, "My hour is not yet come." The Gospel later, however, says, "This beginning of miracles did Jesus in Cana of Galilee; and he manifested his glory, and his disciples believed in him."

This act of love, through the belief of the disciples, became an act of faith. The miracle did not occur in vain; it had its purpose and achieved it. People began to believe in Him.

Christ returned once to Cana, where he had "made the water wine."

"And there was a certain ruler whose son was sick at Capharnaum. . . . He went to him and prayed him to come down and heal his son, for he was at the point of death. Jesus therefore said to him, Unless you see signs and wonders, you believe not. The ruler said to him, Lord, come down before that my son die. Jesus said to him, Go thy way, thy son liveth. The man believed the word which Jesus said to him, and went his way. . . . And as he was going down his servants met him and brought word saying that his son lived" (John 4:46-51).

Christ's first answer to the official of Capharnaum was tinged more with sadness than with reproach: "Unless you see signs and wonders, you believe not." His words resound through history for everyone, placing all miracles in a proper divine perspective. Do not ask for miracles; *believe!*

Another occasion during which He tested the faith of his disciples upon whom He intended to build His church, is related in the Gospel of St. Luke (5:1-11). He had been speaking to the multitude, and when He ceased He turned to Simon and asked him to cast his net for a catch. Although Simon Peter knew that their strenuous night-long attempts to catch fish had ended in failure he believed: ". . . at thy word I will let down the net."

The miracle that followed this total obedience and childlike confidence brought fish. At the same time the Gospel narrative describes the fear and astonishment that the miracle inspired in the Apostles. Simon Peter fell on his knees, insisting upon his sinfulness and his unworthiness. It was the natural terrifying shock that is produced in the human soul at the sight of supernatural intervention. But peace of soul followed; peace pervaded their minds and spirits, and "leaving all things, they followed him."

One of the most moving and significant events in the life of Jesus is the healing of the centurion's servant at Capharnaum, for it reveals humankind in its finest expression and the victory of God's love in its immediacy and totality.

Upon entering Capharnaum Christ met a centurion, a non-Jew, who came "beseeching him." The anxiety-ridden misery of human existence spoke in the words of the centurion: "Lord, my servant lieth at home sick of the palsy, and is grievously tormented." Seeing this man full of charity who begged for his servant, Jesus did not hesitate. He said to the centurion: "I will come and heal him." The simplicity and goodness of His spirit are expressed in His words. "And the centurion making answer said: Lord, I am not worthy that thou shouldst enter under my roof; but only say the word, and my servant shall be healed" (Matt. 8:5–8).

Mankind at its finest is revealed in the answer of the centurion. It is not an act of degrading self-humiliation, but an expression of total faith, trust, and love.

The calming of the storm climactically stresses the importance of faith.

> "A great tempest arose in the sea, so that the boat was covered with waves; but he was asleep. And they came to him and awaked him, saying; Lord, save us! we perish. And Jesus said to them: Why are you fearful, O ye of little faith? Then rising up he commanded the winds and the sea, and there came a great calm" (Matt. 8:24–26).

The emphasis is not on the miracle. The emphasis is on the person who works it and on its spiritual content. "O ye of little faith . . ."

If we consider one of the last miracles, the healing of Malchus' ear in the garden of Gethsemane, we see even more clearly that the miracle is always an act of supreme charity. When the soldiers came with Judas to take Jesus prisoner, Simon Peter, the most emotional and least stable among the Apostles (until after Pentecoste), "having a sword, drew it, and struck the servant of the high priest, and cut off his right ear. And the name of the servant was Malchus. Jesus therefore said to Peter: Put up they sword into the scabbard. The chalice which my Father hath given me, shall I not drink it?" (John 18:10–11).

Christ in His human nature asked no more from His disciples than the Father had asked of His—namely, to fufill God's plans in utmost obedience in a spirit of love.

"Thinkest thou that I cannot ask my Father, and he will give me presently more than twelve legions of angels?" (Matt. 26:53). In our human words, this means that He does not wish to display His power for power's sake. Power is only secondary in the miraculous performance; the miracle must be the manifestation of goodness. Jesus did not want the twelve legions of angels although He could have marshalled them. He did not punish His enemies: "For all that take the sword shall perish with the sword" (Matt. 26:52). Instead of evading God's will, He used His divine power. He invoked that power to heal his enemy: "And when he had touched his ear, he healed him" (Luke 22:51).

Christ's greatest miracle is His resurrection. On this fact Christianity stands or falls. The multiplication of bread and fish, the calming of the storm, the cure of the paralytic and the many sick and diseased, the blind, the deaf, the dumb, the exorcism of the possessed, and the raising to life of the widow's son and Jairus' daughter and Lazarus,—are all acts of love accompanying the teaching of the new message that salvation, the greatest act of love to be performed by God, is near. The resurrection as an act is the supreme fulfillment and the greatest miracle. God, who became man, at the same time humbled Himself and was destroyed as a man. For a Christian the resurrection of Christ means that Christ is living among us still. The whole Christian doctrine would not be possible or understandable without the resurrection of Christ and without His living presence. Union with Christ who is God is the supreme end of every Christian. This miracle is the greatest reality of history. Thus it is understand-

able that the resurrection of Christ was so carefully described by the
Evangelists and by all of them from different angles. There are six
documentary descriptions in the New Testament of the resurrection,
chronologically in the following places: (1) I Cor. 15; (2) Matt. 28;
(3) Mark 16:1–8; (4) Luke 24; (5) Mark 16:9–20; and finally (6)
John 20 and 21. Its history can be retold, based upon the above documentation, in the following way.

Mary Magdalene, accompanied by other women (who later on go
another way), left her house before the end of the night between
Saturday and Sunday. Alone she walked to the tomb while the
women went to provide herbs and perfume oils. When Mary Magdalene arrived at the tomb, she found it open and without the guards.
And because she did not find the body of her divine Master inside,
she thought that the body had been stolen and she ran to notify
Peter, the Chief of the Apostles. When she left the tomb the other
women arrived. They entered and were greatly shocked because the
body of Christ was not there. At this moment an angel appeared and
informed them that Christ was risen. The women were terrified, and
ran away. No one believed what was told them, and because of this
their speech was blocked. Later, however, they talked. St. Mark in-
forms us about their silence, but St. Luke about what they said.

According to all probability, Peter and John then proceeded to the
sepulcher, and after they examined it they concluded that the Lord
had risen. After Peter and John had left, Mary Magdalene again
went to the tomb and encountered Jesus before the entrance. She
heard his voice. He talked to her and through her sent a message for
the Apostles.

The Gospel narrative makes it clear that the guards were present
when the tombstone that closed the entrance removed itself. Cleo-
phas, and one of his associates, saw and heard the risen Lord. Peter
and James were favored by an apparition.

The day was not yet ended and Christ had already given to all
the Apostles (save one who was absent) and other disciples undeniable proof of his redemption.

And during the subsequent forty days there were many other
manifestations of Christ, all reported by the Evangelists. One of the

most important among them is that describing his appearance before 500 witnesses. This proves that the Evangelists did not invent anything. Another extremely important apparition was that of the miraculous catch of fish, the net remaining intact despite the fact that it pulled 153 fish to shore. This alone proves that the Apostles were not victims of an illusion.

The resurrection of Christ is not, of course, conceivable by the human mind; it has to be accepted as part of our faith in the living God. Although the authenticity of the Bible narrative and other sources is beyond question, efforts have always been made to destroy or weaken the belief in the fact of resurrection. The argument asserting that fraud was used to deceive the people is out of date and is no longer used by the adversaries of Christianity. Another explanation maintains that the Apostles were in such a state of excitement that they had visions of Christ and "imagined" that he was risen. The truth about the state of the Apostles is quite otherwise. After what had happened the Apostles did not expect that Christ would come to life. They did not want to believe the first reports about the resurrection. The Bible, moreover, relates several instances when Christ appeared and showed Himself to many people. He appeared to the Apostles, eating and drinking with them. And he also let Himself be touched—by Thomas the Apostle. If Christ's resurrection had been only a vision, it could not have had the effect on the Apostles that it had. A vision disappears; and although it leaves a deep impression upon the soul, it is still not a material reality. The Apostles enjoyed the return of Christ in their midst, and His resurrection made them in turn rise from their depression and begin a heroic, dynamic apostolate.

Another theory has it that the message of the resurrection of Christ is simply another version of the mythical Oriental mystery cults replete with gods who die and then are raised to life. Modern science, however, has clearly established that at best these religions, through a god, personify the undying idea of and the eternal yearning for eternal life. The late Josef Leo Seifert, outstanding disciple of the great historian of religions, Father Wilhelm Schmidt, S.V.D., has proved in his unique work on the meaning of myth[6] that the idea of the Trinity, and the hope and symbols of salvation, were parts of the religions of primitive peoples. On the other hand, we know that revelation did not start with the Bible: "This communication of heavenly knowledge began to be made from the day of man's creation . . . The preparation of the redeemer's coming was a progressive revelation, but the definitive manifestation of all God's purpose on behalf of the human race was made by the Son of God incarnate in the fullness of time. A living teaching authority is prior to every single book of divine scripture . . . Whatever divine revelation or communication there was in the early days of the human race, probably took place by word of mouth only, and was handed on orally from generation to generation."[7]

Thus, the resurrection of Christ as a unique historical fact is in no way in conflict with any myth that may have reached into any religion through these pre-Biblical revelations.

From the first century on, the resurrection was the central, focal point of Christian faith. Patristic literature gives ample evidence of its influence upon the first Christians. The examples given here are based chiefly on the work of Père de Grandmaison.

Clement of Rome, in a letter dated around A.D. 92 or 101, wrote that the resurrection of Christ presents a continuous hope for our resurrection in the future.

Ignatius of Antioch (died 110) in several of his letters always returns to this greatest fact of Christianity. "Christ is risen from dead, really and truly. He was risen by the Father and one day we will be risen too." In another letter he says: "Jesus Christ possessed a human body after His resurrection; he told the Apostles, touch me, feel me, and you will see that I am not a bodiless spirit. . . ." St. Polycarp of Smyrna (died 155) declared that "the solid root of Christian faith is that . . . Jesus Christ was resurrected by God after He died for our sins."

St. Justin Martyr wrote, around 455: "When Christ was crucified all His disciples abandoned and denied Him. Later, when He was risen from death and had shown himself to them, and taught them to read the prophecies which had predicted these facts, they believed."

Origen asked how anyone could doubt the fact of crucifixion and resurrection of Christ, "since He was crucified before the very eyes of all Judea and His body was removed from the cross in the presence of so many witnesses . . ." How is it possible to imagine that the Apostles, who had abandoned Him after the crucifixion, suddenly became courageous, enthusiastic to the point of expounding His doctrine despite the greatest dangers and at a time when people were not well disposed to listen? It is inconceivable that the Apostles invented the resurrection. Such a collective lie could not have been maintained for so long a time by so many people.

St. Augustine's point is the most important for the Christian: "The heathens, too, believe that Christ died; the belief, the faith in his resurrection makes the Christian Christian . . . It is faith in this resurrection that justifies us" (*Contra Faustum Manichaeum,* XXIX).

Why is resurrection so important for the Christian? Romano Guardini, the German theologian, gives the answer:

"Death came into the world through sin. This is the answer Christianity makes to the question of death. It is a bold answer, which troubles the mind and stirs up opposition. . . . The Christian religion is certain that death in itself and as such (not 'the end') has no proper meaning, and justifies the protest against it. But it also recognizes death as a real thing and acknowledges all its harshness. . . . Death has its origin not in an inner necessity of human existence, but in sin, the sin of all men, which is also the sin of each individual. . . . But Christianity knows something further. In the chapter of Romans, Paul says: 'For if by one man's offense death reigned through one; much more they who receive abundance of grace, and of the gift, and of justice, shall [even now] reign in life through one, [that is] Jesus Christ. Therefore, as by the offense of one, unto all men to condemnation [and to death]; so also by the justice of one, unto all men to justification of life' (Rom. 5:17–19). When Christ died something happened to death. . . . The word resurrection is as strange to modern feeling as the idea that death is not necessary. We still use it as an inheritance from the age of faith, but in a different sense. In contemporary language, it signifies the return of life in spring after the torpor of winter, or some new accession of energy in a man after a period of stagnation. . . . There is nothing of this

in the resurrection of Christ, and through him of redeemed mankind.
. . . It means that Christ, after his death, raised himself up by the
sovereign power of the living God to a new and truly human life. . . .
It means that his body, after it had died, lived on in a higher way; that
he saw by the power of the Holy Spirit, penetrated and transformed
his body; that he entered upon eternal glory in the fullness of his divine
and human nature. This doctrine is not a legendary apotheosis, not a
later, mythical structure put on a purely human life, but is found everywhere in the original sources. Christ's resurrection is as essential a part
of the Gospel, throughout, as his redeeming death. The fact that he
rose is as much a fact as that he lived at all. Paul leaves us in no doubt:
'and if Christ be not risen again, then is our preaching vain. . . . if
Christ be not risen [and through him we ourselves] . . . if in this life
only we have hope in Christ, we are of all men most miserable' (Rom.
I, 4, I Cor. 15:14–19). Without the resurrection of Christ there is no
Christianity. Without the resurrection Christianity would become
something apt to make anyone capable of serious and profound reasoning 'of all men the most miserable.' With Christ's death and resurrection something happened to death. It ceased to be the mere executing
of God's justice. . . . Christ's death has given it a new character, which
does not change its form but does alter its meaning and restore it to
what it should have been for the first man—the passage into a new,
eternally human life."[8]

But Christ's resurrection has more meanings for the Christian. In
another chapter we shall discuss the mystery and miracle of the
Eucharist. Here, we have to remind ourselves only that Christ's
eucharistic presence with us unto the end was made possible only
through His resurrection. The two mysteries are close to each other.
According to Thomas Merton, "The real presence of Christ in the
Host is the necessary and immediate consequence of transubstantiation."[9] But the real presence and the transubstantiation are "a consequence of the resurrection." If, as Guardini says, without the resurrection of Christ there is no Christianity, it is equally true that the
Eucharist, in Merton's words, "is (therefore) the very heart of Christianity." "Christianity is a religion of life, not of death. It is the religion of the transcendant, living God," continues Merton. And this
continuity that is expressed by the words "living God" manifests it-

St. Catherine of Genoa. Contemporary (artist unknown) painting
in the Hospital of Pammatone, Genoa, Italy.

(*Alinari, Rome*)

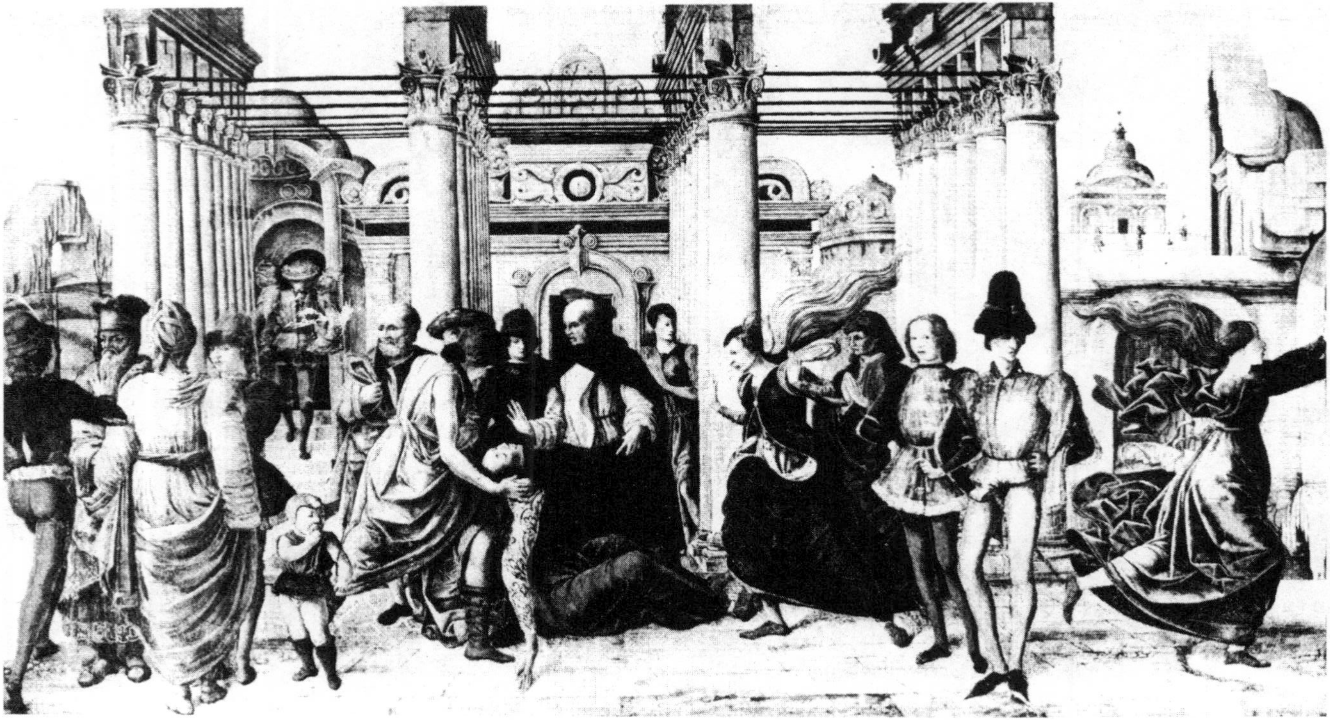

Left: St. Vincent Ferrer healing the sick. Painting by Francesco del Cossa, attributed also to Ercole de'Roberti, in the Vatican.

Photograph during the ceremony of the liquefaction of the blood of St. Gennaro in the Cathedral of Naples.

St. Teresa of Jesus (St. Teresa of Avila), portrait by Fr. Juan de la Miseria in the Carmelite convent of Valladolid.

St. Benedict Joseph Labre. Portrait by Antonio Cavallucci in the National Gallery in Rome.

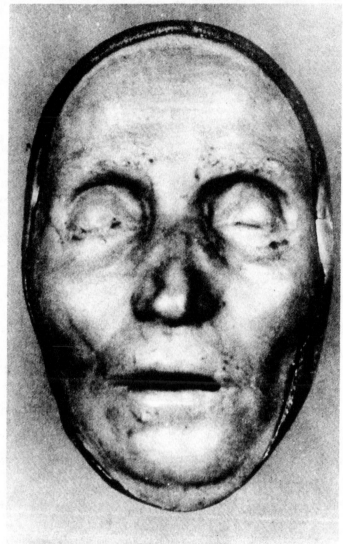

St. Veronica Giuliani. Death mask in the possession
of the Capuchin nuns in Città di Castello.

St. Mary Magdalen de'Pazzi. Portrait by unknown artist in the Carmelite convent in Florence-Careggi.

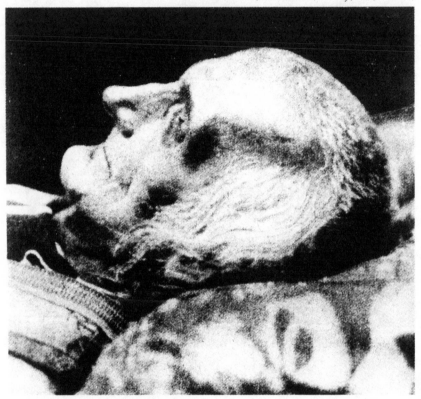

St. John Vianney, photograph of the saint on his deathbed.

self in the continuous death and resurrection of Christ on the altar, and an assurance "of the general resurrection and our entrance into glory."

The mystery of the Eucharist consists in the changing of the substance of the bread and wine into the body and blood of Christ. It is not a miracle in the strictest sense of the word, for the mystery happens outside sentient experience. This is why the Eucharist is a mystery and not a miracle. Nevertheless, it can be called the greatest mystery of all, and "a miracle" that is within our reach although not within the range of our perception. The faithful, the believer who participates in the Mass and witnesses one of the thousands of transubstantiations that occur daily, the communicant who is fed with this Living Bread, the priest who holds the mystery in his hands and who is the instrument of it all, should be aware that they are participating in the greatest mystery of the universe. All believers should be careful to avoid an attitude or state of mind that takes this tremendous mystery for granted.

Miracles in connection with the Eucharist remind us that we are face to face with the most glorious, the greatest event in history, which promises the solution of every problem. Such miraculous occurrences have taken place ever since the earliest Christian ages. St. Gregory Nazianzen was suddenly healed after receiving Communion. A similar event occurred in the life of St. Cyprian. St. Gregory the Great once celebrated Mass before a crowd of people who did not believe in the mystery of transubstantiation. When the sainted bishop lifted up the Host during the Offertory, it was transformed suddenly into the Child Jesus. About one hundred and thirty miracles of the Eucharist are noted in Church history. There are precise reports of cases where blood dropped from the Host at the moment of elevation. Such cases were reported in Ferrara in 1171, in Florence in 1230, in Bolsena in 1263.

The case of Bolsena is the most important because it was the occasion for Pope Urban IV to extend the feast of Corpus Christi to the Universal church. The Pope commissioned St. Thomas Aquinas to write the Mass and the Office for the occasion.

Bolsena is a small city on the shores of a lake of the same name. In

1263 a German priest, Peter of Prague, on his way to Rome, stopped at Bolsena, already famous because it contained the tomb of St. Christina Virgin and Martyr in the church of the city. Peter of Prague was a pious priest, but he found it very hard to believe that Christ was actually present in the Host. He celebrated his Mass at an altar upon the tomb of St. Christina and when, still doubting, he broke the Host, it became flesh and blood, dropping on the altar cloth and the corporal. He tried to hide what had happened, but a few seconds later, frightened, he interrupted the Mass and asked to be taken immediately to neighboring Orvieto, where Pope Urban IV had taken refuge at that time. The Pope listened to the priest and absolved him in confession from his doubts and then investigated the case. When all the facts were ascertained he ordered the bishop of the diocese to bring the Host of Bolsena and the linen that bore the traces of blood in solemn procession to Orvieto. He enshrined it in the cathedral of the city, where it is still conserved intact in a side chapel. And in his bull *Transiturus* of August, 1264, he instituted the feast of Corpus Christi, now celebrated all over the world.

Other miracles in connection with the Eucharist: The consecrated Host appeared surrounded by a great light in Turin, Italy, in 1453, and in Paterno near Naples in 1772. Hosts were miraculously conserved from decay in Morrovalle, Italy, in 1562, in Favernay, France, in 1618, and other places. Many miraculous cures are connected with the Holy Communion, among them those at Loreto, Fatima, and Lourdes.

CHAPTER 8

Centuries of Miracles

"A Saint is a person whose holiness of life and heroic virtue have
been confirmed and recognized by the Church's official processes of
beatification and canonization, or by the continued existence of an
approved cultus and feast. To such only may public veneration and
liturgical honor be given; but the Church also produces numerous
other saints who remain unknown and unrecognized."[1]

As is the case with the definitions in other authorized encyclo-
pedias, this precise and authoritative definition of sainthood does
not mention that a saint becomes a saint because he produces miracles
or because miracles occur upon his intercession. It says simply that
saints are persons who have lived a holy life and exercised certain
virtues on an heroic scale. If the Church publicly recognizes the
achievement of such persons they become officially venerated as
saints. But the Church does not exclude the possibility that there are
hundreds, perhaps thousands, of hidden saints among us in this our
modern society, whom God considers to be saints because they too
live a holy life and their virtues are heroic. Again there is no mention
of miracles.

The importance of this fact cannot be emphasized strongly enough.
The blessed and the saints are selected examples, torches of light
so that everyone may see the power of grace and the power of man's
free will upon which grace operates. It would be erroneous to think
that saints are at best only great men whose social work and charitable impulses helped their fellow human beings on the purely
humanitarian level. Without denying the greatness and importance

of these humanitarian "saints," we must realize that the real saint is something quite different. On the other hand, the holiness of the life led and the heroic virtue practiced are not selfish, leading to self-righteous indulgence, or to the conceit that one has direct contact with God, unlike the mediocre mass of people unable to arrive at such a peak of perfection. A saint is an image of Christ. As Saint Paul says, he is "alter Christus." The measure of a saint, therefore, is Christ. The life of Christ as his human nature lived it, its main characteristics, can be summed up in the two Commandments: Love thy God with all thy strength, and love thy neighbor as thou lovest thyself.

The unique harmony expressed in this really threefold commandment has been so often disregarded and forgotten: God, one's neighbor, and one's very own self. No saint can be imagined who loved his neighbor but who did not love God, or who said that he "loved" God but ignored his neighbor. And what kind of love of God does one possess if one indulges in a pietistic emotionalism and fake mystical experience but fails to love himself by failure to recognize his own sins and faults—that is, by failing to be constantly humble? It would not be love of God if one deliberately aimed at destroying himself because of a neurotic, unauthentic humility. In other words, if one takes the life of Christ as an example and scrutinizes each phase of His life and teaching, one cannot fail to discover this complete harmony. It should not be thought, however, that this harmony is a constant earthy "beatific vision." To love God and one's neighbor on an heroic level means to discern the harmony of suffering, if one is afflicted. Acceptance of suffering again does not mean that one should suffer at any cost. Christ in the Garden of Gethsemane asked the Father that the chalice of suffering should be taken away from Him. Nevertheless, He also asked that the will of the Father be done.

Saints are men, normal, sinning, penitent, men who also sin again and again. Nevertheless, they live in this constant harmony. They live a full life and they have their frustrations, tempers, and problems. In short, they are not angelic, perennially placid, bodiless, exclusively spiritual creatures, but persons of flesh and blood. They might even have characteristics or habits that one might not like or even find irritating. They are in no sense angels on earth, but rather prospective angels whose fight with evil is more acute, more tenacious, and more conscious than that of their fellow human beings. Saints are chosen. No one can become a saint simply because he wants to be a saint. But if God wants him among the chosen he will feel the heavy but loving hand of God on his shoulders.

Still no word has been said about the connection of sanctity and miracles—and rightly so, for miracles are not the indispensable attributes of sainthood. But it would be inconceivable to imagine that God should perform miracles on earth and disregard those who, while on this earth, were among His most faithful allies and collaborators, men and women who could hardly wait for the ultimate union with Him. If saints are chosen people, as they doubtless are, it is logical that God should let the world know that His elected son or daughter enjoys His total confidence. This is why it is said that a miracle happens because of the intercession of a saint. This is one of the meanings of the Communion of Saints: "The unity under and in Christ of the faithful on earth (the Church Militant), the souls in Purgatory (the Church suffering), and the blessed in Heaven (the Church Triumphant); it is shared in by the angels and by those non-Catholics in good faith who belong to the Church invisibly."[2]

This great union, this invisible yet existing and most active communion, is held together on the wings of prayer. Miracles and intercessions of saints occur most often in response to prayer. As it was beautifully expressed at the Council of Trent, we are connected with each other through the "bond of faith, hope, and charity."

The miracles wrought by God through the intercession of saints are visible signs and proofs of this communion, although we must believe in the existence of this communion without any miracles or proofs. These miracles are gifts, they are performed for us, for our good and welfare. They are not spectacular prodigious events to startle or shock us. Although we personally might not be able to believe in some of the miracles that followed after the death of the last of the Apostles, we should still respectfully assume that those responsible for the government of the Church for the past nineteen centuries have been as conscientious as ourselves and have had more occasion and opportunity to ponder circumstances and evidence than one single member of the faithful.

Biographies of saints are frequently criticized as being naïve and credulous. It is thought that lives of the saints, by definition, must always be pious recitals, deprived of any critical spirit and overladen with innumerable miracles, mostly legendary. On the basis of such a prejudice it is asserted that the early centuries of Christianity and the Middle Ages were characterized by a facile credulousness. As proof it is cited that during the Middle Ages there was widespread belief in the Apocryphal Gospels and the Golden Legends. Other critics charge that the first Christians had no greater sense of reality and truthfulness than those of the Middle Ages. As evidence they cite the so-called miracles of Apollonius of Tyana, which the early Christians attributed to the devil, rather than reject them *in toto*.

This, of course, is a superficial view, even though it is quite true that people in all ages have tended to be credulous, even overcredulous. But edifying lives of saints, devoid of criticism, are scarcer than skeptics would like to believe. It is true that during the Middle Ages many legends and popular tales were accepted as historical fact. Early medieval literature was replete with vivid tales of the martyrdom of saints who miraculously escaped from barrels of boiling oil, from lions, and from sundry instruments of torture. It should be pointed out, however, that these stories were written many centuries after the martyrdoms occurred. What is really important, however, is that almost the same facts are contained in the reports of the contemporaries of the same martyrs, very often written by eye witnesses whose good faith, truthfulness, and sense of responsibility bear comparison with the best of historical documents. In other words, there were enough persons in the primitive communities capable of recording actual events correctly. This, of course, was also their duty, since ecclesiastical authority was ever-vigilant in this respect from the very first days.

Not only did the first Christian apologists reject as lies and witchcraft so-called miracles of the pagans, but they also denounced them as the work of the devil. Now after so many centuries of scientific development and progress it can be said that the early belief that these so-called miracles were wrought by Satan is not so absurd after all. Indeed, it is corroborated by the reports of missionaries of all faiths. For instance, the secret society of the primitive African sorcerers requires candidates for membership to submit to an initiation ceremony during which the most horrendous crimes are committed. Furthermore, members of the society perform acts that are difficult to explain according to the laws of nature.

The Middle Ages tended toward a greater credulousness than did the ancient world because it was a society in which everything bore a Christian stamp, and no one doubted or contested the authority of the Church nor was it then considered necessary to be critical about reported miracles, for miraculous occurrences elevated the thought and sustained the hope of the faithful. So convinced was the medieval average man that God had wrought miracles and that He could make them at will, it hardly seemed to matter whether the birds had really listened to St. Francis of Assisi, or whether some pieces of cloth really came from Mt. Tabor, and were parts of the tent the three apostles set up there. It was more than sufficient that these beautiful tales should delight the people by depicting and glorifying the power of God. It is inherent in human nature to cherish any tangible evidence or relic of the past, be it an old uniform or a piece of furniture, even if its authenticity is questioned. The important thing is the desire to perpetuate the memory of those persons with whom cherished objects are associated.

After such admissions it must also be emphasized that even in those remote ages there were plenty of people in the Church endowed with innate good taste, excellent knowledge of theology, and a passion for certitude. They were the real disciples of the saints, whose authentic belongings and relics they sought to preserve for posterity.

The first recital concerning the martyrdom and miracles of a saint dates from February 22, A.D. 156. It is one of the most moving and at the same time most precise testimonies of this kind. In it the Christian community of Smyrna describes the martyrdom of Bishop Polycarp. This official document was written by his clergy immediately after his death. It reads like the minutes of a trial. Three days before his arrest the bishop dreamed that his face had caught fire. Upon awakening he told his priests, "I will be burned alive." And he was. As he was being tied to the stake, eye witnesses claimed that his body seemed suddenly to be surrounded by a blanket of air stirred up by a barely perceptible wind which seemingly protected his body from the flames. Yet his body perished.

Another such document is the description by the Christians of Lyons in A.D. 177 of the horrifying crimes and miraculous events that took place during the persecutions there. Even the skeptic Renan was convinced of the authenticity of this document, and he quoted it in his book on Marcus Aurelius. The document deals with the tortures inflicted upon members of the Christian community for six consecutive days, surpassing even the modern terror of Nazi and Communist concentration camps. Yet the victims of the anti-Christian terror did not give up their faith.

Before discussing more of these documents it is first necessary to separate those that report legends from those that truthfully report facts. Millions of people are familiar with the figure of St. George astride his horse slaying the dragon. This figure became a symbol of knighthood. St. George is the patron saint of England, and there are many people who like to believe that he was an Englishman.

According to legend there was a desolate city in Lybia, in North Africa, seemingly forsaken by man and God. A dragon dwelt in the marshes in the vicinity of the city, laying waste the surrounding land and constantly menacing the lives of the citizens. The dragon came up to the very gates of this city and poured his venomous breath into the streets and the houses of the frightened inhabitants. Flowers and trees died; the water in the wells became stagnant, and then epidemics decimated the population. To appease the hunger of the monster it had been agreed that each day a citizen was to be delivered up to be devoured by the dragon. One day it was the daughter of the king himself whom blind fate chose to be the victim of the dragon, and she was prepared to immolate herself for the community. As she was being escorted to the gate of the city, a knight came riding up the bridge. No one had seen him before. "My name is George," he said, "and I will kill the dragon." And so it came to pass. George liberated the daughter of the king and lifted the nightmarish siege of the city. The king offered the mysterious knight the hand of his daughter and immeasurable treasures, but he gently refused everything and disappeared. This is the legend of St. George.

The historical truth is somewhat different. All that is known is that his tomb was venerated in Lydda, Palestine, and that it has been the goal of many pilgrimages since the fourth century. Otherwise, nothing is known of his personality. Efforts have been made to identify him with one of the martyrs executed during the persecutions of Diocletian, but they have not been too convincing. Efforts have also been made to establish his birthplace in the Orient, close to the Black Sea. The fact that St. George is highly venerated both in the Oriental and Occidental Churches lends some plausibility to this hypothesis. But this is all that is known about him. The cult of St. George received new impetus during the Crusades when he was chosen as patron saint of the cavalry. The legend about the dragon, the besieged city, and the king's daughter dates from the eleventh century. That St. George actually existed is a fact because his tomb in Lydda was a shrine of veneration between the fourth and ninth centuries. Many documents refer to this veneration. The rest is legend. Should St. George for this reason be removed from the roster of the saints of the Church? Such an idea is unthinkable. His figure has ennobled generations of men and has been a perennial source of the highest virtues, even though the miracle of the dragon remains legendary.

Another saint, among many, whose figure gloriously lives on in the imagination of men, mostly in the East, is Achatius. According to the legend, he was the leader of those ten thousand martyrs who were executed during the third century on Mt. Ararat. Miracles attributed to him were numerous during the Middle Ages. He was chief of the fourteen saint helpers ("auxiliary saints") in all emergencies. They were called upon when nothing or no one else could help. Other members of this group were St. Blaise, St. George, St. Erasmus, St. Vitus, St. Margaret, St. Christopher, St. Pantaleon,

St. Cyriacus, St. Aegidius, St. Austachius, St. Dionysius, St. Catherine, and St. Barbara. Most stories about them are legendary.

St. Aegidius was born in Athens in the seventh century. As a
young man he withdrew from the world and became an anchorite
in a forest in southern France. Here he saved a deer pursued by
hunters, and this legendary beast fed him in his hermitage thereafter. St. Cyriacus was a Roman who suffered death during the
persecution of the Emperor Diocletian. In the legend he cured
Artemia, the daughter of the emperor, of an evil spirit. St. Dionysius
was martyred on the hill now known as Montmartre in Paris. Legend
has it that after his head was cut off he walked with his head in his
hands from Montmartre to the place where he wanted to be buried,
now the site of the Abbey of St. Denis in France. St. Vitus, patron
of many professions and of the sick, was once one of the most popular
saints in Western Europe. After his execution, according to the
legend surrounding him, he was lifted up by angels and brought
back to his place of birth to be buried there.

Who is not familiar with the figure of St. Nicholas, the prototype
of Santa Claus? In southern, central, and eastern Europe children
pray to St. Nicholas on the night of December 6 to bring them gifts,
mostly candies and cookies. According to this legend, St. Nicholas
goes from house to house. Where the children have been good he deposits his gifts on their doorsteps; and if they have been naughty he
calls the devil, who accompanies him, and the devil leaves a stick
there instead. The legend of St. Nicholas also says that he raised
three children, killed by a wicked innkeeper, from the dead. Other
stories tell of miracles in which he saved ships in distress on the high
seas. But all that we know about St. Nicholas is that he was Bishop of
Mira during the second half of the fourth century. The rest of his life
is a mixture of legend and fact, many elements of which were taken
from the life of another St. Nicholas who lived in the sixth century,
also in the neighborhood of Mira. He became one of the most popular saints in both the Oriental and the Western Church. In France
and Germany about two thousand churches are dedicated to him,
about four hundred in England, and forty in Iceland.

St. Nicholas is usually represented by the side of a vessel wherein a certain man had concealed the bodies of the three children, whom he had killed but who were restored to life by the saint. The relics of St. Nicholas of Bari were translated there in 1087 and after fifteen centuries "the manna of St. Nicholas still flows from his bones and heals all kinds of sick."

As we have seen, the saints of the Old Testament, like Jacob and many of the prophets, were in communication with God in their dreams. So was St. Joseph, who in a dream was advised what to do with Jesus and Mary. It seems that in the first centuries of Christianity God often communicated with His elect in this way. Mention has been made of the dreams of St. Polycarp. Similar to this are the dreams in the life of St. Cyprian. After arriving in the city of Curubis, St. Cyprian, in a dream, saw a young man who led him into a room where a tribunal had just signed his death sentence. Later, the event took place in exactly the same way as in the dream and Cyprian underwent a martyr's death. This was described by the Deacon Ponzio, a disciple of St. Cyprian, and the authenticity of his description is beyond doubt. Another saint of the third century, St. Perpetua, received a vision while in prison. In this vision she witnessed her own execution and her reception into heaven. Before her martyrdom she recounted her vision in detail to Deacon Ponzio.

Many other authentic miracles could be cited from the fourth and fifth centuries. It suffices for our purpose, however, to refer only to one whose authenticity is confirmed by friend and foe: the miracle of St. Augustine, the Bishop of Hippo. St. Augustine, in *De Civitate Dei*, relates the events of his time in Africa and in Milan. His description is deliberately exact and detailed—as though he knew that later ages might question the facts. In connection with a miraculous cure, St. Augustine, like a good reporter, describes the disease of a person in medical terms, and when he has doubts he gives expression to them. He always made a special point of describing miracles that he himself had witnessed, emphasizing that others could give similar eyewitness accounts.

One of the miracles occurred in Milan "while we were there," writes St. Augustine. It concerned a blind man who had regained his sight, and took place in the presence of the Emperor and a great crowd. St. Augustine attributed this miracle to the intervention of two martyr-saints, St. Gervase and St. Protase.

Another miracle (Augustine describes twenty-one of them) occurred in Carthage where an official of the government, a certain Innocent, was cured while "we were present and saw it with our eyes." St. Augustine described Innocent as a very religious man, who for many years had been suffering from an incurable disease. He had a fistula that covered his entire body and was treated by the doctors in the most primitive manner, typical of the age.

St. Augustine describes the exterior location of the fistula. For three pages he deals with attempts of doctors to operate on Innocent and the excruciating pain suffered by the poor man. There was no hope of saving him. When his death seemed near, his friends, the bishop and St. Augustine himself, recited prayers in his room. St. Augustine then wrote as follows: "I do not know what the others prayed for and I do not know whether they noticed the great pain of this man. As far as I was concerned, I was unable to pray. I said only in the intimacy of my heart, What prayers do you listen to if you do not listen to this? I was convinced that nothing more could be said and that the only thing was to ask God that [Innocent] should die praying." The next day Innocent was completely cured. The wounds were healed, and only the scars remained.

There is one miraculous event in the life of St. Augustine himself. He related this in his great work on the Holy Trinity, De Trinitate. One day he was walking along the seashore completely immersed in contemplation of the mystery of the Holy Trinity. He was trying to devise a method for explaining the seeming paradox of the Trinity to the human mind, when suddenly he saw a little child playing in the sand. The child had dug a hole in the sand and with a tiny spoon was trying to fill the hole with water from the ocean. St. Augustine jokingly addressed himself to the child: "You do not mean to put the whole ocean into this little hole, my child?" The child looked up, his angelic eyes staring fixedly into the eyes of the venerable Bishop of Hippo, and answered, "I should be able to do that before you solve the problem of the Trinity." Then the child suddenly disappeared. Although this angelic vision is the only miracle recorded of St. Augustine himself, he never doubted the existence of miracles and wrote one of his greatest essays on them.

As Christianity developed and established itself, most miracles came to be associated with saints who were not martyrs—for example, St. Martin of Tours, whose biographer, Sulpicius Severus, is unfortunately thought to be somewhat overcredulous. St. Martin, the son of a Roman officer and knight, was born in Pannonia (present-day Hungary). Educated as a Christian in Italy, he was very much drawn to monasticism and wanted to become a hermit. But as a son of a veteran of the Imperial Roman Army he was obliged to serve, and he fought valiantly in Gallia, in Noricum, in Raetia, the present territory of France and Germany. Everywhere the people lived in utter misery. At the gates of the city of Amiens a half-naked beggar once asked him for help. Martin took off his mantle, cut it in two with his sword and gave one part of it to the beggar. That same night he dreamed he saw Christ coming down from heaven wearing the same piece of mantle around his shoulders. Christ was surrounded by angels to whom He said: "Martin, who has not yet received baptism, gave me this mantle." Shortly after this vision Martin was baptized. He became a wandering preacher, founded monasteries, and in 371 became Bishop of Tours.

The greatness of Martin, Bishop of Tours, manifested itself very shortly in a crucial question. When an apostate priest, Priscillianus in Spain, founded an heretical sect, many bishops asked the Emperor that he be punished and put to death. The end of the fifth century, not too distant in time from the day when Christians were persecuted and killed for their faith, was a crucial period for Christianity. Martin, the Bishop of Tours, protested and did everything possible to prevent the bishops from carrying out their plan, but to no avail. Priscillianus was tried before an Imperial, not an Ecclesiastical, court, and beheaded in 385. This was the first sentence of blood pronounced and executed by Christians. It was the beginning of many centuries of religious wars, bigotry, and intolerance. As Martin of Tours felt that he could not remain in such a world any longer, he retired to the monastery of Marmoutier and died there twelve years later.

Martin was the first great champion of the freedom of the Church from political power, and at the same time he united in himself the monastic ideal with apostolic activity. Thus it seems quite just that this exceptional figure of early Christianity should have possessed the gift of miracles. Besides the vision that led to this conversion, he raised the dead and healed the sick. This happened during his office of bishop as well as later when as a monk in Marmoutier he Christianized large regions of Western Europe. His biographer has noted particularly that he prayed incessantly for those bishops who refused to heed his words and condemned heretics to death. He prayed also for those druid priests and pagans who were captured and put to trial; and many of them, it is recorded, were saved miraculously by these prayers. His miraculous power was recognized by the Church throughout the centuries. The liturgy of the Mass for his Feast hails him as *Trium mortuorum suscitator* (the man who raised three from the dead).

When we enter the Middle Ages we are faced with a whole thesaurus of miracles. The most important legends of the miraculous of the Middle Ages concern St. Francis of Assisi. His miracles were most significant for the greater glory of the Church, as was the rest of his activity, which brought about a new high level of Christian spirituality. In his life and through his stigmata St. Francis was really a living image of Christ. It is known that he hid his divine wounds and that very few people knew about them during his lifetime.

The most important account of these facts was that of Thomas of Celano who obtained his information from two Franciscan brothers, companions of St. Francis. The stigmata were later viewed by a great crowd that marched before the bier in which his body was exposed after his death. According to Thomas of Celano, the entire city of Assisi ran to Porziuncola in the mountains above Assisi where Francis had died, so that everyone could see the stigmata. Thomas writes that the wounds were filled with hardened blood in the form of nails. These clots looked like real nails, for if they were pressed from one end they came out on the other. Thomas declared that he had seen all this, and had touched the wounds and the nails. These were not simple wounds. Both feet and both hands were completely pierced by these nails of blood, as if someone had literally hammered them into his flesh. Thus the stigmata of St. Francis were not simple phenomena of bleeding as described in our chapter on certain physical phenomena of mysticism.

Although there has been some question about the stigmata of St. Francis of Assisi, we can safely go along with Thomas of Celano's account. Thurston, in his exhaustive scientific essay on stigmata,[3] comes to the conclusion that "the historical evidence leaves us absolutely no ground for doubting the reality of St. Francis' wound marks," and that the stigmata of the Saint of Assisi were probably identical in nature with stigmata observed during the course of history. There is no question about their supernatural nature. These wounds were not self-inflicted. No fraud was involved. Thurston points out that while hysterical patients can sometimes produce similar scars, nothing can be compared with the stigmata of St. Francis of Assisi. Few miraculous cases of the Middle Ages have been studied so deeply and thoroughly as the stigmata of St. Francis.

Renan suspected that one of the heads of the order "made" the wounds after his death. It would have been impossible to create nails of blood and in any case the stigmata were known to only a few of the brothers before the death of St. Francis. The suspicion of Renan may be discarded, since there was no such sign of deceit and hypocrisy in the life of the saint. The life of St. Francis, by the particular grace of God, was so saturated with the miraculous that it seemed that nature herself wanted to glorify him. If St. Francis had been only a simple, hysterical monk, how could his work and his spirit have survived for seven hundred years? His spirit is still alive, and is considered one of the great moral forces, not only of the Church but of all mankind. Countless people outside the Church are attracted by the spirit of simplicity, love, and universal brotherhood preached and lived at a sublime exemplary level by St. Francis. A further proof of his greatness has been the amazing success of the Franciscan Order, its steady growth and enormous importance in the life of the Church and society.

St. Elizabeth of Hungary, the daughter of King Andrew II of Hungary, was betrothed in infancy to Louis, Landgrave of Thuringia, and brought up in his father's court. Later, when she married Louis, she was not content "with receiving daily numbers of poor in her palace, and relieving all in distress, she built several hospitals where she served the sick, dressing the most repulsive sores with her own hands. Once as she was carrying in the folds of her mantle some provisions for the poor, she met her husband returning from the chase. Astonished to see her bending under the weight of her burden, he opened the mantle which she kept pressed against her, and found in it nothing but beautiful red and white roses, although it was not the season for flowers. Bidding her to pursue her way, he took one of the marvelous roses, and kept it all his life. On her husband's death she was cruelly driven from her palace and forced to wander through the streets with her little children, a prey to hunger and cold," but she welcomed all her sufferings. She continued to be the mother of the poor. She died in 123 at the age of 24.

St. Claire of Montefalco, also called Claire of the Cross (1275-1308), belonged to the very severe order of the Augustinian Sisters. After a life of penance she died very young. At her death her heart, extracted from the body, which the sisters had embalmed in a most primitive way, bore the figure of the crucified Christ, the scourge, and the five stigmata, totally impressed in the flesh. It is interesting to note that the heart of St. Veronica Giuliani (1700-27), showed the same mystical signs. Her heart was thoroughly examined by two great physicians in 1920, and it was established then that the marks on her heart are exactly the same as those on St. Claire's.

Saint Vincent Ferrer was called the "angel of judgment" by his contemporaries because in a vision he heard the voice of Our Lord telling him to convert sinners "for my judgment is nigh." Born in 1350, (died 1419) at Valencia in Spain, his entire life was spent in apostolate and preaching all over Europe. He reached small villages as well as towns in England, Ireland, Scotland, Italy, France, Switzerland, Spain and he spoke only his native Spanish but he was understood everywhere in all tongues. He converted thousands. Wherever he went the blind, the lame, and the sick flocked to the church and great miracles followed his appearances.

St. Catherine of Siena (1347–80), had to fight strenuously to achieve her aim of becoming a nun. She dedicated her life completely to charity in the deepest sense of the word: softening the burdens of the poor, nursing even the most repulsively sick, and caring for the wounded on the battlefield. She defended unwed mothers, Jews, and illegitimate children against maddened crowds that sought to stone them. In 1374 she received a vision. She became stigmatized, and Christ told her that she should work for peace, preaching peace to priests, laymen, and even to the hierarchy, and show them a "weak woman can shame the pride of the strong." From this moment Catherine dedicated her entire life to fulfilling the order she received in the vision. She corresponded with princes, bishops, and Popes. She begged, prayed, and threatened in an heroic effort to achieve unity in that chaotic period of the late Middle Ages. Her life was marked by many miraculous events. The evidence of her levitations is overwhelming. The stigmata are proven. In Catherine's body, after her death, one could trace the stigmata by the transparency of the tissues.

She received communion without the Host's being brought to her. During a journey from Avignon to Rome the priest celebrant consecrated the Host and was about to give the general absolution when he noticed that Catherine's face was strangely radiant. When he wanted to touch the consecrated Host, he could not because it had moved forward by itself about three or four inches to the paten and then had leaped to her. On another occasion, Catherine was close to the entrance of the Church while a priest was celebrating the Mass and received Holy Communion there, for, as she said, "It was brought to me by our Divine Lord Himself. . . . He deigned to appear and gave me the particle that you consecrated with His own sacred hands." Once, while working in the kitchen, she sat down by the open fire and fell into ecstasy. When she was found later she was lying on the fire itself and had been lying in it for more than an hour. Neither her clothes nor her body had been injured.

St. John Nepomucene (1345–93), was a martyr to the secrecy of the confessional. King Wenceslaus requested him to disclose what his wife, Queen Joan, had told him in the confessional. When the priest refused he was arrested, dragged through the streets of Prague, bound hand and foot, and thrown into the river Moldau. The tongue of St. John Nepomucene has been entirely preserved. According to Pope Benedict XIV, when the tongue was examined 332 years later, in 1725, the experts declared that it was whole, that it had kept the normal shape, size, and color of the tongue of a living man. In addition, it was soft and flexible. The Church has accepted this as a miracle of the second class, explaining that divine intervention had preserved intact the tongue which refused to disclose a secret of the confessional.

St. Catherine of Bologna (1413–63) became an Abbess of the order of Clarist nuns. A woman of great artistic talent, she composed music, painted, and wrote hymns in Latin. She also wrote about her mystical experiences. Johann Joseph von Görres, the great German Catholic philosopher and writer, describes certain miraculous occurrences involving her as follows: When she died and the grave was dug, the sisters carried her body to be buried without a casket. As the body of the saint was lowered into the grave an incredibly sweet fragrance emanated from it, filling the entire cemetery and regions beyond. . . . After several days, when the sisters visited the tomb, the fragrance was still there. There were no trees, flowers or herbs on the grave or in the vicinity and it was safely established that the scent came from the grave. Soon, about eighteen days after the interment, miracles began to happen at the grave. Persons incurably sick were cured. The sisters suddenly felt guilty because they had buried the body without a casket and that as a result masses of earth might have fallen on her face. They thought the body should be exhumed and placed in a casket. The sisters went for advice to the confessor of the convent, who was quite surprised to learn that after eighteen days the body had not yet started to decay. And when the nuns told him of the fragrance still emanating from the grave, he gave his consent for the exhumation. It was found that St. Catherine's face was only slightly distorted because of the pressure of the earth. Otherwise the body had remained white and fragrant, without any sign of decay. The fragrance became even sweeter, pervading the church and the immediate neighborhood. Then the body that was white as snow turned slowly red and exuded an oily liquid of an ineffable fragrance. Before the body was interred again it was examined by many doctors and ecclesiastical authorities. Exhumed again three months later, it was still found to be intact and giving off the same fragrant scent.

Nicholas of Flue, the patron saint of Switzerland, was the son of peasants. As a youth he tended the fields and livestock on alpine slopes, and in general there was very little extraordinary about his early life. He married, had children, and felt quite satisfied with his life. But he felt also that he had to express his gratitude to God for what had been given him; so he fasted and mortified himself as a sacrifice to God. He fought in the several wars that preserved the freedom of Switzerland. His righteousness and his sense of justice earned him the greatest respect of the people, who wanted to elect him as counsellor and judge. At first he resisted the idea of accepting such a trust, but finally did so out of a sense of duty. When eventually he was allowed to return to the plough he was much happier.

Throughout his life, however, an inner voice urged him to leave his family, whose well-being was permanently assured, and to become a mendicant. He left his family in 1467 and went to live as a hermit in a log cabin he had built himself. He became a joyful helper of the poor and lived in a state of constant penance. Slowly the people began to understand that they had a true saint in their midst. Pilgrimages to him started and a chapel was built near his cabin. Those who had mocked him now seriously sought his advice. He preached the gospel constantly. Once when civil strife threatened it was prevented through his intervention, and since then he has been venerated as the patriarch of Switzerland. One of the most extraordinary miraculous happenings in his life was his very long fast. It is said that he took no food for twenty years—from 1467 until his death in 1487.

St. Catherine of Genoa, who was descended from the Fieschi family which had given two Popes to the Church, was the daughter of the Viceroy of Naples. She wanted to enter a convent but instead her family married her to an influential patrician of Genoa. Catherine suffered much from her husband's brutality, which she bore with exemplary Christian patience. Later, however, in the tenth year of her marriage, she lost all hope. Upon the advice of her sister, a nun, she went to confession and thereafter her life underwent a complete change. She acknowledged her own sins, but at the same time she recognized within herself a unique love of God and this never left her again.

She fasted very severely, and for many years during Lent she nourished herself only with the Host of the Holy Communion. At the same time she cared for her husband and household and dedicated herself to nursing the sick. Her great fasts lasted from 1476 to 1499. During Lent and Advent of these years she took only water mixed with vinegar and pounded salt. After drinking this mixture she would declare that the mixture refreshed rather than harmed her. At the same time she seemed to be afire. Occasionally during these ecstasies she would lose her speech and sight, remaining in this state for about three hours. She indicated with her fingers that she felt as if red hot pincers were clutching at her heart. Sometimes the burning was so intense that she could not stay in bed. "Once a large silver cup was ordered to be brought in which had a very high saucer; the cup was full of cold water for refreshing her hands, the palms of which, because of the great fire that burned within her, pained her terribly. Upon dipping her hands into it, the water became so boiling hot that even the cup and the saucer were heated in turn."[4]

One of her ecstasies was so violent that a rib was forced out of place. (The phenomenon of the displaced rib also occurred, as we shall see, in the life of St. Philip Neri, in an ecstasy during which his heart expanded.) She was described as a seraph by her contemporaries. There was no question that she was burning with the fire of love, *incendium amoris*, known in the mystical lives of saints, and that she bore the stigmata internally. But she never allowed these supernatural phenomena to be known to the outside world.

St. Francis Xavier (1506–52) belongs to the classic great missionaries of Spain. Although many miracles are related by his early biographers, some of them were discarded later because reliable evidence was lacking. His later biographers consider the "real miracle" in St. Francis Xavier's life to have been his manner of expressing love for God and for his fellow man. This was the "magic" that worked upon the Japanese, the Indians, the Chinese, and the natives of the Pacific Islands. Nevertheless, there are attested cases of genuine miraculous events in his life which cannot be overlooked. Cases of levitation were reported about fifty years after his death, but none during his lifetime. This weakens the evidence with respect to levitation but does not completely rule it out. As for the phenomenon of bilocation, even so critical a reviewer of physical phenomena in the lives of the saints as Thurston admits that the "bilocations which are related in the story of St. Francis Xavier would seem to be of quite ordinary occurrence."[5] He was reported to have been at several places at the same time, preaching to the natives.

St. Teresa of Jesus (1515–82), called also St. Teresa of Avila or the great St. Teresa, and St. John of the Cross (1542–91), are the greatest mystical teachers of the Church.

Teresa of Avila was raised from early childhood in a profoundly Christian spirit in which the Passion of Christ and the stories of the martyrs played an important role. At the early age of seven she wanted to leave home, together with her younger brother, to go to Africa and to die there for Christ. At the age of twelve she lost her mother, and in her great and almost unbearable suffering she asked the Mother of Christ to assume her care henceforth. She was convinced that this prayer was decisive in her life. Several months followed, however, during which she was completely under the influence of the romance literature of the age. After a serious illness, during which she read the letters of St. Jerome, she decided to become a nun. She entered the Order of Carmel, which she later reformed with the help of St. John of the Cross. She founded 17 convents for nuns and, together with St. John of the Cross, 15 monasteries for Carmelite monks.

Her life was one continuous desire to live in union with God. Her descriptions of her mystical experience are unique in the history of literature. In her *Autobiography* she describes a vision in which she saw an angel who pierced her heart with a long golden spear with a fiery point. She also wrote a hymn based on this vision. After her death, her heart was extracted and a white horizontal fissure was found in it. This is still in evidence on the relic enshrined in Spain. St. Teresa of Avila is a case in point proving that the mystic is not abnormal but supernormal. She was completely integrated into life, practical, and full of common sense. She not only founded convents and monasteries but also administered them efficiently.

St. John of the Cross, now celebrated as one of the great teachers of the Church and author of some of the classics of Spanish literature, started life as a craftsman. After being discharged several times for incompetence, he became a hospital attendant, and in his free time studied in the school of the Jesuits. He entered the Carmelite Order in 1563 and was ordained in 1567. Arguing that the contemplative life of the order was not adequate, he decided to enter the Carthusian Order. In the end, however, he was persuaded by Teresa of Avila to remain and undertake the difficult task of reforming the order. After his first attempts, he was arrested by a superior of the order, and locked in a cell for nine months. Nevertheless, he succeeded in instituting reforms. He lived in almost complete austerity and ever in mystical ecstasy, yet he did not receive the stigmata. His body was found uncorrupted and fragrant nine months after death. When a finger of his body was cut off, it bled. The body was exhumed several times during the centuries and always found intact, the last time in 1859, almost three hundred years after the first interment.

St. Teresa was beatified in 1614 and canonized eight years later, in 1622. At her beatification and canonization processes abundant evidence was presented of miracles after her death. During the processes the four miracles approved were: the instantaneous cure of a four-year-old child afflicted with encephalitis, the instantaneous cure of a nun with three cancers, the miraculous cure of a priest's incurable stomach ulcer, and the cure of a young layman with a cancer of the throat.

The miracles accepted in the cause of beatification of St. John of the Cross were the instantaneous cure of a complete lethal apoplexy, and the cure of a nun who had been paralyzed for ten years.

St. John of the Cross was beatified in 1674 and canonized fifty-two years later, in 1726.

St. Philip Neri (1515–95), known as the Apostle of Rome, and also the joyous saint of Rome, belonged to the old nobility of the city, but at the invitation of one of his uncles he decided to become a merchant. From early youth Philip was passionately dedicated to the Faith. He heard Savonarola preach and knew Fra Angelico personally. The personality of Fra Angelico, however, had greater attraction for him than did the severity of the Dominican reformer in Florence. Thus slowly he decided that he would, as a layman, devote his life to the people, and particularly to the youth of Rome. The beginnings of his apostolate were inconspicuous. Philip made a practice of conversing with townspeople of every class—with workers, artisans, and even with politicians. His conversations were witty and urbane but he always succeeded in convincing his hearers that the burden of the Lord is sweet. His piety had nothing dour about it, and he sang and laughed easily. In the meantime he secretly studied theology. When this was discovered he protested against the idea of becoming a priest. Out of a sense of humility he feared that as a priest he might not be able to continue his apostolate among all walks of people. Even so, he was ordained at the age of thirty-six.

St. Philip was one of the great attractions of Rome for as long as he lived. Members of the great Roman families, and men like St. Francis de Sales, St. Charles Borromeo, and others, often visited him in his little apartment. He never lost the aim he had set for himself: to restore Rome, then imbued with the spirit of the Renaissance, to the spirit of St. Peter—that is, to make it once more the City of the Apostles. But now he was no longer alone. A large group of friends, both priests and laymen, now carried out this apostolate under his leadership.

St. Philip was endowed with extraordinary supernatural gifts. Levitation seemed to be an almost natural phenomenon in his life during Mass, as well as at other times. He never denied that "it seemed to him as if he had been caught hold of by someone and in some strange way had been lifted by force high above the ground." He never asked for these extraordinary favors and resisted them when they appeared. His cell was often radiant with light that emanated from his body. In 1544, the day before Pentecost, he retired for meditation to the chapel of the catacombs of St. Sebastian. While immersed in contemplation he felt that he was in an extraordinary way "filled with God," and at the same time his chest, above the heart, became enlarged. After his death, medical examination proved that two of his ribs had separated from each other and bent outward without causing him the slightest pain. Evidence also disclosed that after he had died, he raised his arm in benediction for many hours.

One should not make the mistake, however, of assuming that this joyful saint of Rome was one to condone laxity and frivolousness. He expressed his opinions boldly and frankly to youngsters, adults, priests, cardinals, and Popes. Although he was against sadness for the sake of sadness he strongly urged that one should seek mortification by overcoming one's pride and self-will.

Another Italian mystic of the 16th century whose life was richly endowed with the physical phenomena of mysticism was St. Catherine of Ricci (1522–90). A great admirer of Savonarola, she became a Dominican nun. At the beginning, however, she suffered intensely in the convent because the mystical gifts she possessed were not recognized by her superiors. In their opinion her spiritual life was distorted and poisoned, so that they were minded to send her back to the world. But she remained in the community and endured her sufferings and illnesses patiently. Soon she became prioress and remained in that post for twenty-five years until her death.

In 1542 on each week from Thursday afternoon until Friday morning she received the wound marks of Christ's Passion and relived the sufferings of Christ. This created a great sensation all over Italy, and the convent attracted innumerable visitors—both genuine pilgrims and mere curiosity seekers. She fled the curiosity of people, and whenever she learned that people were coming she hid herself in a closet, in the shrubbery of the garden, and once even in the pigeon cote. She did, however, help needy people who had not come as sensation seekers. She prayed to be relieved from these sufferings, but only after twelve years was her prayer answered.

Catherine possessed other mystical gifts, among them the sign of the mystic espousal, a phenomenon to be described in connection with the lives of other saints. She was surrounded by a radiant light when she fell into ecstasy, and at the same time a sweet-scented fragrance filled the room. Also possessing the gift of clairvoyance, she predicted an attempt against the life of St. Charles Borromeo, at that time Archbishop of Milan.

San Bernardino Realino (1530–1616), wanted to become a civil servant in the service of the great ducal family of Este. The brilliant world of the Renaissance, of which he was an authentic representative (he even fought a duel to appease his offended sense of honor), was open before him. In 1564, after a crisis of conscience, he joined the Society of Jesus and became a priest. San Bernardino dedicated his life to the education of youth and to the care of prisoners, slaves, Christians and non-Christians alike. He lived and died as an example of altruistic self-sacrifice for others. According to his biographers no harsh words ever left his lips. It was attested at his process of beatification that a visitor, and later others, had once seen him surrounded by light while sparks of fire emanated from his body. These witnesses asserted that the radiance was so strong they could not clearly see the features of Father Bernardino and had to turn their eyes away. A visitor once called on him in the early morning just before dawn and found him praying on his knees, while the radiance emanating from him lighted up the whole room.

St. Aloysius Gonzaga (1560-91) was a son of the Duke of Mantua. Because of the worldly spirit of his family, immersed as they were in the long and bitter conflicts among the Italian city states, his aim to become a priest was difficult of realization. At last, however, he was able to enter the Society of Jesus, journeying to Rome to enter the novitiate. There he became one of the many victims of the plague—with the difference that he knew the date of his death in advance. But this was not the only miraculous event in his life. Pope Benedict XIV, in his treatise on the beatification and canonization of saints, lists Aloysius Gonzaga among those through whose intercession the convent in which he had lived was provided with abundant food by supernatural means—that is, by multiplication.

St. Louis Bertrand (1530–81) was the son of a notary in Valencia, Spain. At the age of ten he left home in order to make a pilgrimage to the great shrines of Europe. Later he entered the Dominican Order, and the rest of his life was spent in the proximity of the greatest dangers. He had no fear of the plague that decimated his native city and the surrounding area. In 1562 he went to South America and lived among the native Indians of Panama. Among them he went hungry for long periods and marched weeks and weeks on foot through trackless jungle. There, too, several attempts were made on his life. All his life he had the gift of prophecy, and was also responsible for some miraculous cures. Upon returning to Spain he became a close friend of St. Teresa of Avila, who often asked for his advice and assistance.

In the process of beatification it was testified that his cell appeared illuminated as though the strongest lamps were being used. Other witnesses described the moment of his death, when "a brilliant light flashed from his mouth, illuminating the whole cell with its splendour, and this lasted for about the length of time that is needed to recite a Hail Mary. . . . A perfume of astounding fragrance rose from his dead body and heavenly music was heard by many in the church where the body was awaiting burial. . . . Seven hours after his death his body was cold but the limbs were flexible and the flesh felt as if alive. . . . Thirty-six hours after his death, before the interment the body was found unchanged, the flesh white as alabaster and the face shining with a peculiar and attractive beauty while the limbs were perfectly flexible."[6]

St. Mary Magdalen de'Pazzi (1566-1607) led a life of prayer even as a child. At the age of sixteen she entered the Order of Carmel, and while still a novice, preparing for her final vows, she fell sick. Her condition seemed hopeless, and the superiors, feeling that her death was imminent, decided that she should be allowed to take the final vows. The sisters carried her into the church and there she made her final profession. Upon being brought back to her bed she expressed a desire to rest. The curtains of her bed were drawn and everyone expected that she was going to die in peace. After an hour or so, when the sisters opened the curtain, they found to their great surprise that she was in total ecstasy, her features radiant and her eyes fixed on the crucifix. A total change had taken place. She was no longer the pale and anemic Sister Mary Magdalen of an hour ago; she now looked like an angel from paradise. This, her first ecstasy, lasted two hours. And each morning after Communion for forty days thereafter she fell into the same ecstasy. Nevertheless, the ecstasies did not change her personality. (Ecstasies never change the personality of a saint.) Though her health was still affected she worked hard. She became novice mistress and later subprioress.

After 1590 her ecstasies became more and more frequent, and were marked by dialogues with the Holy Spirit, with the Blessed Virgin, or with one of the saints. During these dialogues she asked and answered questions. It was not difficult to discern with whom she was speaking at a particular moment, as her voice changed according to the answers she received. Sometimes her voice was formal, dignified and majestic, at other times warm and full of love; whenever she spoke in her own name her voice would be lower and softer, almost inaudible. In these states of ecstasy, she was seen levitating, and even when not in ecstasy she seemed to be exempt from ordinary physical laws. Her confessor said that she walked with an incredible swiftness. She was raised to dangerous places, once to a height of about thirty feet. When Mary Magdalen de'Pazzi died at the age of forty-one her body remained incorrupt. Sixty years after her death her body was still intact and fresh, and a fragrant oily liquid exuded from it.

The life of St. Joseph Cupertino, who is also known as St. John Joseph of the Cross (1654–1734), furnishes one of the most extraordinary instances of levitation. He was a Franciscan monk who lived a life of penance and possessed the gift of penetrating into the very hearts of those who came to him for confession. One of his great miracles was connected with St. Januarius (Gennaro) whose blood, preserved in the cathedral of Naples, becomes liquid on certain occasions. Some years before his death, he went with the crowd into the cathedral to venerate the blood of St. Januarius. Then an old and feeble man, he used a walking stick for support. He managed to reach the altar, but upon leaving the cathedral somebody knocked the cane out of his hands and he could no longer walk. Then, as he later told his friends, he asked St. Januarius for help. Immediately thereupon he was lifted up above the heads of the crowd and carried out from the cathedral. Once outside he sat down, and after a while his stick moved through the air about a foot and a half above the heads of the people and settled down beside him.

St. Joseph was also seen in levitation at other times. Evidence reveals that he was raised in the air to a height of five and six feet. On one occasion he was lifted to the roof of the church. On another, while people thought he was walking in a procession that extended for two miles, in reality he was in ecstasy and was being carried about a foot above the ground all the time.

St. Veronica Giuliani (1660–1727) entered the convent of the Capuchin nuns at the age of seventeen. Her life was marked by phenomena that are associated with only a very few mystics. She had revelations, visions, ecstasies, and other graces. In 1696 she received "the wound of the Heart," which was discovered only after her death. Two years later she received the stigmata on her hands and feet. The bishop of the city reported everything to Rome and was advised to carry out a very rigorous examination in order to ascertain the authenticity of the phenomena. He went to the convent with several experienced priests and examined the wound marks. Physicians were ordered to "heal" the wounds with special treatment that involved putting bandages and gloves on her hands. The wounds refused to heal, and instead they became larger and larger.

Next, the abbess was directed by the bishop to test Veronica's patience, humility, and obedience with the greatest rigor. She was relieved of her duties as novice mistress, deprived of her vote in the assembly of the nuns, forbidden to associate or talk with any of the sisters. In addition to these prohibitions she was forbidden to participate in the choral office, to hear Mass, and to receive Holy Communion. Further, she was locked for fifty days in a cell that looked more like part of a prison than a convent. Then she was treated as though she were insane or an impostor. She remained steadfast, however, and received the stigmata and shared the experience of the "mystical espousal." In a vision on April 11, 1694, she received the mystical ring from the hand of Christ. As witnesses testified, "This encircled her ring finger as ordinary rings do. On it there appeared to be a raised stone as large as a pea and of a red color." While not ordinarily visible, this ring could be seen quite clearly at times. During her ecstasies a sweet fragrance pervaded the room where she lived.

Veronica Giuliani did not ask for these favors, and endured with great humility the doubts, the accusations, and endless examinations at the hands of her skeptical associates and contemporaries.

St. Benedict Joseph Labre (1748–83) was a beggar, or even, as some might say, a tramp. He came from a well-to-do French family, the eldest of fifteen children. Because of his kindness and apparent piety, his parents sent him very early to one of his uncles, a priest, for his formal education—presumably for the priesthood. Until his sixteenth year he made good progress, but then everything seemed to go awry with him. He could no longer absorb learning, and he wanted to enter a very strict religious order. His state of mind was similar to that which St. John of the Cross has called "the dark night of the soul," during which God prepares His chosen for union with Himself. He sought to enter several religious orders, but his efforts were in vain. He was refused by the Trappists, the Carthusians, and the Cistercians, either because he was too young, or not strong enough, or it was felt that he would be unable to abide by their rule.

Then he decided to go on foot from France to Italy, to Rome itself in search of a monastery with a strict rule. While he wandered thus, he received a vision that enlightened him about his future life. This inner vision revealed that it was God's will that he should leave his country and family and all that is pleasant in life and live a life of penance like St. Alexis. This penitential life was not to be lived in the desert or in a monastery but in the very midst of the world, while he wandered from one sanctuary to another as an eternal pilgrim.

From this moment on, his soul was filled with deepest peace, and all the attempts of his confessors to persuade him to settle down and dedicate himself to some work failed. He began his wanderings, and his life thenceforth was spent on the highways and byways of Europe. During the day he visited the churches that were open, and at night he looked for churches in which perpetual adoration was observed. He quenched his thirst at public wells and stilled the pangs of hunger with the refuse he found on the streets. He slept under bridges and gateways. In Rome he slept in the Colosseum, where he was known as the "poor man of the Colosseum." But his wanderings and pilgrimages were not aimless; he was well-versed in theology and as he wandered he contemplated the great mysteries of faith. Once he said to a priest, "When I meditate upon the crowning of Christ by thorns, I feel that I am lifted up to the Holy Trinity." The priest protested, "You are an uneducated man, my friend; what do you understand of these mysteries?" And the beggar-saint replied: "I do not understand anything, but I feel myself to be drawn to these mysteries."

This was precisely true, for often he became wrapt in ecstasies. One day, while he was praying in the church of the Gesu in Rome, other worshipers began to notice that he was in a kneeling position, levitating in the air. When the sacristan was asked what had happened to this poor beggar, he replied with an altogether Roman calm, "The saint is in ecstasy," and went on sweeping the church as though this were the most common thing in the world. Several instances of bilocation occurred during his life, for it has been attested that he was seen at two places talking at the same time. His funeral drew such crowds as had not been seen in Rome since the burial of St. Philip Neri.

As he lay in state it was very difficult to believe that he was dead. One of the doctors opened his veins to make absolutely certain of it. Still, his body remained warm for many days; the limbs were supple, and his hand grasped onto a bench with the natural gesture of a living person. Rightly does Karl Stern observe in his book *The Third Revolution*, "There always remains an element of madness in the spiritual encounter." He points out that St. Benedict Joseph Labre never did any so-called useful work. "He embraced a peculiar form of poverty. Most of the time he was unkempt, unclean, and covered with vermin. Today there would be a big file on him in one of the social welfare agencies; there would be personality tests and he would be classified in category E by army physicians. When it comes to the life of the spirit, our concept of normalcy breaks down because it is a concept of conformity. . . ."

St. Clement Hofbauer (1751-1820) was the son of a poor and very pious Austrian family, half-Czech, half-German. As a youth he worked as a baker's apprentice, craftsman, and layservant in a monastery. For a time he was also a student, earning his tuition by working for the school. After a pilgrimage to Rome he entered the Redemptorist Order and was ordained in 1785. After two years' work in Vienna he left there because of the anti-Catholic attitude of Emperor Joseph, and settled in Warsaw, where he lived for the next twenty-one years, preaching in both German and Polish, and occasionally in Czech. Here he founded several schools and other institutions for young people.

After his return to Vienna in 1808 he immediately became the center of the spiritual and also the intellectual life of the city. Sometimes he spent as many as eighteen hours in the confessional, forgiving the sins and directing the conscience of the poor and the rich, of the day laborer as of the aristocrat. During the Congress of Vienna in 1815 his influence upon the assembled statesmen, writers, and philosophers was amazing. No one could ignore his superhuman energy. One of the statesmen at the Congress said that he could name only three people with real energy; Napoleon, Goethe, and Clement Hofbauer.

His biographers, as well as witnesses at the process of beatification, note several diabolical attempts to hinder his mission. In 1801 while he was preaching to a great crowd in his Warsaw church on the subject of Holy Communion, the cries of a suffocating child could be heard—but there was no trace of any child in the crowd. At another time, before Communion, one could hear a deep murmuring and then terrible shouting: "A child has been suffocated!" Another voice shouted: "A woman has just died in the crowd!" The whole congregation froze into a frightened silence and searched for the alleged victims, but nothing was found. Then suddenly from hundreds of different points of the church, could be heard shouts of "Fire! Fire! The church is burning!" Everyone saw the smoke and the flames, and the crowd was in the grip of panic. The smoke and flames were also seen from outside. When the firemen arrived, they could find no trace of fire or smoke. The church was completely intact. The incident was attributed to diabolic intervention.

On the same afternoon, as St. Clement prayed before the altar of St. Joseph, hundreds of people saw a cloud forming above the altar, and then enveloping the figure of the saint, who disappeared from their sight. In his place the congregation saw a celestial vision. A woman of great beauty, with radiant features, appeared and smiled at the worshipers, who only a few hours ago had been frightened by the prodigies of the devil. The sanctity of St. Clement was accepted by everyone who encountered him. After his death miraculous cures occurred continuously through his intercession, and people afflicted with incurable diseases asked his help and received grace.

St. Clement appeared several times in a vision to his friends and to people whom he protected. In 1822, he appeared to Zacharie Werner, one of his most intimate collaborators. Father Zacharie had just finished his evening prayers in his room, when suddenly his cell was illuminated by a great light that surpassed the radiance of the sun. In the midst of this light he suddenly saw Clement Hofbauer and heard him say, "Zacharie, come, come, come soon." Then the figure disappeared. Zacharie Werner testified later that he was not dreaming or hallucinating. A few weeks later he died.

Another apparition is related by the sisters of St. Ursula in Vienna. St. Clement appeared to Sister Sebastiana and told her that she was to become a saint. The sister, completely humbled, could not answer at first. Then she told the apparition that she felt unworthy, whereupon St. Clement assured her that he would assist her when she died. Several years later, when Sister Sebastiana lay dying, the nuns around her bed heard her exclaim that St. Clement had kept his promise. And the sisters saw him appear and disappear while Sister Sebastiana passed into eternity.

The bodies of many saints have been immune from natural decay—an immunity that has lasted, in some cases, for several centuries. The preservation of their earthly remains is very often related to other phenomena, sometimes the absence of rigor mortis, sometimes the presence of a delicate fragrance emanating from the body.

This fragrance persists sometimes for years. Another phenomenon is the persistence of warmth and, occasionally, the bleeding of the dead body. In modern times several scientific explanations have been offered to explain this phenomenon of incorruption—and all of them have been inadequate. The most important among them suggests that these saints lived an ascetical life, abstaining from the kinds of food that would increase putrefaction. The fallacy of this theory is evident if we consider that the corpses of the thousands who die during famine are not exempt from decay. Further, the phenomenon is unknown in such regions of the world where the population, because of its extreme poverty, lives year in and year out on a very "ascetical" diet.

The first known case of incorruption was the discovery of the body of the martyr St. Nazarius by St. Ambrose of Milan. After two hundred years the martyr's blood was fresh and his decapitated head incorrupt.

St. Francis Xavier, who died in 1552, was disinterred in 1553 and the body was found fresh. At a new disinterment in 1556 it still had its natural color.

The body of St. John of the Cross, who died in 1591, was found nine months after his death to be incorrupt, and when the fingers were cut the corpse bled. Almost three hundred years later, in 1859, the body was still incorrupt.

St. Charles Borromeo, who died in 1584, was found in 1880 in the same condition as at the burial.

St. Joseph Calasanctius died in 1649. After his death the viscera were removed (not embalmed). His heart and tongue are intact up to this date.

St. Angela Merici died in 1540. Her body remained flexible for thirty days. At the disinterment in 1672 it had a sweet scent, and in 1876 it was still intact.

There are several cases from the 19th and 20th centuries. St. Madeleine Sophie Barat, foundress of the Religious of the Sacred Heart, died in 1865. At the distinterment in 1893 her body was found to be intact though the coffin was decayed.

St. John Vianney died in 1859. His body was intact at the disinterment in 1905.

Although the decomposition of the human body follows a very complicated process that is not yet completely understood, these phenomena cannot be explained entirely by natural causes. And it must also be kept in mind that the bodies of the above-mentioned saints had not been embalmed.

For the last five hundred years the people of Naples have been witnessing a unique and, until now, unsolved phenomenon which is generally accepted to be of supernatural origin. This is the liquefaction of the blood of St. Januarius (San Gennaro). The blood of San Gennaro in coagulated form is contained in two phials, one 36 cubic inches and the other 15.25 cubic inches. They are hermetically sealed and locked in a metal box and safely stored away. Once a year (the date differs from year to year) this solid blood becomes liquid, and the Neapolitans consider this a miracle. Interestingly the prodigy always occurs on some important occasion such as the anniversary of the translation of the body of San Gennaro, or the anniversary of his martyrdom, during the visit of an illustrious personality, or during the public display of the box containing the phials.

The liquefaction occurs under various and mysterious circumstances. Seemingly, no natural or physical cause contributes to it. On certain days the liquefaction occurred when the temperature was 75°; at another time at a temperature of 86°, and another, when the temperature was 67°. The liquefaction does not always occur in a fixed length of time. Sometimes the blood liquefies after only a few minutes of expectation, but there have been cases when the entire congregation waited for three hours. And the volume of liquefaction varies. At certain times, it fills up the phials, at other times it reaches only up to the halfway mark or more. It has also been noted that the weight varies. All these data have been carefully recorded. Thus, in two cases when a phial was filled halfway the weight in each case differed. Chemical examination of the substance has proven that it is blood.

All hypotheses aiming to provide a natural explanation of the prodigy have failed up to now. The question whether the blood is really San Gennaro's could not be definitely answered, but written records going back as far as 1329 explicitly state that on August 17, 1329, the blood of San Gennaro became miraculously liquified. According to tradition and research the blood of San Gennaro was preserved in the basilica of Stefania, Italy, before the 13th century.

San Gennaro had been a bishop of Benevento during the fourth century. He was decapitated together with three others. At first the trio of martyrs had been condemned to be thrown into the amphitheater of Pozzuoli, near Naples, to be devoured by wild bears at a public spectacle. Because of a judicial delay, they were decapitated instead. San Gennaro's name is mentioned in several Church documents in Rome, in Germany, and in other places. There is no doubt about the historical reality of his existence and martyrdom.

San Gennaro is one of the patron saints of Naples—and the most popular of them. In particular he is the protector against fires because of one legendary episode in his life. According to this legend, after his arrest by the persecutors he was thrown into a furnace but remained unscathed. San Gennaro is invoked specifically when an eruption of Vesuvius threatens, or during an eruption. He is also invoked against earthquakes, plagues, and epidemics—in short whenever calamity hovers over Naples. The manifestations in honor of San Gennaro are the most colorful in Naples. But it is not the popular veneration that has attested to the authenticity of the liquefaction, its cause, and its nonnatural origin. Scientists and Church authorities have done considerable research in order to establish the facts.

Many other prodigies or miraculous events involving blood are recorded in the history of saints. In *The Physical Phenomena of Mysticism,* Thurston cites the case of an English hermit of the eleventh century, St. Goderic of Finchale. According to his biography, written by a friend, Goderic was well over ninety when he died. He had been bedridden for about eight years. Before his brethren could bury him, relic-seeking crowds rushed to his hermitage and cut the nails from his toes, even cutting into the flesh. From these cuts there poured out more blood than the human body contains. It is written that the prodigy happened about fourteen hours after death and that people afflicted with grave diseases were instantly cured upon contact with this blood.

A similar case is the completely unexplained prodigy of St. Pacificus di San Severino, who died in 1721. After four years his body was exhumed and found to be incorrupt and giving off a sweet scent. While the body was being moved, the carriers slipped and the head of the saint struck on a stairway, whereupon the head detached itself from the trunk of the body and fresh blood gushed forth from the neck.

All these cases are admittedly unsolved by science.

Elsewhere in this chapter we have mentioned the preservation of the tongue of St. John Nepomucene. There are similar cases of preservation, such as the heart of St. Bridget of Sweden; the right hand of St. Stephen, King of Hungary, whom the entire nation venerates, and the hand of St. Oswald, King of England.

In order to found monasteries of Benedictine nuns, the great apostle of Europe and particularly of Germany, St. Boniface summoned thirty nuns from England, among whom was his niece Walburga. She was the daughter of St. Richard and a sister of his collaborators, Wunibald and Willibald. St. Walburga was appointed Abbess of Heidenheim in Bavaria. She died in 779, after governing the abbey for twenty-five years. Venerated as a saint soon after her death, she has been credited with innumerable miracles, which occur to this day. The greater part of her relics are enshrined at St. Walburga's convent in Eichstadt, Bavaria. Since the year 1042 a miraculous oily fluid, odorless and tasteless, exudes from her bones during four months of each year. This phenomenon has been occurring for almost one thousand years up to the present day.

Another example is that of St. Gerard Majella, who died in 1756. His tomb was opened for the process of beatification in 1856—one hundred years after his death. Official statements ascertained that a mysterious oil flowed in such abundance from his bones and his brain that it filled a basin. About six months later the body was examined again and found to be somewhat damp due to the humidity of the soil. It was then dried and placed in a chest lined with cloth. Several hours later, when the examiners opened the chest, they noticed that the same kind of oil, giving off a sweet odor, seeped out from the bones.

It is of interest to note here that both brothers of St. Walburga were canonized and the earthly remains of St. Willibald remained incorrupt. The convent of the Benedictine nuns in Eichstadt, Bavaria, attracts many pilgrimages and it is a great center of spiritual life for the entire German people. The convent assumed a new importance during the administration of Abbess Marianne Benedicta Spiegel, who was Abbess from 1926 until her death in 1950. During her lifetime and after her death the convent seemed to be favored with extraordinary spiritual endowments which it is claimed are of supernatural origin.

Although he is not canonized, Abbé Olier's case belongs to this chapter. Abbé Olier, the founder of St. Sulpice, was convinced that the religious life of France had to be reformed. Once he participated in a religious retreat under the direction of St. Vincent de Paul. Abbé Olier was in his cell, praying, when suddenly he saw St. Vincent de Paul approaching him. In one hand he held the crucifix and in the other a crown. His guardian angel, whose beauty was beyond description, followed him. Later Olier was in his room immersed in prayer when he saw a vision. A lady of great beauty and majesty approached him holding in one hand the crucifix and in the other a crown. An angel held her mantle and this angel's beauty was also beyond description. The lady's eyes were full of tears. She looked at Olier, her features in great pain and penance, and said the following words: "I shed tears for you . . ." Olier was convinced that he saw the Blessed Virgin.

Nevertheless, he went to the convent at Langeac because he had heard about a nun of great sanctity, Mother Agnes, and he had a presentiment that it was this Mother Agnes whom he had seen in the vision. Mother Agnes at that time was the prioress of the convent and she received Olier in the customary manner, her face covered with a veil. Abbé Olier asked her to remove the veil and then he cried out: "Mother, I have seen you somewhere else." And Mother Agnes answered: "It is true, you have seen me twice in Paris and I appeared to you during the retreat in St. Lazare because I received orders from the Holy Virgin to pray for your conversion because God has chosen you to reorganize all the seminaries in France."

This was not a dream of Olier. The lives of both Olier and Mother Agnes contain sufficient corroborating evidence to substantiate the facts. And Olier succeeded in establishing the seminaries which later on produced sufficient priests for France, for North America, for Indochina and other places.

There are miraculous happenings in the lives (or after) of most of the saints. It was not our intention, nor is it possible here to cite all the saints of history, but the reader will find here a selected list of miracles taken from a selected list of saints. Some readers will miss their favorite saints. We had no room left to describe the prodigies of St. Anthony of Padua. Thus we mention here only the most important miracles from his life. Once when he arrived in Padua he went to stay with a friend. At night this friend saw a brilliant light streaming from under the door where the saint stayed, and surprised by the strange radiance, he looked through the key hole. Then he saw a little child standing upon a book which lay open on the table. The child embraced Anthony, both his arms around the saint's neck. When the vision had vanished, St. Anthony asked his friend not to tell anything about what he had seen until after his death. When he died, voices of children were heard crying in the streets of Padua: "St. Anthony is dead, our father Anthony is dead." We did not list St. Thomas Aquinas or St. Dominic who, according to his biography, in 1218 resuscitated a youth who had been fatally thrown by his horse. Or St. Nicholas of Tolentino who never ate animal food. Instead he restored to life the doves which his fellow monks had brought to him as a delicate morsel during his illness.

In view of the most recent utterances of Pope Pius XII about the importance of the cult of The Most Sacred Heart of Jesus, we felt that the reader is thoroughly acquainted with the life of Mary Margaret Alacoque. From early childhood on, she manifested a deep horror of sin, and after she entered the Order of Visitation, the most important events in her life were the visions of Jesus. In these Christ displayed his Sacred Heart, now burning furnace-like, now torn, bleeding for the sins of the world. In 1675 she was told that she would be the person to institute the veneration of the Sacred Heart—a vision which has been confirmed thoroughly throughout the last three centuries.

Nevertheless the selection of the saints and miracles was not arbitrary in this book. Wherever we could we have chosen those miracles which were witnessed and confirmed by many and which are phenomena of mystics whom Church history calls thaumaturgi or wonderworkers. But not even in this field can we claim this list to be complete.

CHAPTER 9

Saints and Miracles Among Us

It is much easier to accept a St. Paul and a St. Peter or a St. Augustine as a saint, surrounded as they are by the glory of the past, than it is to acknowledge a contemporary saint. Likewise, it is easier to imagine that the grace bestowed upon them made these venerable figures exceptional beings rather than to concede the same thing of persons whom we have known, or who lived among our immediate forefathers. We find it hard to believe that these contemporaries are really saints, that they "worked miracles," that during their lifetime they were in intimate touch with the supernatural, with God.

But the study of saints and miracles of the 19th and the 20th centuries can be highly fruitful for us. No matter how unreservedly we now accept their greatness, we must put ourselves into a proper frame of mind and recognize that these persons whom we venerate as saints, and whom we accept as great and exceptional figures, were usually not considered great and important in the opinion of the world. In turn this gives us a significant insight into the very essence of sainthood.

The lives of 19th- and 20th-century saints provide us with an opportunity to compare them to those persons on whom tradition and history have laid the hand of immortality, as well as to measure their effect and influence upon the community.

From this point of view the last hundred and fifty years provide some revealing facts. This history of this specific time encompasses the lives of our parents and grandparents as well as our own. Thus we almost personally, physically touch the whole period from the end of the 18th century on. These last hundred and fifty years have produced great men and heroes in a secular sense; all over Europe, and even in the New World, there were social revolutions and wars of emancipation. This was also the age bearing the name and the impress of Queen Victoria. Finally, our entire technological and industrial development took place during this period. In no other age has human achievement ever been so zealously fostered, proudly accepted, and universally acclaimed. Men of the 19th and the first half of the 20th century had a much stronger sense of what was specifically human, in the most earthly sense of the word, than of the supernatural.

In the eyes of the world the saints of this period are less than inconspicuous, simple persons of no conceivable consequence. Catherine Labouré was a peasant woman; Bernadette Soubirous, a poor girl from the lowest social stratum. John Vianney, the country priest, was an obscure and awkward figure. Thérèse Martin (St. Thérèse of Lisieux), an average French middle-class girl, chose the obscurity of a Carmelite cloister. The Pope who became a saint during this period, Giuseppe Sarto (Pius X), was a farm boy without any ambitions for material success. Maria Goretti (who died in 1902) was the hardworking young daughter of a wretchedly poor Italian family. Conrad von Parzham, a Bavarian Capuchin laybrother, served throughout his long life as doorkeeper and errand boy of his little community. And Giuseppe Cottolengo gathered the destitute, the crippled, the maimed, and gave them a home—although he did not have the means of making a home for himself.

Many other saints and blessed are even more prosaic figures. The characteristic they have in common is not the performance of miracles, or the fact that miracles occurred after their deaths, but that their very lives were spent in love for neighbor and God which was expressed in a *heroic* degree. These persons were not professional social workers or benefactors of humanity, they were not do-gooders; they simply dedicated their entire lives to God from the "very moment of truth" in which they recognized their true mission. All "moments of truth" are accompanied by a readiness to die, and for this they did "foolish" things (in the Pauline sense): things that seem utterly mad and incongruous to the world.

None of these contemporaries who have been canonized by the Church had any desire to perform miracles (this is also true of all the saints throughout history). Whether it is during the life of each one, or after death, the miracle seems to take place according to a divine plan. Obviously God has chosen the most humble, the most ingenuous persons to teach that His Kingdom is not of this earth, and to hold up these seeming nonentities to a world that has become increasingly hardened by pride, self-sufficiency, status-consciousness —intellectual, material, and even spiritual.

The behavior of Catherine Labouré, the Saint of the Miraculous Medal, is revealing in this respect. She was a strong, healthy peasant girl who worked in the fields and for a while as a waitress in a Parisian inn owned by her uncle. If one can imagine even a respectable place in the Paris of 1828, frequented by all sorts of people—soldiers, workers, vagabonds, minor officials—one realizes that a girl of her age needed both moral balance and physical strength to cope with the situations arising from her job. But nothing was more alien to her than pride of any kind. Upon entering the convent later, she reached a long sought-for and cherished goal. A novice in a convent is on the lowest rung of the spiritual ladder; she must be put to the test and taught to be humble. Thus Catherine Labouré was inconspicuously and completely submerged in the anonymity of the thousands and thousands of novices being prepared for religious life in the convents of the Church.

Yet, it was this wholly insignificant girl whom Divine Grace selected to receive an apparition. One night in 1831 she was suddenly called by an angel and led into the chapel, where she met the Blessed Virgin. This girl, who had not yet been introduced to all the rules of monastic life, and whose knowledge of the world was limited to the simple facts of tending the household, tilling the soil and waiting on tables, was entrusted by the Blessed Virgin with messages of extreme importance: prophecies about France and the world which later became true. And this young woman whose sense of reality was razor-sharp received the great privilege of being allowed to touch the hem of the Virgin's garment during the miraculous occurrence.

But the miracle of Catherine Labouré consists not only in the fact that she received these glorious apparitions; her life became a model of heroic virtue. She accepted these apparitions humbly and not as a reward or distinction for her person. She reported it to her confessor, who thereupon tried to discourage her by suggesting that she was a victim of hallucinations. As a matter of fact, the priest did not accept the apparitions as true, and Catherine did not disclose her secret to anyone else. When her confessor finally consulted the bishop, even the bishop refused to believe a word, and Catherine did not insist.

When the investigation disclosed the facts clearly, and the bishop allowed the medal requested by the Blessed Virgin to be coined, and when the Bishop himself witnesses a great spiritual miracle through the intervention of the Virgin of the Miraculous Medal, Catherine Labouré still remained silent. Once the bishop came to the convent and told the nuns that someone among them was favored by the Blessed Virgin. The Bishop did not disclose Catherine's name, nor did the nuns know who the elected person might be. Yet Catherine Labouré kept her secret. Her entire life remained rooted in this self-effacing simplicity. It might be objected that it ought not have been a great effort for her to withdraw and to keep the mystery to herself. But she managed it for forty-seven years. For forty-six years she remained in the Convent of Enghiens, where she predicted her own death one year before it occurred. On December 31, 1877, one of her fellow religious said to the dying nun, "Sister Catherine, you are leaving us now without telling me a word about the Blessed Virgin." The Sisters by that time knew about the apparition to Catherine. But even on the threshold of death Catherine replied, "It is not I who should speak."

The miracles connected with the great apparitions, the miracles that occurred through her intervention, and her life spent in work and contemplation on a heroic scale have spoken for Catherine. She was canonized in 1947. It was the Blessed Virgin's intervention through Catherine Labouré that led to the conversion of the two Jewish industrialists, the Ratisbon brothers. Alfred Ratisbon's illumination, which occurred in the Santa Maria delle Fratte Church in Rome in 1865, was also a miracle. During the canonization process the Church accepted two miracles that took place through the intervention of Catherine Labouré after her death. One of them occurred in 1929 to six-year-old Jean Ribet, a French boy of Toulouse who was afflicted with Pott's disease, and was instantaneously cured on November 26, 1929. Innumerable spiritual graces have been received all over the world as a consequence of the apparitions in Rue du Bac, when the Blessed Virgin said to Catherine: "Grace will be showered upon all who ask for it with faith and fervor." When Catherine Labouré's body was exhumed nearly fifty years after her death it was found to be in a perfect state. The hands that once were allowed to touch Our Lady had not been allowed to decay.

The world was amazed by the life, works, and miracles of St. John Vianney. Theodore Maynard writes correctly that "the 18th together with the early 19th century produced relatively little sanctity and was the age when the Catholic Church appeared to be at so low an ebb that made many acute observers declare that the world stood at her deathbed." This, however, was only the appearance of things. Hidden sanctity flourished. It is enough to read the case histories of canonized saints, who were born or lived during that period. But even among them, the case of John Vianney is more than exceptional.

He, too, came from a peasant family, poor and struggling, and he had a difficult time finishing his education. Born in 1786, he "grew up as a child under the shadow of the terror of the French Revolution." The little village of Dardilly in the Pyrenees had been entrusted, according to the new laws, to a schismatic priest, so that most of the people ignored his church, going to the neighboring village in order to hear Mass. Dardilly and the house of the Vianney family had another importance for the spiritual development of young John Vianney. It was there one night that his grandfather gave shelter to an unwashed vagabond. And this man, who blessed the house that had given him asylum, was Benedict Joseph Labre, the Beggar Saint, canonized in 1785. John Vianney was far from brilliant, in fact, he failed his examinations several times. When he was finally ordained a priest at the age of 29 (a little later than his fellow seminarians) he was not allowed to hear confessions, only to celebrate Mass. He was assigned the remotest, poorest, most primitive parish in the diocese. Ars, as the parish was called, had only two hundred souls.

Yet, this man, who was called stupid, dull-witted, ignorant, whose few letters written to the bishop were full of mistakes in spelling, is a shining embodiment of St. Augustine's ejaculation: "Behold, the ignorant arise and snatch heaven beneath our eyes."

His life in Ars was a regular sequence of miracles. All of them occurred before the eyes of the inhabitants of Ars, and later before the thousands of people who came to him to learn the wisdom of God. As one of his biographers wrote, he lived in a glass house. An unsophisticated man who had no visions and no apparitions, Jean Vianney worked miracles none the less.

Another biographer rightly observed that "the first miracle of the Curé d'Ars could not be admitted by the Church, for it concerns the influence of John Vianney and the genius of his sermons . . . with his extraordinary power of provoking confession and confidence." This was not considered supernatural. Yet it deserves recounting because it reveals the hand of Providence. At the beginning of his career as pastor, he stopped in the middle of his sermon because he had lost its thread. After much sweating and blushing, he apologized and left the pulpit. This happened so often that eventually none but a few old women went to his church.

Then, suddenly, he no longer prepared his sermons. He spoke from his heart, fumblingly but coherently. He did not elaborate on any great theological conceptions but spoke of love, God, and sinners. "He no longer knew what he said," according to his biographer.

At this moment the miracle of Ars began. Every time Père Vianney preached in his own parish, the crowds overflowed onto the public square fronting the church; and he was insistently invited to preach in the neighboring villages. It was not eloquence that drew such crowds of listeners, but something else—a rare Christlike holiness that opened the hearts of penitents in the confessional and made them leave the church with joy after receiving his absolution. Père Vianney did not threaten people with eternal fire and damnation; rather, he implored God, he talked with Him and wept and repented. All his sermons had essentially one theme: the love of God. If God loves us, how can we keep from loving Him and his redeemed children—our neighbors?

Although it was not miraculous in the technical sense, this love, which revealed the simplicity inherent in true holiness, made the erstwhile "fool" one of the best-known men in all France. Pilgrims jammed the roads to the village. Atheists were converted. Then the other miracles followed—authentic ones accepted by the Church. Père Vianney, it seems, addressed people by their first and last name, when he had never seen them before. A deaf man regained his hearing, a blind person his vision. But Père Vianney attributed these miracles to St. Philomena, to whom he was devoted. He told visitors hidden secrets about their past (in each case before witnesses) and in such number that no clairvoyant could ever dream of succeeding so consistently. One day a young woman obsessed by the fear of death, went to see him. After only one or two minutes of conversation, he told her: "It is death that you are afraid of, my dear daughter."

On another occasion a peasant wanted to find out whether his sick wife would be cured or not, and only for this purpose did he kneel in the confessional before Père Vianney. The peasant had no intention of making a real confession of his own. As soon as the man entered the confessional the Père Vianney told hm: "Please return tomorrow." On the next day, he heard the same injunction: "Return tomorrow." But on the third visit, Père Vianney, in a loving voice tinged with sadness, said to the peasant: "My friend, I think this is enough, you want to cheat God and me."And he went on to tell the astonished peasant about un undisclosed crime he had committed, citing the exact location of the crime, the prison to which he had been sent, and finally the reason he wanted to simulate confession.

To provide for the poor in his parish and in the neighborhood, Père Vianney founded an orphanage and called it "The Providence." One day the Sister Superior of the institution told him that they had no bread and only enough flour to feed about five persons—and eighty hungry mouths had to be fed. (In the village itself there was no baker, since every housewife baked her own bread.) "Put yeast into that little amount of flour you have," Père Vianney advised. The mixture was prepared, and next morning when they started to knead it, the dough kept on increasing until, instead of two loaves sufficient for five, they managed to make ten big loaves, each weighing 22 pounds—as though a whole sack of flour had been used.

On another occasion, the barn was empty: they had no wheat, no flour, and—no money. When John Vianney was informed, he pondered the possibility of distributing the orphans among the neighboring villages because of lack of food. While thus pondering, he went to inspect the barn, accompanied by the sisters. The veracity of the sisters, who had reported that the barn was totally empty, cannot be questioned. Nevertheless, when only a few minutes later Father Vianney arrived with them, the barn was full. Later when he went to see the anxious orphans he announced the miracle with these simple words: "My poor little children, I lost confidence in Divine Providence and I was ready to lose you. . . . So, God had punished me."

St. John Vianney always remembered this miracle, attributing it to St. Francis Regis, whom he had chosen as protector of the orphanage.

Actually, a saint never attributes to himself the miracles that occur during his lifetime, but very often it is to the protector saint on whom he has chosen to model his own life. Don Bosco, one of the great miracle-workers of the 19th century (1815-88), chose St. Francis de Sales, one-time Bishop of Geneva, probably because his amiable character strongly appealed to him. St. Francis de Sales, however, achieved his serene disposition by constant struggle against his own sharp temper. Don Bosco, on the other hand, as Jorgensen, the Danish biographer and poet, wrote: "is a result, the fruit of the people to which he belonged. The Italian people, full of fundamental goodness, have been influenced, formed, changed, perfected, educated and ennobled through centuries and generations by the faith. And this faith is its ferment in its daily life. Don Bosco is a full and perfect blossom of Latin Christianity." This is evident from his great practical love for the young. In understanding youth, handling their problems, and providing for adequate means for their interests, Don Bosco was a genius. But he was a genius in another sense, too. Long before

St. Joseph Benedict Cottolengo. Lithograph by F. Perrin.

St. Gaspar del Bufalo. Painting by Missori.

The martyrdom in Australia of St. Pierre Louis Chanel, painted for the beatification ceremony. Painting (artist unknown).

St. Pierre Louis Chanel. Portrait (artist unknown).

St. John Bosco. Photograph of the saint.

St. Conrad von Parzham. Photograph of the saint on his catafalque.

St. Bernadette Soubirous. Photograph of the saint on her deathbed.

Pope St. Pius X. Photograph.

social problems became acute, he understood that the modern social problem is not simply the problem of being poor or being rich. Modern social problems are of a more complex spiritual-material nature. Don Bosco's parents were Piedmontese peasants, but the father died when the future saint was two years old. He was brought up by a deeply religious mother, with the help of the priest of the neighboring village, who discovered extraordinary qualities in the boy. His memory, for instance, was probably as prodigious as Mozart's. Thus he decided early to study instead of becoming a farmer. Miraculous or near-miraculous events started very early in his life. Despite his interest in study, he was uncertain about his vocation—that is, whether or not to become a priest. One night he had a dream in which the Blessed Virgin told him to "care for her flock of sheep." From this moment on, dreams played an important part in Don Bosco's life.

This son of poor peasants became one of the great reformers within the Church, a man who clearly recognized that without concerted efforts to improve the care of young people, and other necessary social reforms, tremendous political and social catastrophes were inevitable. His idea was to make the millions and millions of boys who are neglected and play abandoned in the streets conscious of God, of their lives, and of the need to be good citizens.

The schools he began to establish in 1841 were not to create intellectual prodigies, but to transform neglected children into good citizens and balanced, industrious adults. The aim of the Society of St. Francis de Sales which he founded was to educate youth at many levels—in grammar schools, in high schools, and in agricultural and trade schools. Don Bosco's success as an educator and a leader of men may be measured by the fact that this religious community ranks third in membership among the religious societies and confraternities of the Church. It should not be forgotten, however, that Don Bosco's community was founded only some hundred and fifteen years ago at this writing. This growth, in itself "a miracle," indicates that Don Bosco was a profound realist, a thoroughly saintly man, and even a good businessman.

His schools have turned out hundreds of thousands of well educated and technically skilled young men all over the world. Don Bosco oratories for boys now number 600, for girls 800. In addition, there are 150 trade schools for girls and 750 trade schools for boys, plus 70 agricultural schools. Don Bosco also established boarding schools, of which there are now about 500 elementary schools, 200 high schools, and 30 colleges. Further, there are 170 houses of study for Salesian fathers and brothers, and 80 for Salesian sisters, which provide trained educators and workers for all these institutions. The growth of this world-wide organization was spontaneous, its administration simple and alien to bureaucracy; and its influence on other religious orders and on Catholic and non-Catholic educational systems has been enormous.

All this must be recounted here in order to put Don Bosco, as a person, in the proper light. If there ever lived a full-blooded man free of neurosis or hysteria, it was Don Bosco.

His life, full of miraculous events, is the more interesting and surprising. The miraculous contact with the supernatural, even in the experience of many saints, is rare and exceptional, but in Bosco's life it was so frequent that it became almost ordinary, common and natural. The extraordinary accomplishments surrounding him, or achieved by him, were so rich in novelty and beauty that "at last their circumstances were dressed in divine elegance," as Pope Pius XI expressed it.

As for his dreams, Don Bosco, very often attributed them to "jokes of the imagination" so as to minimize their importance. But these dreams become something more than "jokes" when it is borne in mind that they were directly connected with Don Bosco's work and that most of these dreams are integral parts of his life. His mother knew that during the night "surprising things" took place in connection with her son. When he was six years old, the mother brought her bed closer to her son's in order to find out what was going on. One night it seemed to her, and to a young relative who was present, that her son was talking with another person. At times he asked questions of this mysterious other person; then again it seemed that he was replying to questions put to him. It was certain that no one else had entered the young boy's room.

In the morning, when he was asked about what had happened, the boy answered that he had had a conversation with a friend. "But this friend has been dead for many years," the mother protested. "Yet I talked with him." He did not explain further, but for days one could see the emotion registered on his face. Moreover, there seems to be little doubt that the Blessed Virgin appeared several times to Don Bosco.

In 1864 he went with two other priests to preach in a village in a region where for the last four months there had not been a drop of rain and a devastating drought threatened many thousands of people. During his three-day mission in this village Don Bosco told the congregation that the Blessed Virgin promised him abundant rain if they would repent of their sins. Thousands upon thousands went to confession, but no rains came. Priests, municipal authorities, and many of the people were disappointed. One of the great landowners said to Don Bosco: "This time, Don Bosco, you are a failure." "If there is no rain," replied Don Bosco, "it will be a sign that we do not deserve it." At the end of the third day, the dry heat continued and the sky remained completely clear. Then amid the demonstrations Don Bosco prayed again and the rain started suddenly within seconds and lasted for hours.

Another miracle that was repeated several times before the eyes of many youngsters and adults was the multiplication of food. It happened that one day in 1860 there was no bread in the institute where Don Bosco was living at the time. They had no money and the baker refused to deliver bread unless the debts were paid. At dinner time Don Bosco was advised of the scarcity of the bread. He told his associates to put all the bread they had in one basket; witnesses under oath later testified that in the basket there was no more than twenty large rolls. Then Don Bosco began to distribute the bread and he gave one roll to each of the three hundred pupils. After he had finished the distribution, there were still twenty pieces left. A similar event happened once during a celebration of Mass when at Communion he suddenly discovered that there were not enough hosts in the chalice. To the great surprise of Don Bosco and the other priests assisting him, the chalice filled instantly and he was able to serve Communion to all the boys. When asked about these incidents, Don Bosco confirmed them.

Don Bosco also possessed prophetic qualities. He foretold events and facts that no human speculation could have predicted. His prophecies would fill an entire volume. In 1844 in the confessional he told the wife of the Portuguese Ambassador to Piedmont that on that very day she would undergo a serious accident. In March, 1845, he predicted the death of one of his pupils, a healthy seventeen-year-old boy, citing the exact date: December 23, 1855. In 1866, September, he again predicted the death of another member of his community. This time, the prophecy leaked out. The police came to question Don Bosco, and the saint told them the name of the person and the date of his death. He was a very young priest, who in fact did die during the same year, on the very day predicted by Don Bosco. Among his other prophecies are those predicting the fate of Paris, in singularly interesting detail, during the Franco-Prussian War.

Don Bosco struggled with diabolical forces too, as many of the saints did. Here we offer other evidence of Don Bosco's supernatural gifts, akin to St. John Vianney's. For Don Bosco also could read and decipher the secrets of his fellow men. One day, in 1850, while another priest was present, a vagrant entered Don Bosco's room and asked for help, pleading that his five or six sons had nothing to eat. Don Bosco helped him. The other priest asked him how he knew that this man was not a professional panhandler who would spend the alms at the next inn. Don Bosco answered, "I have read it in his heart," he said. The same priest later met the man, and the former vagrant told him that with Don Bosco's alms he had provided for his whole family and that their situation had started to improve on that very day. Don Bosco knew exactly what was happening simultaneously in other institutes belonging to his community, no matter how distant they were from Turin, where he lived.

Levitation in a state of ecstasy occurred several times at Mass during Don Bosco's life. One of the witnesses for his levitation, Don Evasio Garrone, declared the following under oath: "In January 1879, Don Bosco celebrated Mass at an altar in his antichamber. I and a friend of mine were present. When the moment of the Elevation of the Host arrived, we saw the face of Don Bosco in ecstasy, reflecting an ineffable joy. At the same time it seemed to us that suddenly the whole room was bathed in light, then slowly his feet detached themselves from the ground and he remained in the air for more than ten minutes. We who served the Mass wanted to hold the hem of his chasuble, as is customary at the Elevation, but he was so high we could not reach it. . . . I witnessed Don Bosco's levitation during the Mass three different times."[1]

Don Bosco never claimed that the miraculous cures were to be attributed to supernatural intervention. None the less, there are certain authenticated miracles—such as the case of a totally blind child whose sight was restored. The miraculous cures claimed by the cured number hundreds. "At other times Don Bosco was not averse to using a little psychological suggestion as when he told a man supposedly suffering from an incurable disease to go to confession and Communion and to pray to Our Lady, at the same time giving him some pills to take. After the man had got well, it was discovered that the pills consisted of nothing but flour."[2]

There are two cases, but not totally authenticated, of resurrection of the dead. The first one is of particular interest. One of Don Bosco's spiritual children, a boy of 16, "died" before he could see the saint, to whom he desired to speak, as Don Bosco was absent from the city. The boy lay "dead" for 24 hours. Upon his return Don Bosco went immediately to the deathbed, and announced that the boy was only asleep. When he loudly called the boy by his first name, the boy's face revived, although his entire body remained cold and deathly. The conversation lasted a few minutes. The boy made his confession to Don Bosco, who asked him whether he wanted to go to Paradise or remain on earth. The boy answered that he wanted to arrive before the sight of God, and then died. As is characteristic with saints, Don Bosco did not divulge this event; he acted with the greatest simplicity and discretion, reiterating that the boy had not been dead.

The other event occurred in 1866 in Florence, when he was called to the deathbed of another young boy. In this case, according to the doctors, the boy was already dead when Don Bosco and other priests entered the room. He immediately began a prayer to Mary

Auxiliatrix, and everyone present prayed with him. The prayer was not yet finished when the presumably dead boy began to breathe. He opened his eyes and lived thereafter. Twenty-one years later, when Don Bosco visited Florence for the last time, he was invited to dinner at the same house. The old lady whose son had been resurrected was still alive, and described the whole event in Don Bosco's presence. Don Bosco, his eyes downcast, modestly added only the following words to the story: "Perhaps he was not dead."

Don Bosco's prophecy concerning Paris was sent to Pope Pius IX immediately after he had spoken it (Feb. 12, 1870). Among other things, he wrote the following: "On the vigil of Epiphany of this year 1870, all material objects disappeared from my room and I found myself observing supernatural events. The visions were brief and intermittent, but I saw a great deal. It is very difficult to communicate through external and sensible signs what I saw, though the form and appearance of everything was clearly outlined. . . . The Pantheon in Paris will fall to ashes. . . . The enemies of France will put her to anguish, famine, and horror. . . . Paris will fall into the hands of the foreigners, your enemies will see the palaces going up in flames, the buildings and houses in ruins, and your sons bathed in blood."[8]

Don Bosco died January 31, 1888, at the age of seventy-three, with the following words on his lips: "Jesus and Mary, I offer you my heart and soul. . . . Mother, open the doors of Paradise for me." After his death many other miraculous events have continued to occur, up to the very present, through his instrumentality. We do not hesitate to call the success of his work miraculous; believers and unbelievers alike admire the achievements of his life. At his death *The Times* (London), in a glowing tribute, stated that Don Bosco was considered the St. Vincent de Paul of the 19th century, his charitable work known and esteemed all over the world.

Because Joseph Benedict Cottolengo was an old friend and a predecessor of Don Bosco, he is worthy of mention after the great Salesian. Cottolengo, a canon of Corpus Domini Church in Turin, Italy, was an intimate friend of all the beggars, crippled, and destitute in his city. In 1827 he was called to assist an old woman who was mortally ill and without means. Since she was a transient, no hospital would take her; so Cottolengo had her put up in an inn. The heartbreaking fate of this woman moved Cottolengo to open a hospital and a hostel that would be open free to everyone at all times. This was Cottolengo's first "little house." In the course of the last hundred and thirty years about two hundred and fifty such homes and hospitals were opened for the crippled, the destitute, and the incurably ill.

Though Giovanni Cottolengo was himself a wonder-worker, the very existence of his "little houses" already constitutes a kind of miracle. These houses are operated without a fixed budget, and sometimes the administrators do not know how they can provide for the next week, or even the next day. Cottolengo never permitted the Government to make a count of the inmates living in a house (and his successors have followed his example). Yet these houses always have everything they need—money, medicine, food, clothing, which come to them continuously and mostly anonymously.

In one of the miracles ascribed to Joseph Cottolengo, he bought food on credit for his destitute inmates, and after five or six months the creditor became impatient. He came in person one day shouting angrily that he had enough of promises and that he now demanded cash. Cottolengo opened all the drawers, showed him his empty pockets, and took the man all over the place in search of money, but they did not find a penny. The creditor then fell into a rage, and after threatening Cottolengo, began to beat him up. With a desperate gesture, the priest thrust his hand into his pocket and pulled out several rolls of money in gold. The creditor was even more surprised than Cottolengo, for only a moment before, he himself had searched through all the priest's pockets and suspected hiding places.

Cottolengo spent very little time in his "office." Anyone who wanted to talk to him found him among his protégés, or at some construction site where he helped to carry bricks, or in one of the many workshops where he would help to repair shoes or clothing, always good-humoured, smiling, and laughing.

The fact that Cottolengo's idea was realized in an institutional sense without any kind of planning, campaigning, or organization, and the fact that it has survived, are miraculous. There is no explanation unless one recognizes a "dynamic finality" in it and unless one recognizes behind this finality the hand of God.

One of the greatest miracles of all times relates to the shrine of Lourdes (1858). The peasant girl, Bernadette Soubirous, was of normal disposition, without the slightest inclination to make history. The Soubirous family lived in the cell of a former prison, for Francis Soubirous, the father, a day laborer, earned hardly enough to support them. One of the Soubirous children was once seen eating the wax dripping from the candles in a church to appease his hunger. . . . At the time of her first apparition, Bernardette was fourteen years old, hard-working, and, as has been said, absolutely normal. When Bernardette conveyed the first message of "The Beautiful Lady" to the Dean of Lourdes, he warned her that if she dared to return again with any such message he would chase her out with a broom. Later on, she was thrown into jail.

After the discovery of the spring following the 18th apparition, Bernardette's practical task seemed at an end. Her own life, which continued in the austere convent of the Sisters of Charity of Nevers, was further evidence of a miraculous nature. Bernadette always remained an unspoiled, simple, balanced, human being, the obedient servant. Later on, she bore another sign of being chosen, for while the fame of Lourdes increased from day to day, she was subjected to almost superhuman afflictions. Stricken with tuberculosis of the bone, she died in obscurity in 1879 at the age of thirty-five. She refused to be taken to the miraculous well: "The spring is not for me. . . ."

Her body was exhumed twenty years later, on September 22, 1899, and examined by ecclesiastical authorities and two physicians. The official protocol, prepared under oath by all those present, attested that her body was totally incorrupt; her half-opened mouth showed all her teeth to be in perfect condition; eyes, hands, fingernails were preserved from decay. On her arms the shape of the veins was clearly visible. After the nuns had washed the exhumed body, they dressed it in new ecclesiastical garments. At this writing Bernadette's incorrupt body still lies in the Convent of the Sisters of Charity of Nevers, France.

The Sacred Congregation of Rites has accepted four miracles that occurred through the intervention of Bernardette Soubirous: two for the canonization, two for the beatification.

If ever there was a saint who was realistic in the worldly sense, a saint free of any visible mystical ecstasies or physical phenomena associated with mysticism, a person full of common sense, wit, and humor, it was Thérèse Martin, St. Thérèse of Lisieux. The miracle of her life lies in the example she set of the way one can smilingly endure everyday worries and anxieties, the most common hardships, the "quiet desperation" of the quotidian. She walked along the straight and narrow road to heaven, not the bright, open road lighted up by the stars. The long suffering she underwent during the fatal illness that struck her never changed her inner smile. Pope Pius XI, who canonized her in 1925, called her *Omen Novum,* a new sign on the horizon for the Church; she has been compared to the greatest saints, to St. Francis of Assisi and to St. Ignatius Loyola, because of the new paths she opened in Christian religious life. This simple nun, this nonmystical mystic whose life was not linked with any prodigies, predicted that she would provide those who petitioned her with celestial graces after her death.

The miracles of St. Thérèse are counted by the hundreds. The cult of her veneration spread all over the globe more rapidly than has been the case with any other saint. Though very often she is wrongly represented as a gentle, detached, and pious girl, the fact is that she was the most hard-working young nun in the convent and that for many years she did the heaviest and most menial work of all.

But the line of saints and their miracles never ends. The modern world might deny the achievements of these saints, as did some people in the 17th and 18th centuries and even earlier. Nevertheless, saints exist and their miracles exist. And it may come as a surprise to some that these preternatural events accompany our ancestors, our grandparents, our parents, and even our very own selves.

Here we shall cite a few of the saints canonized during the 19th and 20th centuries:

St. Mary Guiseppe Rossello (1811–80), an Italian nun and founder of the Daughters of Our Lady of Misericordia. One of the miracles that occurred through her intervention effected the instantaneous cure of a fifty-year-old man from meningo-encyphalitis.

St. Gemma Galgani was born in Italy in 1878 and died there in 1903. In addition to her stigmata, which have already been described, many other miracles are attributed to her. One of them occurring in Lucca, Italy, in 1907, involved the sudden conversion of a great enemy of the Church. This person had been a militant atheist and a brutal, vulgar persecutor of the clergy. Some of those who received the grace of seeing the true light, upon the intervention of Gemma Galgani, died very soon afterward, some only a few hours after conversion. This cannot be interpreted to mean that there really was no miracle. The actual miracle was the conversion of the unbeliever. The influence of Gemma Galgani is felt in many countries, most of the miraculous cures being reported from Canada.

St. Pierre-Louis Chanel, a Marist Father, was born in 1803 in France. He went as a missionary to Australia, where he became the first martyr of the continent; after undergoing terrible tortures he was killed by a native tribe in 1841. One of the miracles attributed to him occurred after his death, the restoration of sight to a man who had become blind as the result of a fire that destroyed the retina of both eyes. The cure occurred in 1890.

St. Conrad von Parzham (1839–94) was a member of the German Capuchin order. He was the handy man and porter of the monastery in Altötting in Bavaria, which contains one of the most famous Marian shrines. He possessed the gift of clairvoyance. Once two novices were taken for a medical examination upon which depended their admission to the order. While passing through Brother Conrad's little chamber near the front entrance one of the novices asked him to pray for success. "Be calm and go," answered Brother Conrad, "you will be approved, the other not." The results of the examinations were just as Brother Conrad had foreseen.

On another occasion Brother Conrad asked one of the Capuchin Fathers to visit a sick man, and he gave the Father the precise address. The priest left immediately but upon arriving at the home of the sick man, he was very much surprised when he was told that no one had asked for a priest, since the illness was not serious. Nevertheless, they led the priest to the sick person, who received him calmly and in good spirit. After making his confession, the man suddenly died while kissing the crucifix. When the Capuchin Father returned to the monastery he asked Brother Conrad whether anybody had requested a priest. Brother Conrad, replied, "No one, but an inner voice suggested it to me."

He could read the most intimate thoughts of those whom he met. One of his fellow monks was full of resentment and sometimes even hated the father superior of the Capuchin monastery. But he managed to keep these feelings to himself. Once when he was particularly under the sway of such feelings he happened to meet Brother Conrad, who looked at him sternly and said, "For a monk, it is a shame. Go immediately and kiss the hands of Father Superior."

After his death, miracles continued all over the world. Brother Conrad was long dead by 1920 but his memory was kept alive and venerated by the Bavarian peasants in the neighborhood, when a three-year-old girl was healed suddenly. The girl had been born with one leg shorter than the other, as well as with other defects. On January 17, 1920, when the whole town of Vasserburg was awaiting the arrival of the bishop, the father of the girl sighed and loudly declared that it would be a wonderful thing if his daughter could march with them in the procession like the other girls. And he added the pious wish that maybe Brother Conrad would help. At this very moment the semiparalyzed child rose to her feet, walked around and shouted with joy: "Look, Father, I can do the same as the others!"

There are more prodigious events in the lives of modern saints. The cases of levitation in the lives of St. John Bosco and St. Joseph Cottolengo have already been described. Another saint, André Hubert Fournet, a Frenchman who died in 1921, had been seen to be lifted up in the air, a fact that was reported in the canonization process.

Once St. Joseph Cottolengo was given a small basket of cherries, and began at once to distribute them to the children. He gave a handful to each child and the basket sufficed for all of them, even though the "amount thus distributed was quite out of proportion of anything the basket could have possibly contained."

St. Gaspar del Bufalo and his early companions had a hard struggle with poverty in founding the Congregation of the Precious Blood, which, from 1815 onward, did so much to revive religious fervor in the more neglected parishes of rural Italy. Father Blaise Velentini (who was later on superior general), giving evidence in the process of beatification, records how, when he himself was in charge of the motherhouse of San Felice at Giano during Don Gaspar's absence, he wrote to the founder that it was impossible to pay his way. There were, he declared, no other resources but the stones with which the place abounded. He received in reply only the message: "Bless the stones and they will turn into *piastres*." Though he took this answer for a jest, it happened shortly afterwards that he was pressed for the immediate payment of a debt. He called the young man who acted as bursar and they looked in the money-box together. There they found fifty *bajocchi* (let us say ten cents and no more) and this was hopelessly insufficient for their purpose. So Father Valentini, at his wits' end, bethought him of the message he had received, and in a spirit of faith pronounced a blessing over the coppers before him. Then they proceeded to count the money once more, and behold they found there five *piastres* and five *paoli**— the exact sum that was needed. The piastres were coins from the mint of Pius VII, and Father Valentini, in his sworn deposition, insists forcibly upon the impossibility of any oversight or trickery by way of explaining the mystery.

The life of Gaspar del Bufalo was characterized by many other mystical phenomena and miracles. His biographer recounts that once while he was preaching to a great crowd before the church, a torrential downpour of rain started. Holding an image of the Blessed Virgin in his hands, he blessed the air, and the rain immediately stopped. Not a single drop fell on the crowd, although it continued to rain all around the crowd and in the city at large. During one of his sermons the entire congregation saw a luminous cross upon his

---

* The currencies of the land at that time.

head; and often his ecstasies were accompanied by levitation. During another open-air sermon, the bishop and the entire crowd witnessed three radiant stars appearing around his head. Furthermore, he possessed the gift of knowing the secrets of the heart and could predict the future. Once he wrote another priest to come and meet him. The priest came and they had a pleasant time together; but after dinner the saint called him into his office and revealed secrets to him that the priest thought only he himself knew. St. Gaspar reminded the priest that he had some unconfessed sins, and that he did not always behave with prudence while hearing confessions.

Once a woman whom he had never met before entered his confessional, yet he addressed her by name and told her about the very oppressive problems she was going to confess. During a mission in an Italian city he was with a group of priests, two of them young priests, the rest very old. While talking with the priests Gaspar said, "I wonder who among us will be the first to reach eternity?" And then after a few moments of silence he added, "Who would believe it! The two youngest will pass into eternity this very year." Although these two young priests were quite healthy and full of activity both died during the same year.

His bishop once said to one of his priests: "My tenure as bishop will be short. I will remain in the diocese of Terracina only for seven years and then I shall die." Skeptically, the priest asked, "Who told you this, Monsignor? Who can predict such things?" In reply the bishop said, "It was Canon del Bufalo who told me, and he is a saint." The bishop did in fact die after seven years.

Numerous miraculous cures were attributed to him. But one of the greatest miracles in his life was the following:

Don Gaspar was hearing the confession of a man while other penitents were waiting patiently in line. When the first one had finished, the next one confronted Don Gaspar and in the presence of the others demanded to know whether the man who had just left had confessed to a robbery commited against the speaker. In the politest manner, Don Gaspar explained that no priest can reveal confessional confidence, and then tried unsuccessfully to calm the excited man. Suddenly he took out a pistol and pressed it against

Don Gaspar, who by this time had stepped out of the confessional. The man pulled the trigger and shot him in the chest. The bullet did not even burn his soutane, and fell at the feet of the priest.

Pope Pius X, the first pontiff to be canonized since 1512, was the prototype of the good, simple, understanding country priest, a loving shepherd of his flock. This good pastor never wanted to become a bishop; yet he was appointed to the highest ecclesiastical post in the Italian hierarchy—that of Patriarch Archbishop of Venice and a cardinal. He never dreamed of the possibility of being elected to the papacy. When he left Venice for the Conclave in 1903, he bought a return ticket at the railroad station, but he never returned to Venice. He became one of the greatest of the Popes, and only 40 years after his death he was placed upon the altars of the Universal Church. Forty years seems a short time in Church history when one considers that the beatification process of another Pope, Innocent XI, begun 250 years ago, is not yet concluded. There was no rush to make Pope Pius X a saint. None the less, the signs of saintliness were so numerous and so obvious that his canonization did not surprise any one.

Jean Carrère, a French writer, after a private audience with Pius X in 1910, described him in *Le Temps* of Paris as a person whose presence not only suggested sanctity but filled the visitor with it. At his death *The Times* (London) wrote: "All those who know what sanctity is will unite themselves with the Catholic Church in mourning Pius X who was a saint, priest, a great Bishop and a great Pope."

This great Pope was a mystic: those who knew him, knew before he died that he had supernatural gifts. We do not consider it miraculous that the house in which he was born in the village of Riese was the only one to be saved during the battles of World War I. Before fleeing from the invading armies the unfortunate inhabitants of that village inscribed with chalk on the walls of this house the legend: "This is where Piux X was born." Artillery shells have no eyes, yet the house of Pius X was spared.

Aside from this and similar incidents, not extraordinary or miraculous in themselves, many other facts attested during his lifetime and after his death can be considered supernatural. Pius X used to smile upon being told a few years before his death that miraculous cures had occurred when somebody touched his vestments. "As if I had nothing else to do than perform miracles," he said. During an audience a lady from a northern country told him in the matter-of-fact manner of her race: "It is reported that Your Holiness is a saint and can work miracles." Pius X answered with a joke, he said: "Please do not confound the consonants. My family name is *Sarto* with an 'r' and not *Santo* with 'n.'" (In Italian *Santo* means saint.)

Charles du Bois, the Belgian Consul General in Rome, who suffered from an incurable illness, attested under oath that he had asked the Pope to pray for him and that shortly thereafter he was instantly cured. In 1910, a peasant woman from Rocca di Papa was received in general audience together with her two small sons, both deaf and dumb. She did not ask the Pope to intervene, only to bless them. Pius X laid his hands upon the heads of the boys and then whispered to the mother that one of the boys was incurably ill and would soon die, but that the other would regain his faculties and live. And so it came to pass.

In 1913, a nun with an incurable cancer asked and received permission to see the Pope "before I die." Pius X entered the room where the sick nun waited, and addressed her in these words: "Sister, what do you want? You are much better off than I." The medical check that immediately followed yielded no trace of disease in the nun who a few hours before was dying of cancer.

Pius X did not allow this and other news of alleged cures to be divulged. "It is not I who have done it, it is the power of the Supreme Key of St. Peter, the Benediction. . . . It is faith that heals those who ask for grace."

The story of St. Maria Goretti, whom many of the faithful call the St. Agnes of the 20th century, is as close to us in time as the life of Pius X. Born in October, 1890, she might be considered our contemporary. Her mother is still living among us. Her story will not interest anyone who has no understanding of authentic innocence, because similar tragedies happen in the world by the hundreds each year and are categorized as sex crimes.

Maria Goretti, an innocent twelve-year-old girl, daughter of day laborers, was killed by a man because she defended her purity. The murderer was caught and sentenced for life. In any other case this would be the end of the story—as is the fate of any such news item. Avid readers wait for the next crime and then forget it. Why was Maria Goretti different from any other victim of murderers' hands? Do they not share with her the glory of innocence and martyrdom?

The miraculous in the life of Maria Goretti is that she was a heroine before reaching martyrdom. How can a girl who died at the age of twelve years be called a heroine? Certainly through the grace that gave her the strength to exercise certain virtues on a heroic level. The process of canonization proved that her love of God and her love of her neighbor cannot be explained by a child's simple non-questioning faith. Her behavior and her words, expressing movingly tender desire to receive Communion, immediately raised her above the ordinary. When her father died and the family remained without help, the mother was faced with the seemingly insurmountable task of caring for six children and their little property. Thus the entire household was left in the care of ten-year-old Maria.

The circumstances of the murder are another sign of her sanctity. After receiving the mortal knife-wounds she did not lose consciousness or complain about anything. Her only concern was that the murderer should see his crime and repent. She was taken to the hospital, but no medical science could help her. One of the doctors said to the Franciscan priest who came to assist her: "Father, there is very little we doctors can do, but you will find here an angel while we leave a corpse." She died on July 6, 1902, while praying not for herself but for the murderer. These facts are of extraordinary importance because the murderer had stabbed her 18 times. No vital part of her body was without wounds. The man whom she had forgiven repented—and this was the next "miracle." He was one of those dispossessed persons who grew up without love, without care: an orphan who felt that the world had maltreated and rejected him, and he hated the world for it. It was certainly diabolical that his violent criminal outburst, protesting his lack of love, should strike at the most innocent creature in the whole community. Released after 25 years in a penitentiary, her murderer retired from the world and dedicated himself to work, prayer, and penance.

The process of canonization revealed that the intervention of Maria Goretti saved a stonemason hit by a falling roof; the mason testified, under oath, that he saw a vision in which she appeared to him. Most of the other miraculous cures (about a hundred) occurred during the years 1945 and 1947. The Italian monthly *Il Crocifisso* every month lists all the cures and favors currently obtained through the intervention of Maria Goretti. The Church elevated her to the ranks of blessed by recognizing her martyrdom, and waived any proofs for attested miracles (as in the case of St. John Fisher and St. Thomas More), holding that her martyrdom was sufficient proof of her sanctity. This, however, did not exclude the possibility of miracles, and in fact four years after the decree on her martyrdom, a new decree of canonization approved two miracles: one, the instantaneous healing of the stonemason; the other, the miraculous cure of a woman incurably ill of pleurisy.

Saints are not merely "heroes of the past"; they continue to live a personal life in heaven, and every faithful Christian knows that through the Communion of Saints he is close to them. This is the deepest difference between the veneration of the saints and the veneration of a hero. On the other hand, the veneration of the saints has nothing to do with the adoration due to God alone. Veneration of saints does not diminish the adoration of God, for their favors and graces are not attributed to their own power, but to God. In this way veneration of the saints increases the glory of God rather than diminishes it.

CHAPTER 10

Apparitions and Miraculous Healings in Our Time

Since the Ascension of Christ most of the miraculous apparitions have been of Mary. The unbeliever who seeks to focus his doubt on this fact can easily come up with all sorts of surprising results. Whether it be Henry Adams' beautiful ode to the Virgin of Chartres, or the apparitions at Lourdes, or even if we go back to the sixth or seventh centuries—there will always be people who will dismiss it all as "mariolatry." In their view all devotion to Mary is a form of idolatry, and the numerous apparitions of the Blessed Virgin are nothing more than the product of excited imagination fed by super-stitious women who cannot lift up their eyes to the true majesty of God. Objective criticism, however, has another answer to the ques-tion why the apparitions are mostly apparitions of Mary and why the apparitions that occurred during the 19th and 20th centuries, save for one unconfirmed exception, were miraculous events involv-ing her.

An apparition is a supernatural and sensible manifestation by which a spiritual object, or a spiritual being, appears to the internal or external senses of man. It is stated in the Old Testament that God presented Himself to Moses and to some of the prophets, but we know from the description that God never "appeared." Most theo-logians agree that the substantial appearance of God to a human being would be impossible, since God is pure spirit. As a matter of fact, in the Old Testament God communicated with Moses or with

Jacob through angels. As Cardinal Lépicier has explained, angels are spirits empowered to take on the form and features of human beings. It is therefore almost logical that the Blessed Virgin, through whom God became man and who has been bodily taken into heaven, should be the person who is allowed to communicate with mortals. Her status as a direct participant in salvation makes her the most logical link between man and God. The appearances and messages of the Madonna are not miracles wrought by her; they are wrought upon her request by the love of God.

Nevertheless, we really do not know just what the purpose of an apparition is. Certainly an apparition is a reminder, a warning that we are not condemned to a purely material existence and that we should never forget this. Furthermore, the apparitions of the Virgin have filled the world from time to time with an unspeakable beauty. In their most concrete and lucid statements all those who were favored with a vision, concur that the beauty they have seen, sensed, and perceived cannot be described.

Here we shall not venture to theorize about why one century received more communications from her and another less. We shall merely record the facts. The apparitions of the 19th and 20th centuries are certainly numerous and extremely important. Even if we added that one is allowed to doubt the veracity of these apparitions, one's doubt cannot last for long if the apparitions at Lourdes and their consequences up to this date are considered. Bernadette Soubirous received the privilege and grace of an apparition in 1858, four years after the declaration of the dogma of the Immaculate Conception. The world then was almost totally absorbed in human progress and the seemingly infinite human potentialities, and it was more than ready to discard, forget, or to refute by means of philosophy and science both the declaration of the dogma and the "childish" apparitions at Lourdes. Nevertheless, it was not Lourdes that ceased to exist; the critics and the doubters silenced themselves.

We have chosen Lourdes as an example because we consider Lourdes uniquely important. This does not mean, however, that any other of the apparitions of the 19th and 20th centuries is of lesser significance. The importance of an apparition cannot be measured by the size of the crowds that visit its scene; its importance is endowed by her who graced the particular place of her appearance.

Mention has already been made of St. Catherine Labouré, to whom the Blessed Virgin appeared in 1830 in the chapel of an obscure convent in Paris. Catherine Labouré was 24 years old and a novice. She had no mystical experience, she did not pray to the Madonna to appear to her. Her aim was just to be a simple, steadfast, and humble nun—attributes of character shared by all those who have enjoyed apparitions of the Blessed Virgin. Those elected by her are without exception humble, unimportant persons—unimportant, that is, with respect to their status in a world that judges persons according to social class and outward appearance. There is no unimportant human being, because there is no unimportant human soul. Sometimes it is very hard to understand that each human being has an immortal soul. All these souls are different and all are individually in communion with God. But let us return to Catherine Labouré.

It was July 18, 1830. The novices, among them Catherine, were asleep in the dormitory. Just before midnight a guardian angel awakened Catherine and led her into the chapel.

She was sleeping peacefully when suddenly she heard her name called: "Sister Labouré." Upon opening her eyes she saw a little child four or five years old, dressed in white and surrounded with a supernatural radiance. The child looked at her and then spoke. "Come," said the child, "come to the chapel. The Blessed Virgin expects you. . . . Be calm and quiet. It is 11:30. Everyone is fast asleep. Come."

Sister Labouré obeyed. The lights from the corridors were on, despite the late hour. The child opened the door of the chapel by simply touching the knob. Inside, the chapel was flooded with light. All the candles and votive lights were lighted, as if a midnight Mass were being celebrated. The child took Sister Labouré inside the sanctuary, beyond the communion rail, to the chair used by the spiritual director of the community. Sister Catherine fell to her knees, but the child remained standing. Several moments passed. It seemed like an eternity. Catherine suddenly felt uneasy because she thought that one of the sisters on night duty might discover her. But at this moment the child turned to her and said: "The Blessed Virgin is coming."

Sister Catherine first heard the rustle of silk, then she lifted her eyes and saw a great lady dressed in an ivory-colored robe and a blue mantle, with a white veil on her head. She came from the church, genuflected before the altar and sat down in the chair close to Catherine. The voice of the little child suddenly changed, becoming authoritative. For a minute Catherine wondered who he might be. Was he her guardian angel? But she had no time to reflect. An invisible force pulled her even closer to the Apparition. She fell again to her knees at the feet of the Madonna, and put her hands on the knees of the Great Lady. Never could she forget this moment, the greatest, the sweetest in her life.

Then the Lady began to talk. She told Catherine how she should behave toward her father confessor, and how she should comport herself later in life when suffering would be her lot. The Madonna lifted her right arm, pointed to the altar and said that it was from there that Catherine would receive consolation. Then Sister Catherine suddenly felt at ease. She even dared to ask the Great Lady what all this meant. And a conversation took place between the Great Lady and the little sister. The Blessed Virgin told her that God had entrusted her with a mission that would cause her pain. She foretold that the Church would be persecuted in France, that the entire world would be put to the test; but that one should go on praying. Everyone who asked for graces would receive them. There would be moments of great danger, and people would feel that everything was lost. "But I will be with you. Have confidence. . . . There will be many victims among the clergy of Paris. The Archbishop will die. The cross will be desecrated and thrown into the mud. The streets will be full of blood. The wounds of our Lord will be opened again." When Catherine asked when all this would happen, the Great Lady answered, "in about forty years."

When Catherine lifted her eyes again, the great Lady had disappeared, but the child was still there, and smilingly he said: "She has gone." Then the child, still full of radiance, accompanied Catherine out of the chapel, to the door of the dormitory. By now it was

2 A.M. In the morning, Catherine confessed everything to her spiritual director, who did not believe a word and scolded her instead. Now she was alone with her terrible secret. She could not share it with anyone else, for the Great Lady had ordered her to disclose it only to her confessor. She passed her days in a state of great tension. On November 27, at 5:30 P.M., all the sisters and novices of the convent went as usual to the chapel for their evening meditation. Catherine, deeply immersed in prayer, knelt with them. Suddenly she did not want to believe her ears. She heard the same rustle of silk and, upon lifting her eyes, she saw the Blessed Virgin again dressed in white silk, the long veil reaching down to her knees. Catherine observed her features: Her face was the face of a woman of forty, radiant but with an expression of suffering. Her feet stood upon a luminous globe that seemed to stand firmly in the air. Her hands graciously held another globe and on this small globe there was a cross. Her eyes looked up toward Heaven. Her lips seemed to pray. It was as if she were offering this globe to God. Then the little globe suddenly disappeared from her hands, and it appeared to Catherine that her fingers were covered with the most precious stones irradiating a transcendental light.

At this moment the Blessed Virgin looked at Catherine and she heard a voice speaking in her heart: "This globe represents the entire world in general, France in particular, and everyone, each human being besides." When the light that surrounded her became stronger, she continued: "This is the symbol of the graces that I extend to every person who asks for them." Suddenly a somewhat oval light surrounded the Blessed Virgin, and at the end of the oval Catherine could read the following inscription: "O Mary, conceived without sin, pray for us who have recourse to thee." Then in another vision Catherine saw the same oval form with their letter "M" carrying a cross, and at the bottom of the letter two hearts, one pierced by thorns, the other by a lance. The fringes of the oval were surrounded by twelve stars. This was the vision during which the Blessed Virgin told Catherine that she should coin medals based upon the model of the oval she had just seen. Those who wore one of these medals and prayed would receive abundant grace.

Again Catherine reported everything to the confessor and again he refused to believe in the authenticity of the apparition. This time, however, he suggested that she should pray and follow in the footsteps of the Blessed Virgin, in order to win her protection.

In December, a few days later, the third and last apparition was granted to Sister Catherine. She heard again the rustle of the robe. The Madonna was dressed in the same way as during the second apparition. The radiance surrounding her seemed brighter than ever. Diamond rings reflected a radiant light on her fingers, but some of the stones did not reflect any light. The Holy Virgin remarked: "These stones which do not shine represent the graces no one asks for." Underfoot was a snake, a concrete reminder of the promise of God made in Revelation: "I will put enmity between you and the woman, between your seed and her seed; He shall crush your head."

The Blessed Virgin turned to Catherine and said, "My daughter, you will not see me any more, but you will hear my voice in your prayers."

Catherine's peasant realism manifested itself immediately. In reply she complained: "My best Mother, Father Aladel [her confessor] does not believe me. He does not want to coin your medal." The Great Lady smiled: "Be calm, my child. The day will come when he will do what you ask for. He is my servant. He would not dare to displease me." Then the vision disappeared.

Catherine, as we know, remained silent for 47 years and told her secret only to her confessor and the bishop. She never chattered about her marvelous experience, though it is hard to imagine a healthier, more cheerful and gregarious peasant girl than she. Her description of the vision seems to transcend the limitations of her simple personality, for she found eloquent words to describe the face, hands, and dress of the Madonna. How is it possible, one might ask, that the Blessed Virgin appeared to Catherine in Paris in a heavy, majestic silk robe, when later in LaSalette she appeared to a group of children as a peasant woman sitting in a posture of grief and weeping? There is no contradiction in the different content of the apparitions. The body of the Virgin participates already in the beatific vision. Thus it is not her true body that manifests itself, but a sensible form that represents it. In the Rue du Bac in Paris the Virgin had the same dignity as in any other apparition. But for some particular reason beyond our understanding, the form representing her was clothed in such a way as to impress most vividly the peasant girl to whom she came to talk. Catherine said that she heard the rustle of silk and that she was so close to her that she felt the material of which the garment was made.

All the circumstances of this apparition were very real, and the details deeply impressed themselves on the mind of Catherine Labouré, the former peasant woman Zoe.

LaSalette is a little village in the French Alps in the region of Grenoble. Wild mountain peaks, enveloped in clouds or glittering in the sun, alternate with deep dark valleys. The Alpine landscape is lovely to the very tree line. Pines offer protection against the scorching sun, nor does the deep green-brown coloration of the forest suggest a desert-like darkness. The pine forests seem to be full of life. But then the trees become ever smaller until at a certain point they disappear completely. Naked desert and rocks are the rule at an altitude of 6000 feet. Here and there grass grows on the slopes. Only cattle and the natives can walk safely on these precipitate slopes and narrow paths. Nature can be beautiful here, but it is always unpredictable.

The people of this region are poor and hard-working, as hard as the rocks around them. Children start to work at an early age, and perform heavy and dangerous chores before they learn to read and write.

In 1846 the region seemed to be completely forgotten and abandoned by man and God. In winter families moved into the stable and slept close to the beasts in order to keep warm. The sick were treated in the most primitive way, someone always knowing which herb was supposed to be good for this or that disease.

On September 18, 1846, two children, Melanie Calvat, 15, and Maximin Giraud, 11, went out to tend a herd of cows on one of the distant slopes. For Maximin it was the first time, but for Melanie the task was not new. They did not talk, for these mountain people are a silent lot. Soon they became tired and lay down to sleep. Melanie awoke first. She became frightened because the sun was high, it was very hot, and she could not see the cows. She awakened Maximin and they ran to the edge of the road until they discovered the cows, placidly grazing. But as soon as they turned back they stopped in their tracks. Their legs almost rooted themselves into the rocks. Not far away on the path they saw a bright light at the very spot where they had been asleep. They saw a woman weeping bitterly, her feet resting on the floor of a dried-up stream. The two children were terrified. The woman rose and said: "Why do you not come nearer, my children? Be not frightened. I have come to tell you some great news." At this moment fear fled from the hearts of the children; in its stead were born love and confidence, and they ran toward her like children to their mothers.

She was all light and radiance. There was light in her face, her hands, her eyes, her whole figure, and even in the tears that flowed from her eyes. "The lady wore a long white robe, scattered with gleaming golden sequins. A white scarf, edged with roses of many colors, was draped over her breast, and a bright yellow apron hung from her waist. She was shod with white shoes, studded with pearls. Around the neck of the lady was a chain from which hung a long cross, to the arms of which were affixed emblems of the Passion. The Christ on the cross shone with a brilliance even greater than that surrounding the lady. A corona of light, like a diadem, sprang from a crown of roses on her head. Other rays of light, all of which blended with the aureole surrounding her, darted from the roses at her feet. Questioned later about the intensity of this brilliance the children could only explain that it was brighter, but different from anything in their experience; "brighter than the sun but not to be compared with it."[1]

This is the common experience of all favored by true vision. They see an indescribable light, of solar radiance, yet not to be compared to the sun. The two peasant children expressed their reactions articulately, even though they were not bright, educated, or carefully reared children. Maximin could not read or write. Melanie, like her companion, had been working since she was six years old. Nor did they speak French; they knew only the dialect of the region. Moreover, they had not known each other previously; Maximin's father was a wheelwright who did not live in LaSalette but in a nearby township called Corps, and he had sent the boy to LaSalette to replace a farmer's hired man who had become ill.

It is impossible that these children could have invented this story between them, for they had seen each other for the first time that morning. All these points are extremely important. The lady had talked to them both in French and in their dialect, and they had repeated her statements word for word. Although they did not know French, they understood her meaning. The lady spoke first to both of them, then to each one alone, entrusting each with a secret. This secret was revealed only to Pope Pius IX.

When the children returned to LaSalette, they immediately reported the apparition. According to them the lady had wept. They had seen her tears. And they understood that she was the Mother of God. She had complained about the sins of the people and said that she prayed constantly that her Son will not abandon them. And she had recounted her sufferings. She mentioned that she had given warnings when last year's potato crop was spoiled, but instead of praying the people had cursed. Further, she had predicted new disasters, even famines. But she said that before the famine, children under seven would be seized with palsy and die. She had also prophesied that grapes would rot, but if people changed, the very rocks and stones would turn to heaps of grain. In addition, she complained that only old women went to Mass and that some people ridiculed religion. Then she asked the children whether they said their prayers properly, and demanded gently that they should recite at least one Our Father and one Hail Mary every morning and every evening. Finally, she had requested that all this should be told to the people.

Suddenly she arose and crossed the bed of the dried-up stream. But she did not actually walk, for her feet did not seem to touch the ground. Then she was lifted up into the air and the apparition slowly faded away, the great radiance she had showered about her being absorbed by the darker daylight.

The two children had a difficult task. At home very few believed them. Maximin was beaten by his father. The Mayor of LaSalette threatened them with imprisonment if they stuck to their story of the apparition and promised them a great amount of money if they would retract it. Other unbelievers also promised to shower them with money. When they described their vision to their pastor, Abbé Perrin, he was frightened and cried out: "Oh, my children, we are lost. The good Lord is going to punish us. It was the Blessed Virgin who appeared to you."

In a very short time news of the apparition spread all over France. A train of theological and political discussion was set in motion. The children were subjected to all sorts of questioning. The bishop of Grenoble immediately dispatched a commission to investigate the case. But in the general commotion, the two children remained miraculously calm. They were not only threatened and tempted with bribes, interrogated legally by ecclesiastical authorities and illegally by all sorts of civilian investigation committees, they were mocked, vilified, and exposed to public curiosity. They had to face the elaborate cross-examinations of theologians. But they remained firm.

One investigator declared: "You said that the lady disappeared in a cloud. It is easy to be enveloped in a cloud and disappear." Melanie looked for a moment at the man and answered: "Monsieur, envelope yourself into a cloud and disappear." According to the minutes of one session Melanie was asked: "Now that you have seen the Blessed Virgin, are you wiser?" "Yes, Monsieur, a quarter wiser," she replied. "What do you mean, a quarter? What kind of measure do you use?" the questioner continued. "I love God, Monsieur." Melanie said. "You did not love Him before?" asked the questioner. "I did not know him, Monsieur. If I had known him I would have loved Him . . ." Melanie answered.

The two children behaved like heroes. Their bearing and their answers were full of dignity and precision. They did not reveal the secrets individually entrusted to them. No material advantages accrued to them as a result of their experience. On the contrary, Maximin's situation was particularly difficult because his father, an alcoholic, treated him brutally. But slowly even his father changed.

Meanwhile, proofs authenticating the veracity of the apparition multiplied. Already on the second day after the apparition, when people finally decided to visit the spot, they found the bed of the dried-up stream vigorously flowing with water. Recovery of the incurably sick and the blind followed. Many conversions took place. To this day LaSalette is still one of the centers of grace, a great shrine of Our Lady, a miraculous warning to the people.

Finally in 1850 Melanie and Maximin communicated their secrets to Pope Pius IX. These secrets are in the Vatican archives and have not been revealed. When Melanie wrote down the secret she was asked the meaning of the word infallible. In explanation she used three words: "Will arrive infallibly." At the same time she wanted to know the spelling of the word Anti-Christ. Maximin, who in the meantime had learned to write a little, had some difficulty with the word Pontiff. These are the only words that we know are contained in the secret message.

In 1850 Maximin was taken to Ars to St. John Vianney, who believed in the reality of the apparition. Maximin led a life full of torment and doubt, but remained faithful to the Blessed Virgin. Finally, in November 1874, he returned to his village, and again visited the site of the apparition. He received Communion, again confirming everything he had seen, and fell sick, dying a few months later, in March of 1875.

Melanie entered a convent, became a teaching sister, and traveled in Italy and in Greece. She was often exposed to calumnies by doubters. In 1902 she definitely left France and went to live in southern Italy, where she spent her days in prayer and constant mortification. She died in December, 1904, at the age of 73, her hands clasping the crucifix.

Each year sees millions of pilgrims from all corners of the earth arriving at the grotto of Massabielle and its miraculous spring. At this grotto, now flanked by two basilicas, Bernadette Soubirous saw Our Lady in a vision that first appeared to her on a cold February night in the year 1858. And Bernadette saw the same vision seventeen times thereafter, the last time on July 16, 1858.

Before these world-shaking events catapulted Lourdes to its present prominence, it was but a minor city among the minor cities of

France. Though the city of Lourdes and its people were deeply rooted in the history of France, and the region of which it forms a part, in no sense was it prepared either to accept or play the role assigned to it by the inscrutable divine Will. Nor could any of the inhabitants of the most wretched quarter of this city—poor beyond belief—ever imagine that this divine Will would focus His sanctifying and liberating grace upon one of them.

Those who see the grotto of Massabielle in its full glory of today would find it difficult to imagine it in its original state. The area immediately surrounding it was wild and deserted, a favorite haunt of wild swine and snakes. It was once a sewer-like cavern in which the River Gave emptied all manner of refuse and debris.

In this wasteland, and amid its desolation, the Blessed Virgin chose to appear to Bernadette Soubirous, the fourteen-year-old daughter of a desperately poor day laborer. Bernadette had come there on February 11, 1858, with a young sister and a friend, to gather some firewood, one of her many daily chores around the house. The grotto drew the attention of Bernadette when she suddenly noticed that it was filled with a bright, cloud-like light. Curious, the girl approached the grotto and there saw a beautiful lady, youthful in appearance, who smiled at her.

This was the first of the eighteen appearances of Our Lady to Bernadette. But an unbelieving world greeted her first appearance with shouts of denial and derision. The resurrection of superstition and hysteria in the modern age of science was at once denounced and deplored, forcing the closing of the grotto, until it was reopened later by order of Napoleon III, Emperor of France.

Even the clergy was ill-disposed toward the phenomenon at first. When poor Bernadette conveyed the first message of the "Beautiful Lady" to the Dean of Lourdes, he dismissed her. Ten years went by before the visions seen by Bernadette were confirmed by the Church as true apparitions of the Blessed Virgin.

In the meantime a dramatic, often violent public debate had been unleashed. The rational, positivist spirit of the times was disturbed and annoyed by talk of supernatural beings, of God and of the Virgin. In the course of time, however, even the most militantly incredulous had to bow their heads in wonder and amazement, if not in belief, in the face of the irrefutable evidence accumulated. The Austrian novelist, Franz Werfel, a Jew, wrote: ". . . What is true, what invented? My answer is this: all the memorable happenings . . . took place in the world of reality. Since their beginning dates back no longer than eighty years there beats upon them the bright light of modern history, and their truth has been confirmed by friend and foe and by cool observers through faithful testimonies."[2]

No greater or more eloquent confirmation of the authenticity of the apparitions could be offered than the fact that Bernadette has been elevated to sainthood.—But not only because she saw the Virgin: she was beatified and canonized because her life was indeed a saintly one. It can be said, in fact, that the second miracle of Lourdes is Bernadette herself, chosen by the Blessed Virgin to call a sinful world to penance and prayer.

The first visitor to Lourdes to be miraculously cured was the four-year-old Justin Bouhohorts. He was brought dying of tuberculosis to the well and immersed in icy waters on February 28, 1858. He was completely cured, and died at a ripe old age in 1935, after having worked as a gardener all his life.

From 1858 to 1914 the *Annales de Lourdes* recorded 6,000 healings or remarkable improvements. But after a careful study of the records, the present chief of the Medical Bureau of Lourdes reduced this figure to 1,600. From 1914 to 1955 the Medical Bureau attested, and the ecclesiastical authorities approved, a total of 262 miraculous cures.

The *Bureau Médical* of Lourdes has existed since 1884, but even before this date the bishop had organized an official controlling body composed of local doctors. It should not be forgtten that Bernadette's mental soundness was confirmed by three independent psychiatrists ordered to examine her by Baron Massy, the top government official of the district. The present medical bureau works together with an international study center established in 1904. The Medical Bureau has a different function from that of the International Study Center. It examines the sick before and after the healing, keeps records, makes the diagnosis. Further, it follows the course of a visiting patient's disease or cure, and collects data on the patient's family, background and medical history.

The Medical Bureau expresses no opinion on any healing—miraculous or non-miraculous—before the end of the second year after the patient involved has come to Lourdes and claimed to have been cured there. Newspaper accounts of miraculous cures at Lourdes are merely personal descriptions and subjective opinions. The Medical Bureau's detailed clinical, scientific verdict is never disclosed before the end of the second year. Then the whole case goes to the bishop, or ordinary of the diocese to which the sick person belongs, and only this bishop can issue a decree declaring a cure miraculous. The International Study Center assists the visiting physicians, who come from all over the world, and in a way acts as a supervisory body over the Medical Bureau. During the existence of the Medical Bureau and the International Study Center, thirty thousand physicians have registered as visitors. The number of physicians who actually work with the Medical Bureau ranges from eight hundred to fifteen hundred a year. These two medical institutions are not ecclesiastical or religious bodies. Any doctor of any race, any country, any faith or ideology, has the right to examine the records and raise questions. Only one document is required—the doctor's certified medical diploma. This freedom of access to all the records guarantees an absolute openness and increases the value of the medical examinations. If only Catholic doctors were to sign the minutes of the meetings at which cases are discussed, criticisms or suspicions of their objectivity would be justifiable. But non-believing physicians also affix their signatures to these documents.

It might still be objected that even such persons can err. Of course, one, two, or three doctors might make mistakes in diagnosis. But it is almost inconceivable that sixty or seventy physicians discussing the same case could fall into the same error. This is why the Medical Bureau of Lourdes invites physicians who are nonbelievers and even hostile to the Faith. The documents signed by them are not approvals or certifications of miracles. This word has been banned from the reports of the medical bureau. The task of the doctors is the task of all science—to establish the facts.

During the diagnostic discussions there are always from fifteen to seventy members present. They may be Americans, French, Italians, Belgians, British, Germans, Swiss, Spaniards, Africans, Asians and Australians, Protestants, Jews, Mohammedans, Buddhists, pagans and agnostics. Each year many sick people claim miraculous cures, but only about fifty pass a first screening test, after which their cases are submitted to the assembly of the Medical Bureau for discussion. There are cases where several commissions of specialists scrutinize the documents and when their examination is concluded, the International Committee in turn studies the decisions made. The scientific medical laboratories of this bureau are equipped with the most modern medical research instruments from all over the world, including the United States.

As has been said, from eight hundred to fifteen hundred physicians participate annually in the actual work of consultation. In 1952 there were 41 university professors, 121 hospital directors, 97 surgeons, 64 pediatricians, 63 specialists on tuberculosis, 54 gynecologists, 30 ophthamologists, 20 heart specialists and 604 general practitioners. Numerically the different nationalities were represented as follows: 734 French, 229 Italians, 157 Belgians, 47 British, 25 Germans, 26 Swiss, 21 Americans, 15 Africans, eight Indians, and one Syrian.

The procedure followed is a rigorous one. It is not enough that the recovered patient rise from his wheel chair: he must also prove that he actually has been sick. Then he must undergo long and constant observation. If a patient declares that he is cured he is immediately removed from the curious crowds and brought to the Medical Bureau, where he must submit documents released by hospitals or doctors in whose care he had been previously. Such procedure is the basis for establishing the exact diagnosis of his disease prior to the alleged cure. Based on these documents the physicians of the Medical Bureau immediately begin their diagnosis. When this is completed one physican, elected by all who examined the allegedly cured person, presents the report to the assembly for free discussion. After the facts are ascertained the patient is released and thenceforth he is under the supervision of a physician of his country or region of origin. This is not a difficult task because the International Association of the Physicians of Lourdes has members all over the world. This doctor then examines the patient for a year, after which he submits his detailed report to the Medical Bureau. After a year the patient is invited to Lourdes and again examined, whereupon a new conference of the assembly decides whether the case should be referred to the highest medical committee, consisting of fifteen members elected by the assembly. The verdict of this committee is final.

After at least two years of continuous examination, discussion, and supervision, the decision is made and communicated to the ecclesiastical authorities. The bishops sometimes wait years before making any pronouncement. There have been cases when the statement of the ecclesiastical authorities came five years after the patient claimed to have been miraculously cured.

In 1946 the Medical Bureau examined thirty-six cases. From these only fourteen were re-submitted for new examination one year later, and in the second year there remained only four. These were delivered to the ecclesiastical authorities. In 1947 the Medical Bureau examined seventy-five alleged cures and immediately rejected sixty-four of them. After one year, eleven cases passed the test, but at the end of the second year only six were admitted for final examination. In 1948, 15,000 sick people came to Lourdes. A total of eighty-three cures was claimed but only nine arrived at the final verdict.

In 1947, 750 doctors participated in actual examinations; in 1948, 999; in 1950, 1200; in 1952, 1300; and in 1953 and 1955, 1500. Since the establishment of the Medical Bureau (and later the creation of the International Study Center) a total of 30,000 doctors examined and visited the sick, and studied all relevant documents and records.

Among the doctors who came to Lourdes was Alexis Carrel, a Nobel Prize physicist and a nonbeliever. It is worth while to sketch his life briefly here. Alexis Carrel was born in 1873 and died in 1944. His most important book, *Man the Unknown*,[8] was translated into all the important languages of the world. He received the Nobel Prize for his extraordinary research work as Medical Director of the Rockefeller Institute. Carrel was a rationalist, a nonbeliever, before he went to Lourdes. Yet he was puzzled by the events there and wanted to know what was behind them.

In 1903, he volunteered to work as an accompanying physician on one of the so-called sick trains that every year take thousands of sick persons from all countries to Lourdes. He was determined not to let himself be influenced by what he saw. He wanted to study the whole Lourdes phenomenon as a clinical case, or as a project in laboratory research. In his book *Voyage to Lourdes*[4] he wrote that he went there an open-minded researcher. If the cures were imaginary, he would recognize it immediately and waste no time on them. But if he observed some positive results, this would warrant deeper scientific examination on his part; and if he discovered that the place was full of charlatans, and the diagnoses erroneous, it would be his duty to call attention to them. But if—assuming the impossible—the stories about Lourdes were true, it would mean that he had participated in something very interesting which could lead to highly important conclusions. He knew, he said, that among the followers of the so-called scientific school it was absurd to talk about miracles. There *is* no miracle. The miracle is, without doubt, an absurdity, but if the miraculous has been established in circumstances that exclude with complete certainty the possibility of error, then—accept it. There is no alternative. Against the reality of facts one cannot oppose an anti-thesis, said Dr. Carrel.

Then he established for himself a list of cures that could lead to the acceptance of the miracle on his part. Some of these were the sudden healing of an organic disease; an amputed leg growing anew; a cancerous tumor suddenly disappearing. He told one of his colleagues, as recounted in his book, that should he witness a cure with his own eyes he would become either a fanatical believer or insane. But this would not happen. The force of Lourdes, whatever it may be, cannot compete with organic forces, said Carrel to himself. Then in Lourdes he saw many sick, many hopeful, and many totally desperate cases. One of them did not seem to have a human form. She had been afflicted with tuberculosis of the lung in early youth, but she was half-way cured. Now she arrived at the shrine with peritonitis of tubercular origin. According to all the doctors it was a hopeless case and she was nearing death. Carrel attached himself to this particular case. The nuns decided that she should not be immersed in the basin, as it would harm her. They bathed only her abdomen with the water of the well, and then they took her to the grotto. Carrel watched her constantly. Suddenly it seemed to him as if the features of the sick woman had changed, as if her customary pallor had vanished. But he did not want to believe his eyes. He said that perhaps it was an hallucination—although up to this time he had had no hallucinations. He felt the pulse of the woman and then said to another doctor standing by: "Her breathing is slower." His colleague answered resignedly: "She is dying," Carrel made no comment. This time he knew that something had happened. There, before his very eyes, the condition of this sick woman rapidly and visibly began to change. Now he concentrated all his attention and studied her constantly. Her face continued to change, her eyes fixed on the grotto. Carrel suddenly felt his own face becoming pale because he saw the blanket of the sick woman drop suddenly where it covered her abdomen. After a few minutes it seemed that the large abdominal tumor disappeared.

He stepped up to the young woman, observed her breathing and looked at her neck. "How do you feel?" he asked. "Very well. I'm not strong but I feel that I am cured," she answered. The nurse offered her a cup of milk which she drank with ease. Then she raised her head and turned on her side with no sign of pain. Toward evening Carrel visited the girl in the hospital and found her already sitting up in bed. Her eyes gleamed, her face, though drawn and thin, was already full of life reflected in the color of her cheeks. She was full of confidence. Her breathing was normal, her pulse 80. Carrel removed the blanket and examined the abdomen. It was normal. He pressed it, but the patient felt no pain. There was no sign of a tumor.

That night Carrel stopped before the basilica. He knew that he must draw a conclusion from all this. There was no doubt that a miracle had happened, for this was truly beyond the scope of nature. What kind of miracle he would not know till later, but it was miraculous—of this he was absolutely certain. He entered the basilica and sat down beside a peasant. Covering his face with his hands he sat motionless for quite a long time, then suddenly the prayer broke through from the depth of his soul: "Oh Dearest Virgin, You who help all the miserable, who humbly pray to you, please defend me. I believe in you. You apparently wanted to answer my doubting with a miracle. I do not yet see, I still doubt, but it is my desire and the main goal of all my efforts that I should believe blindly, without arguments and without criticism. My intellectual pride is deep and hard, and the dream, the most enchanting dream of dreams, is still buried beneath my pride. This dream is that I should believe in you, that I should love you the way those of pure heart love you."

By the time he entered his room it seemed to him that he had arrived at the certainty that he was suddenly able to clear his soul from recurring doubts; and he was filled with peaceful joy.

The experience of Alexis Carrel is only one of many. How many people visit Lourdes? Millions. In 1949, 1,600,000 came from all over the world. In 1952 about two million came, and since then the number has fluctuated between two and three million. In 1954, there were four million pilgrims. Not all the sick are cured, as we have seen, but all leave Lourdes spiritually strengthened. This tremendous mass of people, many of whom are sick, are transformed when they arrive in Lourdes and leave as new men. In her book *The Miracles of Lourdes,* the non-Catholic Ruth Cranston writes: "The greatest thing about Lourdes is the spirit in which life is lived there: The brotherhood of men in actual performance, the Beloved Community, *the human dream come true.*"[5] We can add to this that the Miracle of Lourdes consists of several miracles. First was the apparition and the sanctity of Bernadette; second, the actual miracles, the cures that take place there, cures not always contingent upon immersion into the water of the well. And the third miracle is the spiritual climate that impresses the cured and the non-cured. No one leaves Lourdes disappointed.

A great historian, for a long time a nonbeliever, made the following disclosure to me after he visited in Lourdes: "I feel that only in Lourdes did I understand what prayer means, and I learned to pray for the first time there. The person who is not cured knows that well.

The prayer in Lourdes is not a series of requests for God's favor. It is a conversation with God. . . . No matter how often you prayed the Rosary before, here you live through every mystery of the Rosary and your soul is filled with it. You get a foretaste of the delight that the angels must feel when they praise God. In Lourdes one does not pray in the first person singular, but for all the sick, for the welfare of the community. All the prayers converge in one great universal stream toward Heaven. The man who has not been cured in Lourdes takes this spirit home and this spirit remains with him and returns whenever he prays the Ave Maria."

The practical expression of the spirit of Lourdes on the spot appears in the activity of the voluntary helpers who take care of this enormous mass of people, particularly the sick. The members of this voluntary organization—Hospitalité Notre-Dame de Lourdes, commonly called *brancardiers* (stretcher-bearers)—come from all over the world and number about two thousand men. They receive no pay. The aspirants who wish to serve in this international corps are admitted only after a period of training. It is a great honor to become a member of this corps. They take care of the sick from the moment they arrive at the railway station or the airport. The *brancardiers* take them to the well and the church, and perform the immersions into the well.

Even though discipline is maintained among the masses of people in Lourdes, if a patient suddenly cries out that a miracle has happened and that he has been cured, a spontaneous feeling seems to seize the entire crowd and pushes it toward the person claiming the miracle. The calm and determined behavior of the *brancardiers* often prevents panic.

The well is the center of the cures. Ever since 1858 the water of the pool has been scientifically examined to determine whether it has any kind of healing effect. The most accurate scientific analysis always arrives at the conclusion that the water of the well is pure and simple, a common potable water. Secular, non-Catholic laboratories have established the following facts: The water of the well is ice-cold, yet no sick person contracts pneumonia and no healthy person has become ill after sudden immersion in it. The water should be full of bacteria of the most atrocious diseases, contaminated by the thousands of sick who come to Lourdes. Nevertheless, the water does not infect any one; when samples of the well were analyzed after the immersion of hundreds of sick the water showed no signs of containing bacteria. Then samples of the water of the well were mixed with samples of the water of the river Gave, which flows through Lourdes, and the sample from the Gave proved to be infected with the bacteria. Animals, too, have been injected with the seemingly infected water of the well without any ill effects. Later, the same animals were injected with the water of the Gave (mixed with the seemingly infected water of the well) and this time the animals became sick, and some died.

Another analysis of the well (taken before it reached the basin), for the purpose of ascertaining its mineralogical composition, ended each time with the finding that the water of the well of Lourdes has no therapeutic value. It is not radioactive, antibiotic, or antiseptic. It is simply a pure, potable water. And it is potable even in its polluted state. "The healing spring of Massabielle is tangibly the frontier between the natural and the supernatural. Here the Unknowable makes bold to assert that the earth is partly its province."[6]

Detailed medical description of all the miraculous cures at Lourdes would fill several volumes. Here we quote only a few. But the reader is reminded that all these cases are meticulously certified by Catholic and non-Catholic doctors united in the Medical Bureau of Lourdes. The facts of these cures have not been challenged.

What, then, are the criteria for determining from a medical point of view whether or not a cure is miraculous?

1. The existence of a disease or illness, prior to the visit to Lourdes or any other shrine, must be absolutely established and certified. This presupposes a detailed, expert diagnosis by physicians.

2. The disease must have an abnormal aspect. A disease is abnormal if the patient is afflicted with an incurable malady. If in certain cases such an affliction may be curable it has reached, nevertheless, such a state that a sudden healing by natural forces would be impossible.

3. The Medical Bureau lists certain phenomena that accompany a miraculous cure. These are:

a. The patient is suddenly beset with a sudden fear and anxiety never experienced before. Often, death is feared to be imminent. But this state changes, from one moment to another, to one of great relief and relaxation.

b. Often the patient feels an intense pain in that very part of the body where the disease is located. The pain then suddenly disappears.

c. In the case of miraculous cure the healing is not followed by any physiological phenomena. Thus, if a tumor disappears there are no signs of uremic intoxication caused by the disintegrating products of the tumor; nor does the temperature of the patient rise as a result of the combustion usually caused by disintegration of tumor cells.

d. A total absence of a convalescent period. The patient immediately feels the effects of healing. His organs immediately start to function in a normal way. A person miraculously cured of cancer, ulcers, or intestinal tuberculosis is able to eat and digest any kind of food.

4. Finally, the Church requires a waiting period of at least one year to ascertain that there is no relapse. In cases of relapse, causes other than miraculous might have effected the cure.

The facts speak for themselves. From the many confirmed miraculous cures that have occurred in Lourdes, we have selected the most important and recent cases. In these cases the blind see again, former deaf-mutes hear and speak, paralyzed persons walk, and cancerous growths disappear. All this seems incredible both to the believer and the unbeliever. There is simply no natural explanation for these cures.

Francis Pascal was born in 1934, a completely normal child. In 1937 he was afflicted with contagious meningitis. His life was saved, but as a result of the disease he became completely blind. In addition, by June of 1938 the four-year-old child was totally paralyzed, and could move neither his arms nor his legs. In August of 1938 he was brought to Lourdes, and after two immersions into the icy water of the basin of Massabielle he instantly regained his complete health. This was one of the most dramatic healings in Lourdes. After the second immersion, when his mother carried him back to the hospital, the child moved his arm and pointed to a tricycle and said: "Mother, look there. Isn't it nice?"

At this writing Francis Pascal is a completely normal young man. Members of the Medical Bureau and other experts have confirmed that both his blindness and paralysis were of an organic nature. There was no hope of cure. Nevertheless, the medical investigation, the checks and re-checks, lasted more than ten years. The Archbishop of Aix-en-Provence declared the cure miraculous on May 31, 1949.

Gerard Baillie was born in 1941. At the age of two and one-half he was afflicted with bilateral chorioretinitis and double optic atrophy. This is an absolutely incurable eye disease. He lost his sight after an operation and, as a consequence, the optic nerves in both eyes were completely atrophied. Many medical certificates attest to this. Here, too, the case was altogether hopeless.

In September, 1947, he was brought to Lourdes. Nothing happened after his first immersion into the water of the well. The next day, however, while his mother and he walked the Way of the Cross leading down from Calvary, the boy, whom the mother led by the hand, suddenly bent down and picked up a piece of wood. He looked up to his mother, smiled, and said, "Mother, you are so beautiful."

The case of Gerard is doubly unexplained. He is cured because he sees; yet when the doctors of the Medical Bureau, and many others, examined him, they all stated: "This boy cannot see. The test shows that he has bilateral chorioretinitis and double optic atrophy." In 1948 he was examined again and the diagnosis was confirmed but none the less he could see objects and persons clearly. The doctors could say nothing except that this was a miracle, since his infirmity by medical definition was technically incurable. Medical science had never known a similar case; after four years of destruction of the internal tissues of the eye and after four years of atrophy of the optic nerve, his retina and his optic nerve was regenerated.

The Church, however, did not accept this as a miracle. Cardinal Lienart of Lille, in whose diocese the boy resided, declared that the canonical commission did not find the cure complete because technically the disease still existed. Nevertheless, the boy who should be blind, sees!

Rose Evrard had been a deaf-mute from birth. Medical examination attested that this was an organic disease. In August, 1897, she was immersed into the well, and when she left she could both speak and hear. The ecclesiastical authority confirmed her case to be an authentic miracle.

Gabrielle Clauzel, a Frenchwoman from Oran, North Africa, had rheumatic spondilitis and had been operated on several times. She had been under treatment since 1938 in different hospitals of France without any beneficial result. In 1943 her condition was positively critical. She weighed seventy pounds, her heart was failing at a catastrophic rate, and in the opinion of all the doctors she was near death. The family brought her, with extreme difficulty, to Lourdes in August, 1943. After immersion into the basin, she was brought into the church and then to the hotel. There suddenly she sat down at the dining table and ate a hearty meal which only a few hours before certainly would have killed her. She regained her strength instantaneously. No trace of disease remained. The Bishop of Oran, in a decree of March 18, 1948, declared the cure miraculous.

When she returned to North Africa the Arab workers who had known her in her pitiable state studied her, and one of them said: "Mademoiselle, we know very well who cured you. Not the doctors but Miriam, the Mother of the Prophet Jesus to whom you prayed so much and whom you serve." (Islam considers Christ a great prophet and calls the Blessed Virgin "Miriam" and venerates her more and more.)

Gabriel Gargam was a postal worker assigned to the Bordeaux-Paris express trains. In a railway wreck on December 18, 1899, he was thrown about sixty feet from the tracks by the force of the collision. Upon being brought to the hospital, it was found that he had broken his clavicle, his legs, and that he also had received some head injuries. All these were healed soon. But the shock had created serious internal troubles, and he was paralyzed from his hips down. He could not eat, and by another year—in December 1900—his weight had gone down from 160 to 72 pounds. At the medical examination conducted by the doctors of the railroad, it was learned that he was a total disability case. All his organs were afflicted, and only his mind was left intact.

In 1901, although his condition was hopeless, his mother took him to Lourdes. He was immersed in the water, apparently without result. His nurse quipped that there was no reason for him to be blessed by the Sacrament during the procession because by that time he would be dead. At this moment the man declared dead rose, and in his bare feet, clad only in his long shirt, he walked behind the baldachin placed over the Eucharist. Immediately, 63 doctors examined this "human ghost"—as they called him—and checked the official diagnosis, which stated that his entire organism was destroyed. His heart, liver, kidneys had malfunctioned, yet without convalescence he had been totally and entirely cured, between one moment and another. And he died in 1953 at the rather ripe age of 80. After his miraculous cure he became one of the *brancardiers* in Lourdes, performing the heaviest and most difficult work. For the rest of his life he continued to be a robust man. The ecclesiastical authorities declared the cure miraculous.

Mary Theresa Canin came from a very sick family. Both her father and mother had died of tuberculosis. The girl, born in 1900, had peritonitis of tubercular origin and Pott's disease. Her condition worsened from year to year without any hope of recovery. She was cured in October of 1947 after an immersion, and the Archbishop of Marseilles, in a decree of February 21, 1950, declared the cure miraculous. She became a nun in the convent of the Little Sisters of the Assumption in Lyon, France.

Paul Pellegrin was a colonel in the French Army. He had fought in Africa, in Indo-China, and in both world wars. In 1949, when he was 51, he became suddenly ill, but his life-experience as a soldier caused him to pay little or no attention to his illness. His condition deteriorated further, and eventually it was diagnosed as an incurable disease: an abscess of the liver which had developed into a chronic fistula. He was treated with all possible skill and with the most modern drugs available. In October of 1950 he went to Lourdes and was instantly cured. The Archbishop of Toulon accepted the recovery as miraculous in his decree of December 7, 1953.

Rose Martin was cured at the age of 45 in June, 1947. She had cancer of the uterus and of the rectum, each growth the size of an orange. Several previous operations had proved useless. She lived, but only with constant morphine injections to relieve the pain. Science could not help her. After the third immersion, she stood up in the basin, walked home, felt no more pain, and ate normally. Medical examinations attested to the complete disappearance of the tumors as well as their functional symptoms. On May 3, 1949, the Bishop of Nice declared the curing of Rose Martin miraculous. Ever since she has been in good health, and takes good care of her family. This woman, who had received five thousand morphine injections and had weighed less than seventy pounds, now weighs twice as much.

Gertrude Fulda was a Viennese dancer who had attained a great success in Europe. In 1937 she fell ill. Under treatment for years, operated on frequently, she lived a shadowy invalid's life. Finally the disease was diagnosed as Addison's disease, incurable. At the age of 36 she arrived in Lourdes in August of 1950 in a hopeless condition. She was taken in a wheelchair to the well and was instantly cured. Five years later, in April, 1955, Cardinal Archbishop Innitzer proclaimed hers a miraculous cure.

The most recent cure was that of *Evasio Ganora*, an Italian farm hand from northern Italy. He had been sick since 1949, with internal diseases of such a nature that even medical science could not diagnose them. He had malignant lymphogranulomatose with great ganglions and, in addition, his liver tended to grow larger and larger. The disease spread and afflicted all the other organs. In one year he received twenty-five blood transfusions. The case was declared hopeless. On May 31, 1950, he was brought with great difficulty to Lourdes. After immersion in the well he felt that his whole body was pervaded with a great heat. He rose to his feet, and he walked. The Medical Bureau immediately stated that the liver and other organs were normal, the ganglia had lost their inflammation, and that the patient was cured. On the third day he was helping to carry the sick to the well. The medical investigation lasted five years, and on May 31, 1955, the Bishop of Casale-Monferrato declared the cure of Evasio Ganora miraculous.

Three other apparitions which occurred in the 19th century have also been approved by ecclesiastical authorities. On January 17, 1871, one took place in Pontmain, France; on August 23, 1876, in Pellevoisin, also in France; and on August 21, 1879, in Knock, County Mayo, Ireland.

In Pontmain, in the Brittany region of France, a twelve-year-old boy named Eugene Barbedette, together with some of his little friends, saw the Queen of Heaven during a winter night. This happened during the Franco-Prussian war when Pontmain feared a sudden German attack. The Barbedette children and their father were working in a barn cutting fodder. Eugene, urged by some unknown impulse, suddenly left the barn to check the weather. As he looked into the sky, gleaming with stars in the wintry night, he saw "between a triangle of specially brilliant stars the figure of a beautiful woman smiling at him." He described her as "a tall beautiful lady in a blue dress covered with stars. She had blue shoes with gold buckles . . . with a black veil around her head on which was set a crown."[7] Later, a red cross appeared on the Lady's breast. As people gathered around the boy an inscription was visible to the children at the feet of the Lady reading, "Pray, my children. . . . God will soon answer your prayers. . . . My Son allows Himself to be moved in compassion." Then the Lady raised her hands, palms outward, shoulder-high, and smiled. But then she became sad and the red crucifix appeared, followed by the name of Jesus Christ in red letters. While the sadness passed from the face of Our Lady the inscriptions slowly disappeared, and the apparition faded out.

The cult of Our Lady of Pontmain was authorized in 1877, after a very rigorous investigation. After fifty-one years Pope Pius XI acknowledged the authenticity of the apparition in a unique manner: by authorizing an office and a Mass proper to Our Lady of Pontmain. Miraculous cures are constantly claimed, and Pontmain is now one of the great national pilgrimage sites of France.

The apparition of Pellevoisin was accorded to Estelle Faguette, an incurably sick woman, in February, 1876. During the night of the

14th and 15th of February Estelle was on the verge of death because of acute peritonitis. It seemed to her then that a demon visited her. Then she claimed that the Blessed Virgin approached her bed and told her to have no fear, for she was the Blessed Virgin's beloved child. She had several other apparitions, in one of which Our Lady told her that she is all-merciful. Anyone who desired to serve her should be simple and make his words and deeds conform. . . . Everyone can be saved in any state of life.

The recognition of the apparition of Pellevoisin encountered many difficulties. The Archbishop of Bourges appointed a commission of fifty-six ecclesiastics. Although their affirmative decision was almost unanimous, the archbishop pronounced no opinion. The case remained unclear for several years. Finally in 1907 Cardinal Merry del Val wrote to the Cardinal of Lyons and the Archbishop of Bourges that the decrees of the Holy See dealing with the case of Pellevoisin neither directly nor indirectly approved or disapproved these apparitions. The sole prohibition was that it should not be stated these apparitions were approved by the Holy See.

Ireland endured great hardships while fighting for its Faith and for its national integrity. As long as the monasteries and holy places flourished, they remained the main source of spiritual energy and comfort to the people. While the wars raged throughout the centuries, the people and the clergy united more closely in spirit and resolution, and came to rely more and more on the help of the Blessed Virgin. During these long years the people felt her aid in innumerable personal graces, accorded to those who showed particular devotion to her. In 1697, the image of Our Lady, taken from Clonfert to faraway Hungary, shed blood and tears for three hours. The image wept for the besieged people of Ireland whose priests, by decree of Parliament, had been expelled, and whose dead could not be buried in the religion of their forefathers.

But finally, after centuries of desolation, the Blessed Virgin visited Ireland in a spectacular manner. The day of August 21, 1879, had been an ordinary one for the inhabitants of the village of Knock, in County Mayo. Only a few people were on the streets. Knock is an ordinary village, inhabited by normal, God-fearing, hard-working peasant farmers. Yet one of these simple but stolid men was the first to notice that evening that the gable end of the chapel was bathed in a soft, white, flickering light. The wall was surmounted by brilliant stars, twinkling as on a fine frosty night. Fifteen people subsequently saw the lights and then Our Lady appeared with St. Joseph and St. John the Evangelist. One of the first persons to witness the miracle, an elderly lady, approached the Blessed Virgin with outstretched arms: the figure of the Madonna receded, although smiling at her. Another man ran excitedly into the dark streets of the village, shouting that all should come to the chapel to see the vision. It was estimated that the visitation lasted two hours. Immediately a commission of inquiry was set up by the Archbishop of Tuam to establish the facts.

While the inquiry was still in process, another apparition took place on January 6, 1880, followed by two more on February 10 and 12 of the same year, which were seen by numerous people. This vision was like the first. Our Lady stood in the center of a group, her hands raised to the height of her shoulders. On her head she wore a brilliant crown that blazed like fire. St. Joseph stood on the right and St. John on the left. To the left of the group there was an altar with a large cross; and at the foot of the cross a lamb. The altar had no adornments, but behind the cross the onlookers could see angels in postures of adoration and prayer. Witnesses swore that the figures had no resemblance to a painting; the figures of Mary, Joseph, and John were distinct, and the observers could move around them.

After the commission submitted a thoroughly favorable report, the fame of Knock spread throughout Ireland, and the influx of pilgrims grew constantly. Knock soon became celebrated as one of the great Marian shrines. It has been the scene of hundreds of cures, all carefully attested to and recorded by a commission of doctors, many of them non-Catholic. Here the visitor encounters scenes similar to those in Lourdes. At the annual pilgrimages, thousands move toward the church and the shine, which depicts the actual scene of the apparitions wherein the humble folk had seen Mary as Queen of the Angels.

In 1917, when three Portuguese children reported that the Blessed

Virgin had appeared to them, Portugal was a country torn by civil strife and ruled by elements hostile to the Catholic Church. After the fall of the monarchy and the proclamation of the Portuguese Republic, the Portuguese government, in 1911, had severed its diplomatic relations with the Catholic Church and declared that thenceforth religion would play no great role in Portuguese life. Its place would be taken by science, philosophy, and reason. For a nation that for centuries had been devoutly Catholic and loyal to Rome this was a tragic event.

On May 13, 1917, Lucia Dos Santos, ten years old, and Francis and Jacinta Marto, who were nine and seven respectively, were tending sheep in a valley called Cova de Iria. It was high noon and the day was warm and pleasant. The sky was cloudless and radiant. Suddenly the three children saw two flashes of lightning. They had hardly recovered from the shock when they beheld a radiance streaming from a globe of light on the foliage of an oak tree. In the middle of this globe, surrounded by rays more radiant than the sun, was a beautiful lady. The children stood still for several seconds; then the Lady addressed them in a soft, and gentle voice: "Be not frightened. I shall not harm you." The Lady seemed to be less than 18 years old. She wore a white robe, and her head was covered with a white veil. Her hands, clasped in prayer, held a rosary. With this apparition there began a sequence of events for which there is no other explanation than that of supernatural intervention.

Paul Blanshard, in his *American Freedom and Catholic Power*[8] wrote: "In recent years priestly promotion in the field of Mariology has centered on Fatima, the Portuguese hamlet where the Virgin Mary made six appearances to three peasant children in 1917 just before the Bolshevik revolution. The messages she delivered to these children were most timely; in fact, they show the considerable comprehension of the delicate position of the Vatican in European politics. Her political forebodings were conveyed to three shepherd children . . . who had never gone to school." Blanshard later added that the Catholic hierarchy did not appreciate the importance of these miracles and five years after the apparition the *Catholic Encyclopaedia Supplement* "did not even mention it."

Lourdes, the Grotto of the Apparitions today.

Entrance to the baths where the sick are immersed into the miraculous water.

Holy Mass for the sick at Lourdes.

A pilgrim being examined by the doctors in the Medical Bureau at Lourdes.

(Viron, Lourdes, France)

Francis Pascal before his miraculous cure at Lourdes (Aug. 18, 1938).

(Viron, Lourdes, France)

Francis Pascal after his miraculous cure at Lourdes (Aug. 18, 1938).

(Viron, Lourdes, France)

Paul Pellegrin, miraculously cured at Lourdes (Oct. 3, 1950).

Rose Martin, miraculously cured at Lourdes (July 3, 1947).

Gabrielle Clauzel before her miraculous cure at Lourdes (Aug. 14, 1943).

Gabrielle Clauzel after her miraculous cure at Lourdes (Aug. 14, 1943).

Gabriel Gargam before his miraculous cure at Lourdes (Aug. 20, 1901).

Gabriel Gargam after his miraculous cure at Lourdes (Aug. 20, 1901).

Lucia dos Santos to whom the Blessed Virgin appeared
in Fatima in 1917. She is now a nun in Portugal.

Blessing the sick at Knock Shrine, Ireland.

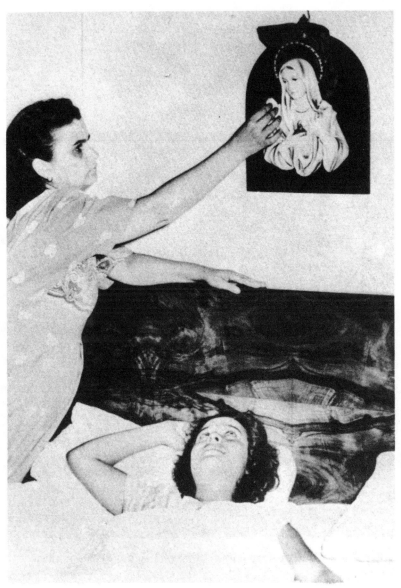

The Weeping Madonna, Siracusa, Italy. This marble statue of Our Lady has become a shrine for pilgrims from many parts of Italy since the sick girl in whose room it stands said it began to shed tears after she prayed to the Madonna (August 1953). Photo shows the girl, Antonina Giusto, on her sick bed, while her mother wipes the face of the statue.

Papal Mass during a canonization process at St. Peter's Basilica.

This passage from the book of this well-known critic of the Catholic Church has been cited only because his statement is an excellent example of the way facts can be completely overlooked, by error or deliberately.

Fatima is situated 62 miles north of Lisbon. The name of Fatima is of Arab origin, for Portugal, like Spain, was once overrun by the Arabs. Fatima was the daughter of an Arab chieftan in Spain, and she had been taken prisoner by Portuguese knights. One of these knights married her after she had become a Christian. After her death her Arab name was given to one of the estates of her husband, and her Christian name, Oureanan, to the county town which became Ourem. In 1917 Fatima was an insignificant hamlet whose inhabitants were as poor as the rest of the population of the country. Cova da Iria, where the actual apparition occurred, is in the immediate neighborhood of this hamlet. The three children had seen apparitions on May 13, June 13, July 13, August 19, September 13, and October 13 of 1917. Two of the children are now dead. Francis Marto died in 1919 and Jacinta Marto in 1920. Both knew in advance the date of their death, which had been revealed to them in a vision. One of the children, Lucia Dos Santos, who is now 49 years old, became a Carmelite nun in Coimbra, Portugal.

It is true that the apparitions occurred just before the outbreak of the Russian Revolution. But it is the wildest misrepresentation to suggest, as Blanshard does, that the Catholic Church planned in advance an apparition to be exploited later for political ends. If the messages given to the children were "most timely" and if "they showed a considerable comprehension of the delicate position of the Vatican in European politics," those messages should have been made public immediately. The Catholic Church certainly was equipped to launch an elaborate Fatima campaign at once in 1917. Instead, the whole story of Fatima reveals just the opposite intention. Blanshard himself admits that "the campaign for Fatima began under Pius XII, who had become Pope in 1939." Thus, more than 20 years passed before the world really became acquainted with all the details. This fact in itself is not unusual. The time lag is inherent in the routine procedure of the Catholic Church. Visions are never accepted immediately, and Fatima was no exception.

In the beginning, after the first apparition, no one was inclined to believe the story told by the children. They were threatened, called liars, and even beaten. Jacinta Marto was told by her mother that she was mad, that it was impossible that she could have seen the Blessed Virgin because the child was not a saint. But the three children were unanimous in insisting that the vision was true, and that the Blessed Virgin asked them to recite the Rosary every day. The parents were embarrassed. When the secret leaked out it became a public scandal. These poor families considered the vision as one more burden to be added to the others already crushing them. When a priest told the mother of the Marto children that what had occurred was a blessing, she answered that it was no blessing to have a lying daughter.

The children told their parents that the Blessed Virgin had asked them to come to the same place one month later. The children went there without their parents, the latter being embarrassed and afraid. Sixty people gathered at Cova da Iria. The vision and the dialogue lasted ten minutes. During this vision Lucia also received a secret message that she revealed later. This was the message that Jacinta and Francis would die before her. Just as during the first apparition, the Blessed Virgin had a heart pierced with thorns, which she held in her right hand.

At the third vision there were 5,000 spectators. This time the parents were also there, but still they refused to believe that their children had stated the truth. Those who accompanied the children did not see the apparition, nor did they hear what the Lady said to Lucia Dos Santos, but they did notice that the sun dimmed and they heard a loud sound, followed by a sudden white cloud. And all noticed that the branches of the oak were bent under an invisible weight. On this day Lucia was again asked by the Lady to recite the Rosary every day, and to learn how to read. All the children were illiterate.

At the next vision, on July 13, the Lady repeated her request that the Rosary be recited daily, and she added that the faithful should make sacrifice for sinners and do penance for the offenses committed against the Immaculate Heart of Mary. She promised that she would come every month and that in October she would identify herself and work a miracle. When Lucia asked her to cure a poor cripple the apparition answered that she would not do that but that the cripple should say the Rosary every day. The Lady promised that others would obtain many favors during the year, and reiterated that all should recite the Rosary.

But the most extraordinary aspect of the July 13 apparition is the prophecies that the Lady made to these simple Portuguese children who did not have the remotest idea of happenings in the outside world. She told them that the war begun in 1914 was drawing to an end (Portugal was not at war). "But if men do not cease offending God, in the next pontificate a worse one will begin." She predicted that God was going to punish the world by war, famine, and persecution of the Church, and that in order to prevent this from happening, people should repent and the world be consecrated to her Immaculate Heart. Then she said: "If my requests are heeded, Russia will be converted and there will be peace. Otherwise Russia will spread her errors in all the world, causing wars and persecution of the Church. Many good men will suffer martyrdom, the Holy Father will have much to suffer. Certain nations will be annihilated. In the end my Immaculate Heart will triumph. The consecration to my Immaculate Heart will be made, Russia will be converted, and a period of peace will be granted to the world."

On August 13, the three children could not go to the Cova da Iria. The Portuguese civil authorities, then violently antireligious, ordered the children arrested and thrown into jail. The chief of police threatened them with death if they did not retract. They were led to a kettle of boiling water and told that they would be thrown into it. But the children remained firm. At this time about 20,000 people went to the Cova da Iria. They saw the white cloud and the lightning, but with the children absent no apparition occurred. The chief of police released the children on August 15 and they were accorded another vision on August 19, when the Lady asked them again to pray and make sacrifices for sinners. Immediately after the children arrived there occurred the same atmospheric disturbances as before. When the vision vanished Jacinta cut off the branch of the tree on which the feet of the apparition had rested.

The fifth apparition occurred on September 13. An estimated crowd of 40,000 gathered in front of the evergreen oak. This time a globe of light appeared on the tree, followed by the white cloud and the rain, which began to fall from a clear sky. Witnesses described it as "a luminous globe coming from the east and moving to the west, gliding slowly and maestically through space. . . . Suddenly this globe, giving off an extraordinary light, disappeared."[9]

The miracle of October 13, 1917, was of such a splendor that nothing like it has been recorded since ancient times. No other apparition has been observed with such care by thousands of people in every walk of life, believers and unbelievers alike. A total of 70,000 people were there. They heard the thunder, saw the lightning, and noticed the parting of the clouds. The Lady identified herself to the children, saying that she was the Lady of the Rosary. She warned that people must change and repent. On this day the children received a vision not only of the Blessed Virgin but also of Christ and St. Joseph standing beside the figure of Our Lady of Sorrows, and finally of Our Lady of Mount Carmel with the Scapular.

As before, the apparitions were seen only by the children, and the messages were given to them alone. But while the children listened enraptured, the crowd witnessed something else. After the Rosary had been recited by the multitude, the dark sky opened, and the sun, appearing in a clear blue sky, suddenly began to tremble and shake, and turn about swiftly like a great wheel of fire, casting off long shafts of light which colored the sky and earth. This spectacle continued for ten minutes and was observed at a distance of twenty-five miles. Then the sun broke loose from the sky and plunged downward through space directly over the people, who fell at once to their knees, crying for forgiveness for their sins.

At this time all Portugal was in an uproar. Journalists rushed to the site. Though most of them were not believers they did want to be objective. The editor of the Lisbon daily *O Seculo* described the event at great length. He telephoned his article from the county capital on the same evening, under the head: Amazing Phenomenon; How the Sun Danced at Fatima at Mid-day.

This was a prodigy that had never occurred before. It was neither a mirage nor an eclipse. In fact, it was just the opposite of an eclipse. Only the miracle that appeared to Josue, when the sun stopped, can be compared to this unique miracle. Hallucination, or mass suggestion, is to be excluded, as each of the 70,000 present saw the phenomenon and no case of mass suggestion or mass hallucination of such magnitude has ever occurred. Psychiatry knows of no mass suggestion and mass hallucination that can seize 70,000 people at once.

As has been said, the children during these months were exposed to all sorts of insults. First of all they encountered skepticism everywhere. Their parents had constantly threatened them until the miracle of October 13. The pastor of Fatima was prudent and skeptical. The investigator sent by the Cardinal Patriarch of Lisbon, Canon Formigao, began his inquiry immediately. All the minutes of the interrogation were made public. As in the case of the children of La Salette, civil authorities attempted to persuade them to retract. The chief of police threw them into jail with common criminals, threatening them with death.

Many of the priests who came did not believe, and openly declared the Fatima events a fraud. Slowly, however, the situation cleared. The first Mass at Cova da Iria was celebrated on October 13, 1921. On November 17, 1921, a spring began to flow at the site of the apparitions. On October 13, 1930, the bishops of Portugal, after fifteen years of investigation (the routine and rule of the Church in these matters), confirmed the apparitions and gave official authorization to the cult of Our Lady of Fatima. No authorization could be given as long as one of the bishops of Portugal opposed the cult. Bishop Domingos Frutuoso finally was convinced in January, 1929, by Pius XI. Thus, in 1930 authorization of the cult could be announced. It was not Pius XII who first recognized the importance of Fatima, as claimed by hostile opinion ignorant of the facts: the cult had been authorized ten years earlier, in 1929.

Later Lucia Dos Santos revealed that the apparition on May 13, 1917, had not been the first one. She could not recall the exact date but she stated that it had occurred during the spring of 1916. At that time the three children saw an apparition approaching them which told them, "I am an angel of peace." Two months later the apparition appeared again and asked them to pray very much. The third apparition took place two months thereafter. This time the children saw a chalice in the angel's hand and as the angel knelt the chalice remained in the air and gave them Communion.

All these later revelations of Lucia have been approved by ecclesiastical authorities. But any other revelations, and some of the secrets, have not yet been made public.

Extraordinary cures are taking place continuously at Fatima. Its medical bureau operates like the one established at Lourdes.

Another comment should be made about the miracle of the dancing sun. It has been established that this was not an eclipse, for no observation in Europe recorded an eclipse on that day. Nor can the partial darkness be attributed to a sudden fog. There was no fog in Fatima.

In order to explain the colored sky it has been suggested that it might have been a rainbow of sorts. A rainbow, however, is a static phenomenon. The "colored sky" was a phenomenon during which the entire visible sky was flooded with colors of various hues in constant motion. Finally, the phenomenon of the aurora borealis, or northern lights, is also to be excluded because it cannot be seen during the daytime.

Thus, it is reasonable to admit, after such careful investigation and prudent restraint on the part of the Church, that the miracle of Fatima is of preternatural origin.

Around 6 P.M. on November 29, 1932, four children, Fernande and Alberte Voisin, and Andrée and Gilberte Degeimbre, went to meet Gilberte Voisin and accompany her home from the convent school of the Sisters of Charity of Beauraing. They walked on the main highway toward the railway viaduct and then turned into the garden of the convent. In that garden was a Lourdes grotto, and, as was their custom, they knelt before it. Andrée pulled the cord of the bell on the convent door and they all waited, expecting one of the sisters to open. Suddenly, as Andrée was looking toward the viaduct, she cried out: "I see a light!" "It must be the headlight of a car," answered one of the other children. All looked in the direction of the source of the light. "Something is moving there. Is it a man or what?" they asked each other. Then Albert Voisin shouted, "This is the Blessed Virgin." All looked again and all were convinced that it was the Blessed Virgin walking on the bridge. In the meantime, a sister had opened the door and when she heard these words she thought the children were speaking about the statue in the grotto. Then when she understood that they were talking about the Blessed Virgin walking on the bridge, the sister laughed. "Go home, children. See you tomorrow. Don't tell me stories. A statue that walks. Don't try to fool me, please."

At home their parents smiled benevolently. The Voisin family was a family of believers. The Degeimbre family was split, the father being something of a Marxist. For about a hundred years Belgium had been divided into these two camps, particularly in Flanders, a region of heavy industry and mines, where Beauraing is situated. The next day the children described their experience to their schoolmates. Everyone talked about the incident but no one attached any importance to it. After school, however, at the same hour as the previous day, they again saw the vision of the Lady walking in the air, her hands clasped as if in prayer.

This was the beginning of the 33 apparitions. It was also the beginning of a series of heated discussions in and around Beauraing. At a later date, on January 3, the apparition came closer to them and a conversation ensued between them and the Lady. Though many people, at one time numbering 30,000, crowded around the site during the apparition, only the children were favored.

The children encountered doubting people and general hostility. Their parents were embarrassed and infuriated. Some of the inhabitants in the villages and the neighborhood mocked them. Then there came the usual exploiters of religious sentiment who built a miniature city of vending stands offering everything from soft drinks to religious articles. The pastor, the nuns, their parents, and others, scolded, warned and sometimes even threatened the children. Still they never would recant. The apparition always appeared close to the

May tree. Our Lady was dressed in a white robe and reflected a blue light. She told them that they should be good and that they should say the Rosary. "Pray. Pray very much . . . pray always . . . pray always . . . sacrifice yourself for me."

This is the message at Beauraing in the 20th century in the center of a highly industrialized country to children surrounded by atheists, doubters, militant Marxists, and constantly subjected to hostile interrogations. Even in 1940 a profound believer like Jean Hellé in his book *Miracles* put Beauraing in the category of doubtful miracles, calling it the Beauraing "epidemic." "During 1932 and the second world war," he wrote, "Beauraing was the scene of an absolute epidemic of miracles, or rather of visionary phenomena. . . . Since 1932 many facts unknown at the time have been brought to the notice of the public. A political movement, Degrelles 'Rexism,'[10] took a special interest in Beauraing and chose it as the jumping off place for its propaganda. . . . It has been asserted that Degrelles purchased land at Beauraing." Hellé collected considerable data on the children and their behavior, on their reading, and on experiences that might have influenced them. He asserted that "Fernande Voisin imagined that she could copy Lourdes and Fatima at her leisure."

In the meantime the investigations went on. Cures and conversions continued to occur. And in May of 1943 the bishop of Namur expressed official, albeit reserved, approval of the new cult. In 1946, after the war, a statue of Our Lady of Beauraing was unveiled at the site where people had constantly prayed during the perilous days of World War II. Then in July, 1949, the same bishop of Namur gave his final approbation.

When I went to Beauraing in 1933 I met the children and their families. First I visited the Degeimbre family. Mme. Degeimbre was a widow. The family operated a small dairy farm. "Are you happy?" I asked. "Yes," she answered with visible emotion. I reminded her that during the apparitions she made a statement saying that it was a great misfortune for the family. "What did you mean by this?" I asked. She smiled for a moment, and then reluctantly said that this statement had been interpreted in so many different ways that not even she could explain what she had originally meant by it.

Then I asked the pastor whether the parents in both families were believers. "I could not confirm that," said the pastor. "In any case they are not practicing Catholics."

Then we walked through the village toward the site of the apparitions and to the convent school where Gilberte Voisin and Gilberte Degeimbre are students. Almost everyone greeted the pastor as we walked through the city, attesting to an excellent relation between the faithful and their pastor. At the convent we first met the mother superior, a placid woman with ascetic features. She introduced the two girls immediately. One was now eleven, the other seven years old. Both were remarkably pretty (in contrast to the photographs of Prof. Greef), their eyes clear, blue and innocent. I could not discover any will to deceive or the sign of any shrewdness on their faces.

"Did you see the Blessed Virgin?" I asked.

"Yes, Monsieur," answered both with a conviction that almost jolted me.

"Are you sure of this?" I continued.

"Yes, Monsieur," answered the children without tension or hesitation.

After we ended our conversation the pastor and I resumed our walk through the village to the home of the prosperous, middle-class Voisin family. Monsieur Voisin was a house painter and he also owned a paint shop. First we met Mme. Voisin, a plump, kindly, rosy-cheeked woman. She talked freely and without inhibition. Then we met Alberte Voisin, one of the recipients of the vision, a nice looking girl of 16. There was nothing extraordinary about her. She looked rather naïve, as she came in from the kitchen where she had been peeling potatoes.

I asked her whether she had any of the pamphlets and books that had been written about them.

She answered smilingly, "Some of them, yes, but certainly not the thick ones, because I have no time."

In the meantime M. Voisin arrived and, with great indignation, displayed some of the news photos of his children. He said that those who denied the apparitions made the children deliberately look idiotic in the pictures. Just then the bell rang and Mme. Voisin went to the door, and returned quickly.

"There is a lady here and she asks for your prayers," she announced.

Alberte Voisin went out to meet her and talked with her for a while. She promised to pray for her that night. The whole family was quiet in demeanor and seemed to be the prototype of a self-complacent middle-class family, an impression reinforced by the furnishings of their home.

When the apparitions ended in Beauraing, new apparitions started in another Belgian village called Banneux. They began on January 15, 1933, and lasted until March 2. Mariette Becco, a seven-year-old daughter of a very poor family, received eight visions. During the second apparition the Blessed Virgin led the girl to a well and told her to immerse her hand in the water. "This well belongs to me," said the Lady of the Apparition. From this moment many unexplained miraculous cures have occurred at the well. During the third apparition the Virgin said to Mariette:

"I am the Virgin of the poor. I came for all nations to help the poor and the sick." The cult of the Virgin of the poor in Banneux received full recognition from the diocesan Bishop in August 1949.

The most recent miracle to be approved by ecclesiastical authorities occurred on August 29, 1953. A terra cotta bust of the Blessed Virgin in the home of Angelo and Antonia Giusto, a Sicilian couple who lived near Syracuse (Italy), was discovered to be shedding tears. The phenomenon continued for three days—until September 1. The tears were analyzed, and it was found that they were identical with human tears. Miraculous cures were claimed and crowds of faithful gathered in the town. The bishops of Sicily immediately conducted an investigation, and in a unanimous declaration issued December 12, 1953, concluded that the reality of the weeping statue could not be doubted.

On November 18, 1955, *Oggi*, an Italian picture weekly, published an amazing article. According to the article, the present Pontiff, Pope Pius XII, received a vision during December of 1954, and that in this vision he had seen Christ. All sorts of sensational and unauthorized articles mushroomed in the public prints following disclosure of the incident in *Oggi*. Indeed, a tremendous confusion was created by people who were not familiar with the facts and with the legislation of the Church in such cases. The only authorized story of the vision appeared later—on December 4, 1955—in the *Osservatore della Domenica*, a picture weekly printed in Vatican City, but not a supplement of or otherwise related to *Osservatore Romano,* the semiofficial daily newspaper of the Holy See. The *Osservatore della Domenica* wrote:

"About a year ago [December, 1954], while the Holy Father was sick and suffering he saw the Lord. The world, so completely absorbed in material things, was stunned: some people were moved, others were skeptical. [The Pope's] prayerful and silent love was received with contemptuous, sometimes sardonic irreverence; [his] profound meditation, which took place in the silence of his soul clashed with the uproar of those who deceive themselves, that they can fill the desert of the soul with noise and clamor.

"These attitudes were reflected in newspapers and magazines which, in their eagerness to outdo each other in sensationalism, sometimes did not hesitate to declare themselves improvised authorities on theological and moral questions.

"The Pope himself had related to some of his intimates the story of the consoling vision that visited him. The secret was divulged, and the Pope has certainly suffered because of it. But this does not alter the fact that the truth remains true, and that this episode signifies one of the most sublime moments in the life of the *Pastor Angelicus.*

"Many things have been said about this [vision]. Some commentators have even sought to embroider the magnificent reality. It has been said that the Pope, not only saw Our Lord but even heard His voice. This is inaccurate.

"Toward the end of November, 1954, His Holiness Pius XII left his residence of Castel Gandolfo and returned to the Vatican. He was already sick. During the following days the disease with which he was afflicted became aggravated. As is known, the Holy Father was not able to assist at the usual [advent] retreat, yet in his painful solitude he read in the original Spanish text St. Ignatius, which is so close to the thoughts of Our Master. On December 1, the physical suffering was acute but the spirit alive; the Pope continued to follow the affairs of the Church. The pain stimulated him to meditate upon the suffering and glorious life of Catholicism. And during that day, on December 1, while his spirit was more intent than ever, he heard, very distinctly, a voice saying, 'There will be a vision.'

"The mysterious announcement was confirmed next morning. On December 2, while the darkness was gradually dissolving, just before the first streak of dawn, the Pope had a vision that the Lord was close to him, silent in all His eloquent majesty. He thought that this was the call. Jesus came for him to tell him, just as He had once told Peter; 'Follow me'; and he interpreted the silence to mean: '*Magister adest et vocat te* (the Master is here and calls you).'

" 'Oh, good Jesus,' he responded with all the ardor of his heart and soul—'Oh, good Jesus, harken to me; *Jube me venire ad te* (Bid me come to Thee).'

"That same morning he announced the mystical visit to a very few of his intimates. When the condition of the Pope suddenly worsened, and Rome and the whole world were deeply concerned, these intimates thought for a moment that the Lord had actually commanded His servant to follow Him. But Piux XII was preserved for the Church and for the entire Catholic world. During the night of December 2–3 his condition began to improve, and shortly thereafter his health was restored. The Lord had once again said to Peter: 'Feed my lambs.'

"If we may be permitted to try to decipher the designs of God, we must ever remember that the passion of Jesus is continued in His Mystical Body which is the Church until the end of the world. Just as during the agony of Gethsemane, the Lord is still often forgotten because His disciples, even the most faithful, sleep. In his suffering Pius XII went toward the Master, 'vigilant in his pain, while so many of us were sleeping.' "

There is, moreover, another recorded vision that occurred to a Pope in the Vatican, under different circumstances and not involving Our Lord. It happened on October 7, 1571, to Pope Pius V (St. Pius V, canonized in 1712).

It was 5 P.M. and the Pope was in session with his advisers. At a certain moment he suddenly ran to the window, opened it, and remained there for several minutes in deep concentration. Afterward he returned to the table and, deeply moved, he told his advisers that a great victory had been won for Christianity. He immediately gave orders for thanksgiving. A few days later, the first news about the victory over the Turks at Lepanto arrived in Rome. In the naval battle of Lepanto, the attacking Turks were decisively beaten and Christian Western civilization was temporarily saved from catastrophe.

Vladimir Solovyev (1853–1900), a mystic and one of the greatest Russian philosophers, has dramatically described the advent of the Anti-Christ in his book *Three Conversations*. While he attributed this prophecy to an old Russian monk, his description of the advent of the Anti-Christ is not the product of literary imagination, as one might surmise, but a direct projection of Solovyev's unique *prophetic and visionary* personality. Though this is not a vision in the theological sense of the word, I report it because of the great importance of Solovyev. He called it the "Legend of the Anti-Christ" and wrote it shortly before his death. At this time Solovyev was a Catholic, having embraced the Faith secretly in 1896.

Briefly, the legend of the Anti-Christ foretells certain events that will come to pass in the twentieth century, which was, according to the prophecy, the "last epoch in which great wars, civil disorders, and revolutions occurred." His predictions of coming events were perhaps confused but not without logic. In any event they were not the most important features of the "vision." Solovyev predicted the coming of a man of obscure origins who was to achieve great authority. The aim of this authoritarian personality is to create peace at any cost in the world. Those who opposed his grand design are conquered and subjugated to him one after the other. His propaganda promises universal peace, and through this slogan he succeeds in becoming ruler of almost the entire world. But his greatest goal is to unify all churches and all religions. At this time this personage is already an Emperor residing in Jerusalem, which is almost entirely populated by Jews. Jerusalem is a free city and the Christian sanctuaries are respected. The name of the reigning Pope is Peter II. This pope becomes more and more apprehensive of this Universal Emperor, particularly after the "Emperor" asks him to make his chancellor Appollonius a cardinal. The Pope considers Apollonius an obvious impostor. The head of the Protestants is a German Evangelical professor of theology, Ernest Pauli, a man of great integrity. And the head of the Orthodox Church is a Russian called simply Father John.

The Emperor finally convokes a universal council in which Peter II, Professor Pauli, Father John, and thousands of others participate. The Emperor wants nothing less than spiritual authority over all the faiths. He talks to Catholics, Protestants, and Orthodox as if he were in complete agreement with each of these religious denominations. While great numbers of priests from all the three faiths become followers of the shrewd "Emperor" because some of them fear his limitless power and others are misled by his talk of peace, the head of the Catholic Church, Peter II, and the head of the Protestants, Professor Pauli, and the head of the Orthodox, Father John, refuse to yield. They recognize in the Emperor the Anti-Christ, and each leader in turn excommunicates him.

The first to call him Anti-Christ is Father John, who is thereupon instantly killed after being mysteriously struck by lightning. The Emperor then requests that the entire Christian world accept him as ruler of the universe, as the supreme head and the supreme sovereign of Christianity. Following this Pope Peter II accuses him of being "the vessel of Satan" and declares, "by authority of Christ, I, servant of the servants of God, exclude you forever from the divine city . . . and I abandon you to your father, Satan. Anathema, anathema, anathema." Apollonius, who is seated beside the Emperor, manipulates a device of some kind whereupon the Pope is also struck by lightning. "This is how all my enemies perish through the hand of my Father," says the Emperor. In the ensuing chaos and confusion only Professor Pauli, a serene and steadfast old man, preserves his presence of mind. He declares that the Emperor is Anti-Christ as predicted by Holy Scripture and reaffirms his faith in Jesus Christ. Professor Pauli and a small group of the faithful from all three churches remove the bodies of Peter II and Father John, and the while singing Latin, German, and Slavonic Christian hymns, withdraw into the desert. The Emperor, however, succeeds in his plans and Apollonius is elected Pope. Thereafter the Emperor declares: "I am a true Orthodox and a genuine Evangelical just as I also am a true Catholic," whereupon he also becomes the head of all three religious communities.

While the Emperor, Apollonius, and practically the whole world celebrate the universal peace, Professor Pauli and the true Christians who have prayed for three days and three nights discover that the bodies of Peter II and Father John are not decayed, and that suddenly both ecclestiastics have revived. Professor Pauli takes the hand of the Pope and Father John, and both Father John and Professor Pauli recognize the primacy of the Pope. *"Tu es Petrus,* this had now been radically proven and without any doubt . . . Now, O Father, we are really and truly one in Christ." And all three and the faithful follow in the direction of an apparition that has suddenly appeared. The heavens open wide and a woman sits in the sun, a crown of twelve stars upon her head, and the moon beneath her feet.

All the world now accepts Anti-Christ, who has declared that he opened the road between life on this earth and life beyond the tomb. "In fact communication between the dead and the living and between men and demons became a routine phenomenon. Everywhere new forms of cults, mystical and demoniac orgies were sponsored." The Emperor now thinks that his supremacy is firmly established and that everyone accepts him as the only incarnation of divinity. He does not figure, however, on the "rebellion" of the Jews. First he tells them that he is going to establish Israel all over the world, whereupon the majority of Jews accept him as the Messias. When, however, he declares that he is a true Jew the rebellion starts immediately, first in Jerusalem, then throughout Palestine until it spreads among the thirty million Jews. It is discovered that he lied when he declared himself circumcised. The entire Jewish people, as one man, rises up against the impostor.

The Emperor did not expect such an explosion and did not imagine "that the Jewish soul in its very depths is not addicted to the appetites of Mammon but lives by the strength of a sincere sentiment in the hope and in the fire of its eternal messianic faith." The Emperor loses control of himself, and by a decree condemns all the insubordinate Jews and Christians to death. Tens of thousands of people are massacred, but very soon an army composed of one million Hebrews marches upon Jerusalem. Apollonius, the great magician who fraudulently became Pope, organizes a much greater force. The Hebrews, despite their inferior number, remain firm and the battle is joined. But at the very moment when the advance guards clash, the earth opens under the feet of the armies of Anti-Christ, and to the roar, fire, and smoke of earthquakes and volcanic eruptions, they are swallowed up, together with the Emperor.

The prophecy ends with the resurrection of all the victims of Anti-Christ, and humanity lives for a thousand years under the reign of Christ.[11]

CHAPTER 11

Modern Science and Miracles

When the primitive man saw lightning and heard thunder, he was shaken by fear and called them miracles. It was a long way from the belief that attributed every unexplained force of nature to an intervention of God or a god, to the present day, when science harnesses even the atom, by the very same method that generated the visible universe, namely, atomic explosion.

Events and occurrences that for centuries were unknowable or considered miraculous have been unveiled. Science seems to dominate the thinking of the human race, and according to certain ideologies it is capable of explaining everything. Moreover, some claim that science can create miracles; indeed, if it cannot re-create some of those miracles described in this book, then those occurrences never took place at all. In view of such opinions and attitudes (albeit they are slowly fading out), we must ask whether it is not useless or even childish to attempt to bring the notions of *science* and *miracle* together. Furthermore, there are credulous believers who do not care what science says; and on the other side there are equally credulous agnostics who dismiss the possibility of miracles and believe only in science.

Nevertheless, it is a fatal mistake for either side to ignore the other, since they are not at all mutually exclusive. And the credulous believer who cries out "miracle" almost compulsively would do better to grasp the hand of science, for—and this is one of the great surprises of our times—science can add to his belief in the true miracle, and science can help to determine whether an extraordinary occurrence has been merely the exceptional effect of some natural phenomenon or a prodigy performed by God.

For those who believe in the omnipotence of God and have no doubt that He can suspend the laws of nature, the possibility of the miracle seems easy and obvious. But it is reasonable that not only the skeptic, but also the believer should resort to the aid of science to test the authenticity of any extraordinary occurrence. In addition, there is something genuinely beautiful in the endless endeavor of men to carry on scientific research. To this we owe all our material discoveries, and our entire technological progress. Only the mediocre, the frustrated, and the psychopathic would condemn progress in its entirety. Everything from gunpowder to wonder drugs and atomic energy can be used for good or for evil. Progress is not the problem; it is human inadequacy and imperfection that create the "times of troubles," to use Toynbee's phrase.

Before we proceed, it should be repeated here that every Catholic must adhere to the decision of the Vatican Council (1870) on the subject of the miracle, as follows:

> "If anyone should say that no miracles can be performed . . . or that they can never be known with certainty, or that by them the divine origin of the Christian religion cannot be rightly proved, let him be anathema" (Vatican Council, session III., Canon 3, 4).

Furthermore, four essential points must again be stressed: 1) The concept of miracle is bound to the existence of a personal God and must be accepted by anyone who is aware of the spiritual life and its true nature; 2) The hostility of determinism to the miracle is based solely upon prejudice; 3) Even if a miracle is not always clearly discernible, it is often understandable either from a scientific or, more often, from a philosophical or theological point of view, for its content clearly indicates an intervention of God: a miracle is always a sign of God's love. Before his death Moses told the Jewish people how God loved them, arguing that the miracles were the testimony and the guarantee of His love (Deut. 29 and 30). And Christ said to Nicodemus: "God so loved the world as to give His only-begotten

Son" (John 3:16). This signifies in other words that the love of God and the miracle of the Incarnation are the substrata of religion.

While most scientists and intellectuals of the 19th century exalted science as the foe of religion, the Vatican Council, despised and belittled because of its pronouncement of the dogma of Papal Infallibility, quietly and with great dignity declared that there is a substantial compatibility and helpful exchange between human, experimental sciences and theology. Therefore, when the subject of research permits, it is always possible that we shall find in natural sciences an aid for the study of revelation.

Obviously, theologians and scientists have different tasks. The scientist moves in the field of controlled experiment and he cannot enter the field of metaphysics. On the differences between the supernatural and the modal supernatural (i.e., the miracle) F. X. Marquart writes:

"The word 'supernatural' is a theological one, bearing an analogical meaning: the essential supernatural and the modal supernatural. The distinction is capital and governs the whole problem of the marvelous. Only the essential supernatural is the supernatural properly so called, the supernatural simply. It points to a reality that surpasses nature. It is totally inaccessible to science, unknowable by natural means. Its very existence is not to be known with certainty save by way of revelation.

"The study of the essential supernatural belongs exclusively to the sphere of faith and theology. Science cannot study it, even indirectly, in its effects, since grace does not suppress nature. Doubtless it corrects the failings of nature and helps it to its proper perfection; but in doing so it respects all the hesitations, all the devious findings of this poor psychology of ours. It is, therefore, not to be expected that the method of elimination used by the doctors of the Bureau de Constatation at Lourdes, if applied to the study of the duality in the soul of the converts, could ever lead to conclude that empirical facts of this sort are due to a transcendent intervention: God acting in the soul of the convert. . . . The case of the modal supernatural, to which category the marvelous belongs, is altogether different. It is supernatural only, as the name indicates, in its mode of production. It is essentially a natural phenomenon, but instead of being affected in conformity with the laws of nature, it comes about in an extraordinary way. . . . Whether slow or instantaneous, the reconstruction of tissue can be observed and can be registered by radiography. . . . Thus the marvelous occurrence is observable, not simply as an occurrence but also as marvelous, that is to say, as having been produced in opposition to, or outside the scope of the laws of nature. We see, then, that the supernatural mode itself can be negatively established by science. We say 'negatively' because science, which is confined to the observable, can ascertain only that the phenomenon is produced in a way which, *as far as our present knowledge goes, is naturally inexplicable.* (Italics added.) The mission of science is to explain observed phenomenon, and either succeeds or does not succeed."[1]

From this logically follows the question: How is it possible that in centuries less scientific than ours theologians sometimes entered the field of science (as in many cases now the scientist tries to enter the field of theology) and with the authority of theology denied science the right to state certain facts established through empirical research and observation? The answer is that the aim of theology was not to destroy science but rather to defend revelation, which seemed to be in contrast with certain discoveries. If we accept the Bible as a source of revelation and the facts that are declared articles of faith are challenged, the theologian cannot enter discussion. For him there is but one way to stress his point. It was not and is not the task of theology to approach science and prove that there is no contrast between revealed truth and scientific result; it is, rather, the task of science to dig deeper and deeper into the phenomena of the world and seek to establish all the facts as far as possible.

The law of finality, however, worked, both on the side of physical scientists and on the side of theological researchers. The teaching that the world was created in six consecutive *days* was superseded when scholars discovered that the Old Testament expression which they had translated as "day" could actually mean a prolonged period of time. The revealed truth remained the same. The mistake had been caused by human inadequacy. Physical science, meanwhile, had searched the earth, dissected living bodies, and experimented with minerals, herbs, plunged to the very depths of the sea, and penetrated the uppermost reaches of the sky. And this venerable army of scholars, dedicated to finding the truth, arrived at the conclusion that the creation of the world did occur in exactly the same way as it is described in the Book of Genesis. Instead of "days," however, one should read "periods" that may have lasted millions of years.

Only determinists and materialists refuse to concede any point in the discussion of miracles, for their position is purely and simply one that denies all miracles. Theirs is the view of Renan: "Only what is natural is scientific." For the materialist holds that "miracles" occurring at the present time, which may be witnessed by a scientist, are tinged with error or are capable of being scientifically explained, or they will eventually become explainable.

The fact that science is not unchangeable but is always evolving is a source of joy to the materialists, for it appears to furnish a satisfactory explanation of supernatural phenomena. Sooner or later, they claim, science will reveal every mystery to them. And the nonscientific freethinker at Lourdes merely waits for some discovery that the waters of the grotto actually possess properties that are both extraordinary and natural, and he continues to hope for the day when the most marvelous event will seem no more astonishing than an eclipse of the sun.

Authentic scientists, however, realize that a halt must be called to reasoning of this kind. They know that science analyzes, but creates nothing. Science remains linked to the natural order and its limits are known in advance. To bestow excessive powers on science amounts to a denial of science. After the latest discoveries in modern physics, many modern scientists agree with the German C. F. von Weizsäcker, who writes as follows:[2]

"Knowledge, science, and power have been our gods and they were clothed with the glory of the infinite and the absolute. Today it begins to be revealed just *how far we can really reach. We cannot reach the absolute.* What we can do is to achieve an insight into the conditions of our knowledge and of our power."

The German theologian and physicist, Heimo Dolch, adds this comment:

Newton was a believer, and not knowing everything was not a

burden for him because he mastered this burden by trusting God. After Newton, however, knowledge and power to an increasing measure have become gods for the scientist; gods that carried the halo of the infinite and the absolute; and when the foundations of this knowledge were subverted, they ceased to remain pillars and principles of an unshakable *Weltanschauung*. Subsequently many modern scientists fell into utter resignation and depression when their gods were overthrown."[3]

Later on in this chapter we shall describe the revolution in modern physics that shook the world. Weizsäcker gives the best picture of this situation: "Modern science found itself in total nihilism and in utter pain and tended to wallow in a sense of guilt, resignation, and the meaninglessness of existence." For the modern scientist who had proved capable of producing the same kind of atomic reaction that marked the creation of the universe arrived at the top without being able to see the next step and without having the power to create.

All great scientists, however, believers or nonbelievers, are basically humble men. The physicist Weizsäcker gave expression to his humility in these words:

"I believe that first we must look into the abyss and that we must be able to bear the sight of the void that opens before us. And I believe that this void does not signify *an end* but a *call for decision*." (Italics added.)

Modern science at this moment is in a process of objective reappraisal or self-criticism. The old structure of physics and science in general has collapsed; and while the scientists, true to their mission, continue the research that has led to the discoveries formulated in the thermonuclear and other theories, they are aware that elements of the supernatural have slipped through their fingers. There is reason to hope that they will find a way to a further explanation of the world and the universe which will not exclude the existence of the supernatural. But, as Dolch warns us,

". . . the possibility of a depressed sense of resignation exists because many scientists have been evicted from the cherished havens of their former *Weltanschauung*. In the words of the Bible they have been exiled from the 'cities' that they built into the desert. It still would be premature and unreal to believe that the present situation, by its inner necessity, would lead the agnostic scientist to the recognition of the true God who is not only the God of the philosophers, but the God of Abraham, Isaac, and Jacob, God of all men and of the whole universe."[4]

Nevertheless, there is hope in the words of the searchers.

"Doesn't God speak to us any more? Our *Ersatz-symbolism* has collapsed, not because it was symbolism, but because it was *Ersatz*. Already the silence that has taken its place (that is, the place of the collapsed Ersatz-symbolism, in which scientific achievement became god) speaks loudly enough. It puts our true situation before us. But first of all we should decide whether we want to listen to God. Listen not to what we desire to hear, but what He says to us."[5]

While modern science and scientists, standing on the brink of the abysmal void, have to face such a decision, the Church does not beat the drums in triumph or derision. These were and are all deeply honest human beings for whom the Church has the greatest respect. If there has been reason to rejoice, it lies in the fact that all their discoveries actually facilitated rather than hampered the task of the Church, and have furnished ample documentation for what the Vatican Council envisioned in the following terms: ". . . when the subject of research permits, it is always possible that we shall find the natural sciences a helpful aid for the study of revelation." Science will never be able to demonstrate how God communicated the revelation to Moses. It is an article of faith. But it could establish the fact that the universe was actually formed in accordance with the statements in the Bible. The actual procedure of creation is, however, another question. We are going to describe several theories from the vast empirical experience of science, which tend to prove that there is no fundamental conflict between theology and science. Before entering this field, however, three important points should be kept in mind:

1. As we have seen, there are miracles that constitute articles of faith. If science declares that these cosmic events actually happened in accordance with revelation we rejoice and take legitimate pride in

human progress. But our faith does not depend upon the approval of science.

2. The theories or proofs furnished by science on the basis of which such results are obtained are not absolute. Further investigation could broaden the theory or cause it to be superseded by another theory that proves the same.

3. On the modal supernatural, and miracles themselves, science is uncovering more and more material. Many of the existing and future facts explain or will explain the fundamental thesis that when God performs a miracle He does not destroy nature, but merely intervenes in it, suspending its laws or accelerating its processes. We "understand" or seem to understand how God acts, without stating that science (i.e., man) could do the same. As regards the miracles that occurred after the death of the last of the Apostles, there are certain cases concerning which science will provide more and more explanatory data. Since not all these miracles constitute an article of faith, it is conceivable that the expected explanations may deprive these cases of some of their miraculous elements. But the miracles constituting articles of faith are exempted. There will never come a time when science will be able to lift the last veil. Science can merely confirm that even these miracles were wrought without destroying nature. For this reason, the theories and their results to be discussed here are submitted with caution, since they are subject to future modification.

Werner Heisenberg, one of the greatest living physicists, has written extensively on the changeability of scientific theory, in his *"Abgeschlossene Theorie."*[8] He maintains that there are certain "closed theories"—a statement of great importance in view of the revolution that shook classical physics. This is the way he describes these closed theories:

A. The closed theory is valid for all times; on the basis of a closed theory, empirical results can be described, even for the most distant future. The laws of this theory will always prove their validity.

B. The closed theory does not contain any completely certain prediction about the empirical world. For it remains in the strictest sense uncertain and contingent upon the degree of our success in explaining future phenomena according to the concepts of this theory.

C. Despite this uncertainty the closed theory remains part of our scientific language and therefore it constitutes an integral and permanent part of our understanding of the world.

Heimo Dolch, whose field is in the relation between theology and science, says rightly that paragraph A appears naïvely optimistic but that actually it is not. By a closed theory the physicist does not mean that all phenomena may be described with immutable certainty. This would lead to a too technical explanation of what is closed and what is open. Actually, Heisenberg considers only four great "disciplines" as closed theories: Newtonian mechanics; the Maxwellian theory together with the special theory of relativity; thermodynamics and statistical mechanics; and finally quantum mechanics (without relativity), together with nuclear physics and chemistry. All these theories are in the relatively closed state and separated from other theories, and each of them can be formulated upon the basis of a few principles and conceptions. It is significant that universal experience cannot be described by one all-embracing homogenous theory. Albert Einstein worked on this all his life without result. The universal experience falls apart in several disciplines, and each one of them perforce is limited to describing only certain groups of phenomena.

In our brief acquaintance with these interesting and sometimes fascinating scientific theories and explanations we must always keep these points in mind. They fill us with reverence and gratitude towards the scientists. Regardless of whether the scientist is a believer or nonbeliever, we need him.

Many theories of modern cosmology agree even with the minutest details of the Biblical account about the creation of the universe. The Bible and theologians have been ridiculed for standing firm on the Mosaic version, which asserts that on the first day God created light. How is it possible to create light on the first day when the sun, the moon, and the stars were created later, i.e., on the fourth day? Modern cosmology, however, offers the following confirmation.

Before the world existed space was filled by a gaseous, cold, and extremely rarefied mass, submerged in total darkness. Then, slowly—and here *slowly* means millions of years—this gaseous mass condensed into billions of small globes. Now it is known to physics that condensation causes an increase of temperature. Because of the heat and the enormous pressure (through the condensation) this gaseous mass produced the first *nuclear reactions*, which increased the temperature even more. The continuing increase of temperature, together with the nuclear reactions, made the first primitive globes (stars) *incandescent*. Thus, there was light for the first time. This was not the light of the sun or of the moon; it was light, material light, the same light as is produced by atomic fission.

When it was stated that the first act of creation was the condensation of that gaseous, rarefied, cold mass immersed in total darkness and that this condensation initiated the creative process, modern science did not exclude God. First of all because that dark mass had to be created by someone, and condensation means *motion*. Then, someone *touched* that mass, and this touch was an act of God.[7]

Not so long ago scientists accepted a certain thesis as a dogma. This thesis lay at the basis of classical physics and became the fundamental attitude of a scientific world-view. According to this thesis, the atom was inalterable, indestructible, and indivisible. Since 1896, however, a revolution has been taking place in science. The first step of this revolution bears the name of *radioactivity*. The second was the quantum theory, and the third the system of relativity, developed between 1900 and 1927. The discovery that radioactive bodies irradiate rays (alpha, beta, and gamma rays) destroyed the whole construction so meticulously built by generations and generations of physicists and chemists. The atom revealed itself *essentially* as empty space. Each atom is composed of a central part called its nucleus and an external part. The nucleus consists of neutrons and protons; the external part of electrons.[8] Furthermore, there are electromagnetic and nuclear fields in the atom, and in the active state of the atom there are positrons, mesons, antiprotons, and other electrons. The protons have a positive charge of electricity, the neutrons have no charge, and the electrons carry a negative charge.

The significance of this discovery lay in the fact that it destroyed the thesis of the continuity and solidity of matter, proving as it did that matter is composed of infinitesimal particles separated from each other by great empty spaces. In other words, matter has a granular structure. Exceedingly intense electrical forces establish the cohesion between these particles in order to form atoms in the various solid, liquid, or gaseous substances.

If we could observe the human body in its "nuclear" form—i.e., through an immense magnifying glass—we would discover that the seemingly cohesive human body is also, like the rest of matter, granular in structure. Through that gigantic magnifying glass, the human body would appear to us as billions and billions of particles in exceedingly rapid motion, and between them we would see great empty spaces.

After this discovery had been validated by experiment, scientists asked themselves the following question: Given these empty spaces between the particles and atoms, why cannot one particle of matter penetrate another, or why cannot a human body go through brick or steel or any other solid substance? The answer they came up with has affected our conception about every miracle, for they maintain that the forces of energy which keep these particles (separated from each other by empty spaces) in a cohesive state constitute an impenetrable net.

But our knowledge of the nature of the neutrons opens up a surprising perspective. The neutrons are insensible to these forces of energy, and can without any difficulty pass over those barriers of energy. (Incidentally, the construction of the atomic pile is based upon this phenomenon.)

Bearing in mind this characteristic of the *neutrons*, certain scholars have applied their theory to one of the miracles of Christ, namely, when He entered into the Cenacle through closed doors after His resurrection. According to their speculations, without changing the atom or its nature it would require only a *small* modification of the energy connections to overcome the obstacle that cohesive energy opposes to the passage of one body through the other. Thus, by a *temporary modification* of the laws of nature that govern the structure of matter, Christ could enter the Cenacle through closed doors.

The Vatican daily newspaper, *Osservatore Romano*, recently published a study in which the author explained the presence of Christ in the Eucharist, i.e., in the bread and wine, by applying the new facts about the structure of matter.

"The atom has no *solid* structure; it is composed of protons, neutrons, positrons, mesons, and antiprotons. In between are empty spaces held together by cohesive, invisible energy. The electron has a negative charge and it weighs one billionth of one billionth of one billionth gram; its diameter is one hundredth of one thousandath of one billionth part of a centimeter. The positron is an electron with a positive charge, and it has a very short existence; when positron and electron collide they produce the so-called gamma ray. The proton is charged positively and weighs 1840 times more than the electron. The neutron has all the characteristics of the proton but is without electrical charge. The protons and neutrons constitute the very mass of the atom, they are interchangeable between themselves, and it appears that they are two different states of energy of the same nuclear particle. The antiproton is the most recent discovery, it being the negative proton. There is sufficient evidence to state that following collision, proton and antiproton become electrical energy. The mesons originate in the nucleus from a collision between protons and electrons. The volume of the mesons differs greatly; they can become, for example, 25 hundred times the volume of the electron and can be electrically positive, negative, or neutral.

"According to quantum mechanics, these particles are accompanied by a wave *the nature of which is totally unknown*. It is assumed that there is a connection between it and the behavior of the particles. In any case, according to quantum mechanics, the particles that unite in order to form a complex system (the atom or the molecule) fuse into a new physical reality; they lose their own characteristics and obey new laws. These laws are connected with the complex electromagnetic gravitational and nuclear fields within the atom.

"The species, or the appearance, of bread and wine originate from their innermost structure as roughly described here. The *fragility* and elasticity of the Host depend on the cohesive forces of the molecules that constitute bread. The *weight* is a consequence of the reciprocal attraction between the mass of the body and the mass of the earth. The *heat* is a result of the rapid, agitating motion of the molecules perceived by our senses as heat. The *color* comes from certain electromagnetic radiations produced upon the retina of our eye. The color of the red wine is caused by the fact that this particular wine, because of its intimate atomic constitution, absorbs all the light that penetrates it, save for red radiation which this particular wine (because of its particular atomic construction), instead of absorbing, *reflects* and *emanates*. Certain chemical characteristics of bread and of the Host are due to the disposition of the external electrons of its atoms.

"In other words it is possible to analyze the species of the bread and the wine. There is, however, beneath this species a *substance* that is hidden from any kind of experimental probing. This substance (from the Latin sub-stat) is the underlying essence of which the appearance, the species, or its molecular-nuclear construction is only the coating.

"Physics being an experimental science knows only the palpable appearances and the *physical* fundamentals of these perceivable, sensible appearances of matter, their atomic, sub-atomic, and energetic structure."

"About the *substance*, per se, physics claims to know nothing.

"Modern physics would be contrary to the dogma of the Eucharist if physics stated that *material substance* does not exist, or if physics asserted that there is no distinction between the material substance and its accidentals. Physics, however, *does not state* that the substance is identical with the structure of particles and energies; it *does not state* that the *substance* of bread (Host) and wine are the electrons, the protons, the neutrons, the electrical fields, etc.

"Physics does not put forward such facts as would indicate that it *denies* the existence of material substance, for this would be totally beyond the research field of physics.

"That matter exists is of metaphysical evidence, and no experimental physics can say the contrary—i.e., if matter *exists* then material *substance* also exists. The problem is, what *is* material substance? Is it the quantity, or is it energy, or is it something else that lies beneath these accidentals?

"Physics does not provide any such elements from which one might conclude that the substance of a body is its extension. Modern physics even excludes this theory, which was the view of the philosophical school of mechanism; nor does physics point to any fact by which it would demonstrate that substance is energy. On the contrary: energy continuously changes its form: therefore, it cannot be the material substance.

"Furthermore, modern physics teaches that in the same object or body there is a succession of several different properties: physical, chemical, energetic, extension, etc. One may thus say that all these properties are accidentals existing in a substance and substance is what remains and animates all these properties metaphysically. Therefore, there is a substance that exists beyond the appearance and accidentals, and it differs from their reality. One could object here that physics demonstrates that matter transforms itself into energy. We have already stated that the collision of antiproton and proton produces electrical energy, while both proton and antiproton dissolve. After this someone might still insist that since matter transforms itself into energy, and matter itself is a substance, energy thus is also substance.

"But this objection has been overcome. The answer is that in this transformation into energy the ponderable matter transforms itself into imponderable matter without body, and because it has no mass it is beyond experimental analysis; therefore, it can be said to have seemingly disappeared. But there is in the transformation a determined quantity of energy. One could also say that the ponderable matter and energy are two properties of the same substance, which remains immutable during the successive manifestations of its properties. In any case the classical concept of substance remains intact; therefore, no objection is raised by modern physics against the conception of substance and against the conception of the substance of bread and wine. Thus, modern physics can be said to have no objection to transubstantiation.

"In transubstanitation only the *substance* changes, and this is precisely what the dogma states. All the accidentals and appearances, i.e., the species of the bread and wine, *remain*. What also remains is their physico-chemical structure with all its particular characteristics, the protons, neutrons, electrons, positrons, antiprotons, mesons, the molecules, crystals, and the electromagnetic nuclear fields, as well as the photons, the quanti, the laws of physics, and the color, taste and smell.

"Since physics cannot experience substance, consequently, it cannot register the transubstantiation, and, therefore, cannot observe and confirm the presence of the Body of Christ in the substance. But since the substance holds and animates the entire physico-chemical structure of the body, it can be said that the transubstantiation occurred within all the elements indicated by physics and sustained by the substance in the existence.

"The transubstantiation is a change in substance, i.e., the change of the substance of the bread into the Body, and the substance of the wine into the Blood of Christ. Chemico-physical analysis shows that bread is not *one* substance in the philosophical sense but a complex of substances that are united. This is also the case with wine. Therefore, in the transubstantiation, the substances that constitute bread change into one unified substance of the Body of Christ and the different substances constituting wine change into the unified substance of the Blood of Christ.

"Theology teaches that the actual presence of the Body of Christ ceases whenever the species of the original substance of bread and wine are destroyed: when, for instance, the bread is pulverized and mixed with other substances or when the wine evaporates. Transubstantiation thus is bound to the substance of the bread and wine.

"Modern physics does *not* oppose the dogma of the Eucharist, but actually it is of great *use* and help in making certain important points more clear and precise."[9]

And here is Einstein's view on substance:

"Yet the fundamental mystery remains. The whole march of science toward the unification of concept—the reduction of all matter to elements and then to a few types of particles, the reduction of these "forces" to the single concept "energy," and then the reduction of matter *and* energy to a single basic quantity—leads still to the unknown. The many questions merge into one, *to which there may never be an answer: what is the essence of this mass-energy substance, what is the underlying stratum of physical reality which science seeks to explore?"* (Italics added.)[10]

Let us now take an argument of the determinists, who assert that a miracle is not an extraordinary event and that it is pure and simple *chance* occurring within the laws of nature and explainable by the statistical laws of probability.

We have an answer to this objection. Jean Perrin, Nobel prize physicist, calculated the probability that a brick weighing two pounds could lift itself from the ground up to the height of the second floor without being touched by anyone. It would be carried upwards by the molecules of the air. Such an operation would of course require a number of years—indeed, so many years that the zeros, *billions of zeros,* required to express the waiting time would fill many volumes.

In time it would take more years than the age of the world. Now, such a mathematical probability is equal to the impossible. But from the point of view of physics, even this possibility becomes nil. Admitting that such an instant could arrive in which billions and billions of molecules would move to lift the brick, their very *motion* would involve *other motions* in many different directions, and these would *nullify* the elevating force of the lifting molecules.

Thus, the methods of modern science, in this case mathematics and physics, exclude the possibility that a miracle could be a *chance* case within the laws of nature, calculable by the laws of probability. Other discoveries in modern science open even more astonishing perspectives to us.

One of the theories of Einstein involves the speculative possibility of *four* dimensions. We live in a world of *three* dimensions as expressed for the first time through the geometry of the Greek philosopher and mathematician Euclid. These three dimensions, which we can easily measure, are length, width, and depth. Our body, the objects, the furniture in our rooms, our buildings, are of three dimensions. The shadow of objects and the screen image in a movie has only *two* dimensions; depth is lacking.

Since we live in a three-dimensional world we can measure length, width, and depth automatically. If the images of people on the screen were to be suddenly capable of *stepping out* into our world, these phantoms would be absolutely unable even to imagine what a globe, a cube, or an object of three dimensions might be because they, these phantoms, are of two dimensions and perceive only two dimensions. They would be able to understand such things as the flat square or the circle, but nothing else. If these phantoms were to walk on their imaginary flat plain always going straight ahead, they would never return to their starting point. The three-dimensional being, however, could make the trip around the world and arrive at the very same point where he started.

If it were impossible for these imaginary two-dimensional beings to return to their own two-dimensional space and as a result they were compelled to live in our three-dimensional setting, they would be unable to conceive our world. After adequate research, observation, and meditation they would resign themselves, declaring that their science was inadequate; and they would possibly adopt our geometry and our physics.

The great mathematicians of our world since the 17th century have been criticizing the uniqueness of three-dimensional geometry. Gauss, Lambert, Helmholtz, and in modern times Henri Poincaré conceived the idea before Einstein of the possibility of new spaces; spaces of four, five, six dimensions.

It is impossible to understand a multidimensional world; a world where parallels meet and where it is not valid that a curved line is longer than a straight one. Poincaré, the great French mathematician, said: "Don't break your head trying to imagine the fourth dimension, *it is absolutely impossible to imagine it;* nevertheless, the fourth dimension and the hyper-spaces exist and their existence is *incontestable.*"

Poincaré is right, for to understand and to *see* the hyper-spaces we should need more perfect senses, we would have to *step out* from our own space; to see the four-dimensional world and to understand it we should *cease to be human beings.* The British mathematician Howard Hinton, a disciple of Einstein and an interpreter of his thought, considers the human being a potential four-dimensional being. We live only temporarily in a three-dimensional world, but actually we are four-dimensional beings walking through a world of three dimensions, and there comes a time for everyone to leave the world of three dimensions.

All this would sound more than fantastic were the theory of the hyper-spaces not upheld by Gauss, Lambert, Helmholtz, Poincaré, Einstein, and others—in other words, by the greatest mathematicians of the world. But what is the opinion of the Church on this subject? How does this theory affect our conception of miracles?

At this point let us again quote from the *Osservatore Romano,* the Vatican organ, which has published an article entitled "The Hyperspaces and the Gospel."[11]

"The Gospel of St. John says twice that after the Resurrection Christ entered a room the doors of which were closed. First, when he appeared to the Apostles who were gathered there, and then eight days later when He reappeared in order to be recognized by St. Thomas, who had been absent the first time.

"The Gospel of St. Luke says that Jesus had appeared to two of His disciples who were walking towards Emmaus, and then suddenly disappeared. But Jesus made Himself invisible at other times, too, even before the Resurrection. For example, when the Jews wanted to stone Him.

"Such events are usually explained the way St. Paul does in his first letter to the Corinthians; he attributes the possibility of being invisible to those bodies which have been gloriously resurrected. . . .

"Today, however, we can explain it through the geometry of hyperspace with which mathematicians are already familiar, although we admit that we deal with speculative studies because they are not subject to our senses and to our experience."

After this the *Osservatore Romano* goes right to the heart of the matter:

"The existence of a three-dimensional body and any point upon it is conceivable to everybody. To create (generate) a space of *four* dimensions we need only to suppose the existence of a point, an actually existing point not belonging to the three-dimension body and therefore inaccessible to our senses. The totality of all points on all straight lines leading from that point in the fourth dimension to all points, i.e., to the whole surface of a three-dimensional body creates a four-dimensional space. All these points coming from the point in the fourth dimension are real and existing because they connect real points. But only those points are subject to our senses which are on the three-dimensional body. Any solid body can move in the space of four dimensions, but it would be visible to our eyes and accessible to our senses only and insofar as it enters the three-dimensional space. . . . It is quite possible, that the three-dimensional space could change position and generate a fourth-dimensional space. This changing of position of three-dimensional space would not be sensed by us, just as a man who stands on a boat does not sense when the boat starts moving unless he looks to fixed points which are outside of the boat.

"But we cannot fix our eyes up on any fixed points that exist in S 4 because our senses perceive only points on S 3.

"This above-mentioned S 4 thus would be, in substance, the space-time of the theory of Einstein; this would be the integral work of creation. . . . Since our senses are limited we can have only an abstract speculative conception of this point in the four-dimensional space. And we do not have any empirical proof of its existence. . . .

"It is quite natural that the passage through walls and the sudden invisibility should seem absurd to us and physically impossible, *nevertheless*, it can be actualized through temporary evasion from three-dimensional space that is submerged in the four-dimensional. . . . Despite the explanation given by us, the cited events in the life of Jesus remain miraculous as other similar events are miraculous; because the miraculous is the temporary suspension of the ordinary physical laws; it is a stepping out from our own three-dimensional space."

The transformation of water into wine at the wedding of Cana, the first miracle wrought by Christ, has the following scientific "explanation": This miracle shows a transformation of one matter into another. From water that is composed of hydrogen and oxygen (H_2O), other elements were generated, elements that constitute wine. Since 1919, modern science knows through the discovery of the great British physicist, Lord Rutherford, the chemistry of transmutations. Lord Rutherford bombarded pure nitrogen and oxygen with alpha rays. He observed that under intense bombardment the atomic nuclei of the nitrogen and oxygen disintegrated; the hydrogen nuclei of the nitrogen were expelled from the azote. In 1934 Frederic and Irene Jolliot-Curie bombarded aluminum with alpha rays of radioactive polonium. To their great surprise the atoms of the aluminum were transformed into phosphorous and were radioactive.

The fundamental discovery in these experiments was that these elements are not stable and under bombardment become unstable, i.e., radioactive. The results of this discovery were also extended to biology.

In Cana one substance was transformed into another substance. The fact is not a contradiction of the present knowledge of science because it has been demonstrated that one element can be transformed into another. But in Cana there were no great complicated instruments to enable Christ or His followers to bombard water with alpha or other rays. It was a miracle because it could happen only under certain circumstances and conditions exclusively through the grace of God.

A similar interpretation may be given to the multiplication of bread and fish. Christ in this case did not create any new substance but increased the already existing substance. This miracle could be interpreted according to a hypothesis which holds that foodstuff has a yet unknown capacity (action) with crystallizing effect, upon the atomic and molecular elements attracted from the immediate environment of the original substance (foodstuff). In other words, under certain circumstances and conditions the foodstuff, in this case bread, would attract and crystallize those elements from its environment (air, trees, etc.) which are necessary to the increase of the original foodstuff. But this could happen only through the intervention of a miracle.

Science knows that there is a fundamental union in the visible universe. Our globe and the stars and all the innumerable sun systems are formed of the same atoms as all the worlds of the entire space. The death of the body is nothing but a physico-chemical transformation. The atoms that constitute the human body assume incoherent motions and orientation that are outside the laws of life; but the important thing is that the living body's atoms have a coherent and discernible orientation and motion. And the miracle in the case of Lazarus was Christ's intervention to re-establish the coherent function of these atoms.

Other discoveries have changed our conception of time. We know that it is the motion of the earth that gives us the possibility of measuring time. We know that for a pilot of a jet airplane flying in the opposite direction to the rotation of the earth with the same speed as the rotation of the earth-time (that is, the time of the clock) would be neutralized, nonexistent. What is time then?

Modern scientific thought (chiefly that of Einstein) has conceived a unitary complex conception; space-time, for which science presupposes the existence of a universe composed of events and not only things; in other words, we should imagine time as distance, a distance that separates events in the order of their succession and at the same time operates as a tie that binds. This distance must be conceived in a direction that is nonexistent in our space, i.e., as a new dimension.

We always think, says the Italian mathematician Fantappiè, that past, nonexistent happenings determine the present. We say that these occurrences, because they happened in the past, do not exist. Nevertheless, their influence is felt upon present existing things and beings. If this is true there is no reason to wonder that future events that are equally nonexistent should have an influence upon the present. But it could be objected that past events and things no longer exist and that future events and things do not yet exist. Thus, we link the attribute of existence to things at "present"—i.e., to things contemporaneous.

But for whom are they contemporaneous? The concept of contemporaneity varies according to the conditions of the observer, according to his position in motion or at rest. If a traveler precedes me by train in the same direction in which I am going by foot, present things for him are future things for me. And when these things become contemporaneous for me, for him they are already experienced, relegated to the past, nonexistent. . . .

When someone dies we usually say that he does not exist. We consider him to have disappeared into the past, into that which does not exist, but it is evident that we are dealing here only with a seeming nonexistence, for the person who dies does not plunge into a void. Nothing that existed and that will exist is going to be lost. All things and beings of this world remain localized in a zone of space and time which for our structure, for our sense, becomes inaccessible. But they exist.

As long as religion alone concerned itself with the existence of the invisible world that is outside of us, it was ridiculed. The theory of space and time is not a concept of theologians. It is the revelation of theoretical mathematicians, scholars of the purest science. And yet, although it is not the work of the theologians, it confirms what theology has thought according to revelation.

Certain theories confirm revelation's teachings concerning the creation of the world and the end of the world as well. According

to the cosmologist George Gamow (Washington, D. C.), when the
universe was only five minutes old its temperature surpassed five
billion degrees C.; at this temperature particles move with extremely
powerful enegry (several million electron volts). Under such conditions nuclear reactions had to occur with increasing speed. "It is
logical to conclude that during the initial state of evolution *all* chemical elements were formed in the same proportion as they exist *now*.
This happened five billion years ago within five minutes. According
to Sir Edmund Whitaker, science may declare, without falling into
error, that those five minutes that occurred five billion years ago
were the minutes of Creation.

The prophecy about the end of the world is contained in the New
Testament in the second Epistle of St. Peter, Chapter III.

All scientists today agree that the universe cannot and will not
exist eternally. The Encyclopedists of the 18th century believed that
the universe could rejuvenate itself through colossal cataclysms, but
now we know that these are only partial, local rejuvenations with
continuously decreasing energy. One of the founders of thermodynamics, Rudolf Clausius, describes the end of the constantly decreasing energy as *Warmetod*, i.e., heat-death, through equalization
of heat, when everywhere in the universe the same temperature will
exist. James Jeans, the renowned British astronomer, arrived at the
same conclusion: The second law of thermodynamics drives the material universe to move constantly in the same direction and on the
same tracks—which can terminate only in death. But Armellini, the
Italian astronomer, claims that the day will arrive when all the stars
will become dark, and energy irradiated by them or which they should
irradiate will fill the whole space and will elevate the temperature of
the space from its present temperature—that is 270° C. below zero—
to 260° C. below zero. All globes and the billions of worlds will
slowly assume this temperature as a consequence of the reduction of
energy.

Other scientists, like Gamow, Bok, and Bethe have made experiments regarding the aging of the sun. The heat of the sun is generated by the slow transformation of hydrogen into helium. Naturally, the sun is losing more and more hydrogen and is being filled

up with helium. The sun will be extinguished when its provisions of hydrogen are exhausted.

Consequently (according to the German astronomer, Stefan), the medium temperature of the earth will increase approximately 300 degrees centigrade; in other words, the temperature on earth will be *the same as the temperature of molten lead,* and so every sign of life will be destroyed.

"And then we will have a total blackout and the death of the sun, which would be preceded by a convulsion that will make from the sun a new star; a terrible convulsion which will bring the solar photosphere into the present orbit of Mars and this cataclysm would suck into the burning abyss the four planets that are closest to it, Mercury, Venus, Earth, and Mars."

The findings of modern science in this case again confirm the words of revelation expressed by St. Peter:

"But the day of the Lord shall come as a thief, in which the heavens shall pass away with great violence, and the elements shall be melted with heat, and the earth and the works which are in it, shall be burnt up" (II Peter 3:10).

"Looking for and hasting unto the coming of the day of the Lord, by which the heavens being on fire shall be dissolved, and the elements shall melt with the burning heat" (*ibid,* v. 12).

The task of science is not to understand and make understandable the *ultimate* things, but to put tools into man's hands so that he can use his freewill and his reason to control evolution. Any simple electrician thinks that he "understands" how an electric battery functions. But the very best physicists of the world do not share this opinion and admit that while they are able to *predict* exactly how it is going to function, they do not fully understand *why* it functions. Man is capable of acting and free to act; he is master of his own destiny and master of the ends of evolution. There are no limits before scientific research within the universe. Lecomte de Noüy rightly says that our science is not yet universal and dominates only inanimate matter. The broadest scope and, at the same time, the limitations of science lie in the law of finality, which Lecomte de Noüy explains for our age in the following terms:

> "We can observe five fundamental, incontestable points: the beginning of life is represented by beings organized in an extremely simple manner; the evolution of life goes on towards more complex forms; the present result of this long process is man and the human brain; the birth of thought and moral and spiritual ideas; the spontaneous and independent development of these ideas in different parts of the earth."

Now the human brain has arrived at the point of being able to tell why a miracle is a miracle and at just what point the laws of nature, i.e., laws of physics and chemistry, are suspended; we can touch and see the miracle. We can penetrate the most intricate parts of human brain and nervous system and describe what phenomena are caused by hysteria, but at the same time we know that no physical law exists which would permit the *instantaneous* growth of a bone in the leg of a human being, as has happened at Lourdes.

And science will never penetrate the final mystery. Rightly says a disciple of Einstein:

> "Man's inescapable impasse is that he himself is part of the world he seeks to explore; his body and proud brain are mosaics of the same elemental particles that compose the dark, drifting dust clouds of interstellar space; he is, in the final analysis, merely an ephemeral conformation of the primordial space-time field. Standing midway between macrocosm and microcosm he finds barriers on every side and can perhaps but marvel as St. Paul did nineteen hundred years ago, that 'the world was created by the word of God so that what is seen was made out of things which do not appear.' "[12]

CHAPTER 12

The Meaning of the Miracle in History

History may be said to be the summation of the actions of man in time. Miracles are God's sovereign interventions into our three-dimensional world, in which this historical process has been, ever since the creation of man, realizing itself. History has a destination, even if we cannot discern it at once, and God is working in history even if his ways are difficult or impossible to recognize. But since history consists of the acts of man and miracles are the acts of God, it may be asked how the two can be brought together, and, how it is possible to prove the influence that miracles have had on the historical process of mankind.

There was a time when the known world consisted only of several countries around the Mediterranean Sea, and those miracles which we accept as articles of faith occurred in and around that Mediterranean world. Nevertheless, the world as we now know it existed and people lived and died on the steppes of Asia, in the remotest corners of the Far East, on the islands of the Pacific Ocean and on the continent of the Western Hemisphere. Were these people affected by the miracles that God wrought for a small group of people, the Jews, inhabiting an insignificant territory smaller than New York State? Or, in our time, does a miracle that involves an obscure nun living in some remote Italian convent, or a miracle brought about by a German peasant become a hard-working Capuchin monk in a Bavarian monastery have any effect on history in the making, with respect, for example, to the immense changes taking place in China, or in the jungles of India and Africa, or anywhere else?

As long as those portions of the world permeated by Christian ideology lived in a relative spiritual unity it can be said that first the supernatural and then the miraculous have had an effect on historical development. Kings and statesmen shared the same belief as the soldier or the serf. The construction of the great cathedrals and churches speaks for itself. In a single century between 1170 and 1270 the French built 80 cathedrals and nearly 500 churches of the cathedral category. Similar data could be produced from the rest of Europe, including the Balkan peninsula and even parts of Russia. Hungary and Albania and the other territories in the East were full of cathedrals similar to those that are still intact in Western Europe. But the constant battles fought with the invaders from the East, Mongols and Turks, destroyed these visible monuments of the Christian Faith. These churches were founded by kings and princes and constantly showered with large endowments. Most of these houses of God were also connected with some miraculous event. For it should not be forgotten that the relic of a saint to whom the faithful prayed for intercession is required for the construction of an altar.

The same spirit was brought by the early missionaries to the Western Hemisphere, to Africa, to the Philippines, to the lands in the East. Wherever they went they carried the images of their beloved saints and set up sanctuaries for them. Soon, in many of these places, the former pagan himself witnessed, or claimed to witness, the miraculous. It is enough to think of the apparitions of Our Lady in Mexico and in other parts of South America, and the shrines of Canada and of the Orthodox Church that reach to the Far East itself.

The people are the real makers of history. Even in those ages when the leaders of a nation or social group did not ask the consensus of the people, they were subject to the people's influence. Better said, there was and there is now a constant interaction, an interchange of influence between the rulers and the ruled, the governors and the governed, the elite and the masses. The only specific miracles that changed the course of history to which we can refer are the miracles of the Old Testament and those of Jesus Christ.

Students of political science and social movement are always deeply concerned with reporting the facts underlying political and economic reality. On the other hand, students of religion have been excessively interested in religious movements to the neglect of religious feelings, so that a comparable study of the influence of faith and the supernatural and even the miraculous in the life of the people, save for some pioneer researches in religious sociology, is still largely missing.

It would be a fallacy to think that only primitive peoples and the more or less primitive ages, in which one used without warrant to include the Middle Ages, lived or live in a climate where the supernatural and the miraculous are taken for granted. It must be stressed here that by the supernatural and the miraculous we do not mean naïve superstitions of the past and the present. There is enough evidence available to validate the thesis that people all over the world desire, indeed yearn, for the miraculous and want to accept it. And the unbeliever or the veritable persecutor is compelled to deal with this massive phenomenon of a faith transformed into an actual historical force.

A few examples will shed more light on this statement. The disciples of Christ and the early Christians drew their greatest strength from their unshakable belief in the resurrection of our Lord. The burden of persecution was easier to bear when one believed in the miracles that happened to the martyrs. Ultimately this deep and abiding faith had tangible results, specifically in the toleration and acceptance of the Christian faith. Whether or not Constantine the Great actually saw the sign of the cross in a vision is irrelevant. What is relevant is the fact that at that point history took a different turn. Since then most of the great missionaries who christianized Europe have been venerated as saints.

When the Turks subjugated the whole Balkan peninsula and the greater part of Hungary, they arrived at the very doors of Vienna and thus menaced the entire western world with destruction. The King of Poland, Jan Sobieski, gathered his knights and his entire army before the miraculous image of Our Lady of Czestochowa and then threw his forces into a last-minute struggle to relieve the besieged city of Vienna and thus save the Western World. It was a crucial historical moment. It is true that many social, economic, political, and other elements created by man converged to precipitate both the pending disaster and the rescue from it which followed. But the imponderable, yet most decisive, element in this struggle was faith in the supernatural, in a God who might, if it so pleased Him, produce a miracle.

The French Revolution of 1789 was determined to dethrone God and put Reason in His stead. The spiritual climate, the political and social conditions were favorable for the realization of this end. Nevertheless, it failed. Was it only the inner conflict of the leaders of the Revolution, their human inadequacies, and the emergence of a strong personality in the person of Bonaparte that changed the course of history? Or had those martyrs who died during the Revolution, those humble insignificant Carmelite nuns in the Compiègne some effect in re-establishing the balance? Admittedly, only those who believe in the power of prayer will agree with such a view. Still, it is both interesting and curious that, in some mysterious way, the tiny minority, which had placed its faith in the supernatural, and not their persecutors, became the crystalizing center around which the new forces of the future gathered. By the beginning of the nineteenth century all France was again in the arms of the Faith, and instead of indulging in the dream of restoring the rule of reason the entire country looked towards a small village in the Alps, toward Ars, where a powerless, obscure person, a shabby country priest, became an instrument in the hands of God to manifest the power of the supernatural.

The skeptic and the unbeliever might ask why God permitted the two world wars and the enormous untold suffering connected with both. Why did He permit a Hitler and the brutal massacre of millions, among them six million Jews? If there was a need for miracles, surely they would have been useful in both cases.

Without in any sense presuming to attempt an explanation of God's inscrutable ways, we may permit ourselves to speculate on such matters. It is not true that there were no miracles. Probably most of us ignored them. Lourdes has existed since 1858—if we limit ourselves to the most spectacular, the most undeniable miracle, the greatest link in the chain of hundreds of miracles. If we believe in the existence of a free will, then we must admit that we were free to ignore the warnings. In that case, of course, we must bear the consequences of our deeds. Or we deny the existence of free will, in which case it is useless to talk about history. And we can also discard the idea of God—for what kind of a God is one who leads the individual and mankind itself into deliberate disasters?

The truth is that there were enough miracles, there were enough manifestations of the supernatural. There were the teachings of Christ, the presence of the Eucharist, and the saints living among us. In 1917 in the apparitions of Fatima we were again reminded of our duties. Indeed we might venture to speculate that the prayers and the actions of the righteous in the mystical realm, in these specific cases, were not able to counterbalance entirely the forces of evil.

The need of miracles cannot be expressed in human terms. Nor can we rightly deplore the absence of a miracle. The only thing we can do is to express our gratitude in recognition and acceptance of it. Many people, for example, consider it as somewhat miraculous that there is still faith and a religious belief in countries like Russia. It is undeniable that in this case we again are face to face with an event, or better still, a chain of events, deeply rooted in the historical process. The religious persecution launched in 1917 when the Bolsheviks took over the Russian empire surpassed the imagination. It was more lethal, more brutal, more complete than the persecution of the early Christians. One could save onself in pagan Rome by exchanging Christ for one of the false pagan deities. But in Russia the alternative was God or nothing. The pressure on the people of Russia resulted in mass destruction of human beings, economic annihilation, and social degradation. Nevertheless, in 1937 a survey conducted by the Soviet government disclosed what proved to be an alarming fact to the persecutors. The faith in a supernatural God lived and worked. This force became so great a hindrance to the atheist rulers that they could no longer cope with it. The only way for them to extricate themselves from an impossible situation was to give in, to camouflage the persecution, and to try to convert people to atheist doctrine.

Father Bissonette, an American Catholic priest, who between 1953 and 1955 was chaplain in Moscow, in his recent book has written that people constantly walk around the Red Square in front of the Kremlin. The reason for their seemingly aimless wandering, however, is not the expectation of being admitted to visit the mausoleum of Lenin and Stalin but to visit the site where once stood the chapel of the Miraculous Image of the Madonna of Iviron, destroyed and removed more than thirty years ago. The faith and perseverance of the Russian people have resulted in a major victory for them. They have no absolute religious freedom yet, but their partial victory is deeply significant. The prevailing powers that be, possessing all the available coercive and corruptive means that matter can offer, withdrew before something invisible, untouchable, inexpressible whose existence is not even admitted by dialectical materialism.

This is the way the supernatural and the individual miracle works in the historical process of mankind. Each would require hundreds of pages of study. But at the end one would still be compelled to ask, why do people believe, why do people accept the supernatural? And why do people not believe?

The answer is that both the believer in God and the unbeliever adhere to a faith, albeit to radically different faiths. It is simply impossible to live without any faith. Chesterton writes: "For some extraordinary reason, there is a fixed notion that it is more liberal to disbelieve in miracles than to believe in them. . . . Men of science believe in such marvels much more than they did; the most perplexing, and even horrible, prodigies of mind and spirit are always being unveiled in modern psychology. Things that the old science at least would frankly have rejected as miracles are hourly being asserted by the new science. The only thing which is still old fashioned enough to reject miracles is the new theology. But in truth this notion that it is 'free' to deny miracles has nothing to do with the evidence for or against them. . . . The man of the nineteenth century did not disbelieve in the resurrection because his liberal Christianity allowed him to doubt it. He disbelieved in it because his very strict materialism did not allow him to believe it. Tennyson . . . said that there was faith in their honest doubt. There was indeed . . . in their doubt of miracles there was faith in a fixed and godless fate."[1]

Thus one can look upon history as a mere sequence of events unrolling in a grim, gray, and dreadful uniformity and monotony. It is as if one stood in a corner of a prison courtyard looking toward the gate as the doomed, drab parade of prisoners sentenced for life marches by in lock step. They know that the monotonous uniformity of their lives can never cease. Nobody can change the color of their uniform, the pace of their steps, and the look of emptiness and disease in their eyes.

Or one can consider history from another vantage point, viewing it as an immense battlefield, as did Matthew Arnold, "where ignorant armies clash by night."

But as one studies this confused picture, from time to time one can see emerging human figures around whom the ground and the smoke clear.

It is hard to believe that the great saints of history influenced only those people who lived in their immediate vicinity, and left untouched those who resisted them or did not know them.

It is not our purpose here to measure the effects of the miracles of a particular saint on his contemporaries or the impact they may have had on the spiritual, moral, or political climate of their age. For it must ever be borne in mind that these single and disparate miracles all have taken place within the framework of the primordial miracle, the advent and the Resurrection of Christ. In our opinion this event, which took place on historical-human and supernatural-divine levels, fundamentally altered the course of history in this world, and it will continue to do so until the end of time. This change, however, was not effected by a direct manipulation by the divine of things or events, but by the Act of Salvation which gave to the lives of men and history a new transfiguring content. Those who bear testimony to Christ by definition acknowledge that He is the Miracle. This Miracle acts as an all pervading ferment operating in the lives of individuals and society. The appearance of Christ on earth and His Real Presence among us miraculously conjoined human history and the supernatural, which is our hope.

Appendix

The Holy See has always exhibited the utmost degree of prudence, and required a scrupulous investigation of the virtues and miracles, real and alleged, of those persons for whom others have sought to obtain beatification or canonization.

Responsibility for the formal proceedings involving the merits of holy persons proposed for beatification or canonization rests with a special section within the Sacred Congregation of Rites. All members of this section are cardinals, but other high Church dignitaries participate in its deliberations, including the traditional "Devil's Advocate." Since 1949 these other participants have included legal and medical experts, postulators and consultors. Among the consultors there is always a Franciscan, a Jesuit, a Dominican, an Augustinian, a Servite, a Conventual Minorite, a Minim, and a Barnabite.

Here it might be useful to explain the difference between beatification and canonization. When a person is beatified (always after death), it means that he or she may be the object of liturgical honors on the part of the faithful. And the brief of beatification does not involve the dogma of papal infallibility. Canonization, on the other hand, involves an official Church pronouncement, in the form of a Bull of Canonization, in which it is declared that the canonized person is a member of the communion of saints. It would be heresy for any Catholic to deny sainthood to a person upon whom the Church has formally conferred this highest of honors.

Any individual Catholic, or group of Catholics, may sponsor a petition requesting beatification proceedings. But the petition itself must be brought before the Congregation of Rites authorities by a *postulator*. A postulator must be a resident priest of Rome, authorized to carry out this function. The first duty of the postulator is to examine the claims put forward in behalf of the candidate, with the assistance of the ordinary or bishop in whose diocese the candidate died. If the Diocesan Commission is not convinced of the orthodoxy or the doctrine of the candidate, his sanctity, his virtues, of the miracles performed through his intercession, or of his martyrdom (if martyrdom is involved), the beatification process can go no further. If this detailed and long-drawn-out informative phase is satisfactory, the cause of the candidate is brought before the Congregation of Rites by one of the member cardinals, appointed by the Pope. As the *relator*, this cardinal must summarize the results of the informative process. If the approval of all is obtained, including the consent of the Pope, the ordinary is authorized to begin the Apostolic Process.

This process repeats, in greater detail and at greater length, the inquiry conducted by the postulator on the doctrine, virtues, miracles, or martyrdom, of the person proposed for canonization. This process cannot take more than two years, and within this time the body of the candidate must be disinterred and examined.

The results of this process are sent to the Congregation of Rites. In three separate meetings, ante-preparatory, preparatory, and general, these results are again discussed and evaluated. A cardinal takes part in the first meeting, all of the cardinals participate in the second, and the Pope himself is present at the third. It is the Pope who actually determines the degree of the candidate's heroic virtue, or confirms the fact of martyrdom. If the Pope decides favorably, the decision is published and the candidate may be called *Venerable*, though no public cult is authorized.

The miracles attributed to the candidate are discussed further, during three other similar meetings held by the same group. Here these claims are scrutinized thoroughly with the assistance of medical experts who pass on the validity of cures allegedly achieved miraculously. Only two miracles are required for beatification. None is required in the case of martyrdom. Upon approval of the miracles another session is held in the presence of the Pope. The case is again summarized and a decree of *de tuto procedi posse* is issued.

Finally, the cause of the candidate is examined in three consistories. The first is a secret one, addressed by the Pope, in which all cardinals present in Rome take part. Again a summary of the case is presented and the cardinals vote *placet* or *non placet*. At the second public consistory the Pope and all the cardinals are also present. The cause of the candidates is upheld by the consistorial advocate to which the secretary of briefs, speaking for the Pope, replies, urging the faithful to pray for divine guidance to the consistory.

The third, semipublic, consistory is virtually a synod. Not only are all the cardinals present but all bishops, archbishops, and patriarchs resident in Rome and adjacent dioceses. Once again the merits of the candidate are discussed and a vote taken. Following a favorable vote, the Pope authorizes canonization, and again all present are exhorted to pray for divine guidance.

The emphasis in canonization and beatification processes is not on the miracle but on the heroic life of the person proposed for veneration or sainthood. It has already been pointed out that the Church admits the possibility that genuine miracles can be performed by persons who do not belong to the body of the Church. St. Thomas declared that even those in a state of grave sin could be used by the divine Power for the purpose of manifesting itself. Pope Benedict XIV in his famous treatise on miracles held that the Jews, the pagans and the heretics were capable of performing true miracles, but that they are not considered saints. A group of monks once venerated a person who had been killed in a state of total drunkenness. Pope Alexander III, in his decree *Audivimus*, reproached the religious community. He told them that though the person in question might have performed many miracles, "you do not have to venerate him as a saint." For this reason great emphasis is placed on evidence of charity and an heroic life. It is not the intention of the Church to recognize miracles for the sake of miracles.

The difference between beatification and canonization, as has been indicated, involves papal infallibility. This infallibility, however, is not extended to miracles approved or disapproved by the Pope. The importance of miracles in beatification and canonization processes can be measured by the fact that Popes, in several cases, have waived the rule on miracles in canonization or beatification process. This has been done primarily in cases where the sanctity, the heroic life of the person is *eo ipso* evident, such as, in the case of a martyr. The most famous cases of this kind were those of St. Thomas More and St. John Fisher. Moreover, there are many saints of the Church whose elevation to the altars was not the result of a papal beatification and canonization process. The present procedure was established only in 1634 under Pope Urban VIII. The infallibility of the Popes of those centuries, even if their private lives were sometimes scandalous, is not to be questioned, for it has been proved that in their official acts, *ex cathedra*, they were true to the true mission of the Church. Thus, if they approved the veneration of a person as a saint their declaration is infallible. While in not all of these cases can the *miracles* be definitely verified, the sanctity of the saints in question still holds. In 1931 Pius XI created a new section within the Sacred Congregation of Rites, the Historical Section, and commissioned it to collect historical data on these early declarations of sainthood.

The miracle is a solemn testimony of the supernatural. The purpose of the miracle is to lead man to the recognition of the supernatural and a personal God. Saints are persons who already have experienced this "shock of recognition," this beatific vision because of their heroic lives of love and charity. This is what is attested to infallibly by the Pope. Most of the saints exercised these heroic virtues without any signs from the Lord in the form of supernatural manifestations. Thus, we should have faith and follow in their footsteps without requiring any special or extraordinary divine intervention.

Notes

CHAPTER 1

1. Jean Hellé, *Miracles* (New York, David McKay Co., 1952).

CHAPTER 2

1. *A Catholic Dictionary* (New York, Macmillan Co., 1954).
2. *A Catholic Commentary on Holy Scripture*, Edited by Dom B. Orchard, Rev. E. F. Sutcliffe, S.J., Rev. R. C. Fuller and Dom R. Russell (New York, Thomas Nelson and Sons, 1953).
3. E. C. Messenger, "The Miraculous Element in the Bible" (ibid.).
4. St. Thomas, II-II, clxxvii, 1; Quoted by D. Attwater, op. cit.
5. "Il vero ed il Falso Sopra-naturale" ("The True and False Supernatural,") in *Osservatore Romano*, Feb. 10, 1951.
6. *Le Miracle* (Descleé de Brouwer, Paris, 1936).
7. Zsolt Aradi, *Shrines to Our Lady* (New York, Farrar, Straus and Cudahy, 1954).
8. *A Catholic Dictionary*.
9. William Doheny, C.S.C. (ed.), *Selected Writings of St. Theresa of Avila* (Milwaukee, Bruce Publishing Co., 1950).
10. Cardinal Lépicier, op. cit.

CHAPTER 3

1. Walter Farrell O.P., "The Devil himself," in *Satan*, see note 3.
2. Giovanni Papini, *Il Diavolo* (Vallecchi-Editore, Firenze, 1953).
3. Henri-Charles Puech, "The Prince of Darkness in his Kingdom," in *Satan*, ed. Bruno de Jésu-Marie, O.C.D. (New York, Sheed and Ward, 1952).
4. Herbert Thurston, S.J., "The Church and Withcraft," in *Satan*.
5. "The Sixteenth Century and Satanism," in *Satan*.
6. Ibid.
7. P. Bruno de Jésu-Marie quoted by P. de Tonquedec, in "La Belle Ascarie," in *Satan*.

297

8. Joseph de Tonquedec, S.J., "Exorcism and Diabolical Manifestation," in *Satan*.

9. Tonquedec, op. cit.

10. Described in: Alberto Vecchi Intervista col Diavolo, Ed. Paoline, Modena 1954.

11. A. M. Lépicier, *The Unseen World* (London, Sheed and Ward, 1936).

12. Cited by Karl Stern, M.D., "Some Spiritual Aspects of Psychotherapy," in *Faith, Reason, and Modern Psychiatry*, ed. F. J. Braceland, M.D. (New York, P. J. Kenedy & Sons, 1955).

13. New York, Pantheon Books, 1944.

14. Tonquedec, op. cit.

CHAPTER 4

1. Herbert Thurston, S.J., *The Church and Spiritism*.

2. P. Lambertini (later Pope Benedict XIV), in "De Beatificatione et Canonizatione," quoted by Herbert Thurston, S.J., in *The Physical Phenomena of Mysticism*, ed. J. H. Crehan, S.J. (Chicago, Henry Regnery Co., 1952).

3. C. A. E. Moberly and E. F. Jourdain, *An Adventure*, ed. Joan Evans (New York, Coward McCann, 1955).

4. Herbert Thurston, S.J., *The Physical Phenomena of Mysticism*.

5. Thurston, ibid.

6. Thurston, ibid.

7. Quoted in Thurston, ibid.

CHAPTER 5

1. Jean Lhermitte, *Mystiques et faux mystiques* (Paris, Bloud et Gay, 1952).

2. *The Third Revolution, Psychiatry and Religion* (New York, Harcourt, 1954).

3. Karl Stern, ibid.

4. Jean Lhermitte, "Pseudo-Possession," in *Satan*.

5. Karl Stern, ibid.

6. Herbert Thurston, S.J., *Surprising Mystics* (Chicago, Henry Regnery Co., 1955).

7. H. Thurston, *Physical Phenomenon of Mysticism*, etc.

8. Ibid.

9. Ibid.

10. Una Carmelitana, *Un Fiore di Passione* (Rome, Pia Societa San Paolo).

11. *Mystiques et faux mystiques* (Paris, Bloud et Gay, 1952).

12. Jean Lhermitte, op. cit.

13. The expression "neurosis" is not used here in the pathological sense of an emotional disturbance commonly called neurosis.

CHAPTER 6

1. Albert Gelin, *The Key Concepts of the Old Testament* (Sheed and Ward, New York, 1955).

2. *A Catholic Commentary on Holy Scripture* (Thomas Nelson and Sons, New York, 1953).

3. Ibid.

4. Ibid.

5. Ibid.

6. Ibid.

CHAPTER 7

1. New York, E. P. Dutton and Co., 1954.

2. Ibid.

3. New York, Longmans Green and Co., 1908.

4. C. Lavergne, "Les miracles du Christ," in *Apologétique* (Paris, Bloud et Gay, 1948).

5. Aelred Graham, O.S.B., "The Person and the Teaching of Jesus Christ," in *A Catholic Commentary on Holy Scripture*.

6. Josef Leo Seifert, *Sinndeutung Des Mythos* (Verlag Herold, Wien, 1954).

7. W. Leonard and B. Orchard, "The Place of the Bible in the Church," in *A Catholic Commentary on Holy Scripture*.

8. Romano Guardini, *The Last Things* (New York, Pantheon Books, 1954).

9. Thomas Merton, *The Living Bread* (New York, Farrar, Straus and Cudahy, 1956).

CHAPTER 8

1. *A Catholic Dictionary*, ed. Donald Attwater, (New York, Macmillan Co., 1954).

2. Ibid.

3. Herbert Thurston, S.J., *The Physical Phenomena of Mysticism*, see note 2, Chapter 4.

4. Baron Friedrich von Hugel, *The Mystical Element of Religion as Studied in St. Catherine of Genoa and Her Friends*, London, 1908.

5. Thurston, op. cit.

6. Thurston, op. cit.

CHAPTER 9

1. Cf. Archbishop (Cardinal) Salotti, *Il Santo Giovanni Bosco* (Turin, 1934).

2. Theodore Maynard, *Saints for Our Times* (New York, Appleton-Century-Crofts, 1951).

3. Salotti, ibid.

CHAPTER 10

1. H. M. Gillett, *Famous Shrines of Our Lady* (Westminster, Newman Press, 1952).
2. *The Song of Bernadette* (New York, Viking, 1942).
3. Alexis Carrel, *Man the Unknown* (New York, Harper and Bros., 1944).
4. Alexis Carrel, *Voyage to Lourdes* (New York, Harper and Bros., 1950).
5. New York, McGraw-Hill Book Co., 1955.
6. Jean Hellé, *Miracles.*
7. H. M. Gillett, op. cit.
8. The Beacon Press, Boston, 1949.
9. Jean Hellé, *Miracles.*
10. Leon Degrelles founded in 1931 a political movement called Rex which was supposed to be a progressive rightist Catholic political movement under the banner of Christus Rex—Christ the King. Its aim was to combat the so-called reactionary anti-social elements in the Belgian Catholic party. Later Degrelles moved far right and was accused of Nazi sympathies. During World War II he actually fought in the German army in German uniform. The movement disintegrated during the war.
11. The quotations are from Vladimir Solovyev: *"L'Avvento Dell'Anticristo"* (Milan, Vita E. Pensiero, 1951), and from *"Vladimir Szolovyev: Antikrisztus-legenda"* (Latomas) (Budapest, Vigilia, 1935). No English translation of the "Three Conversations" exists.

CHAPTER 11

1. F. X. Marquart, "Exorcism and diabolical manifestation" in *Satan.*
2. *Zum Weltbild der Physick* (Leipzig, 1944).
3. *Theologie und Physik* (Freibury, Herder, 1951).
4. Heimo Dolch, op. cit.
5. C. F. von Weizsäcker, op. cit.
6. Der Begriff "Abgeschlossene Theorie" in der modernen Naturwissenschaft, Dialectica, Zürich, 1948.
7. Pius XII in an allocution to the Pontifical Academy of Sciences on "The Existence of God and Modern Science" (Nov. 22, 1951) said among other things: "Modern science has followed the course and direction of cosmic developments and discovered those terms in which the cosmos will end. At the same time modern science has proved that the cosmos was created five billion years ago; furthermore, it has confirmed with the solidity and concreteness peculiar to the scientific method . . . that at about that time the cosmos issued forth from the hands of the Creator."
8. The nucleus of hydrogen is composed of only one proton and one external electron; carbon has six protons and six neutrons in the nucleus and six electrons around them; oxygen has eight protons and eight neutrons in the nucleus and eight external electrons.

9. Roberto Masi, "Fisica moderna ed Eucaristia," Osservatore Romano, Dec. 4, 1955.

10. Lincoln Barnett, *The Universe and Dr. Einstein* (New York, Harper & Bros., 1950). With a Foreword by Albert Einstein.

11. No. 80 (April 6, 1947), p. 3.

12. Lincoln Barnett, *op. cit.*

CHAPTER 12

1. G. K. Chesterton, *Orthodoxy* (New York, Dodd Mead, 1955).

Bibliography

GENERAL REFERENCE WORKS

Attwater, Donald (ed.). *A Catholic Dictionary*. New York, Macmillan Co., 1954.

Sacra Rituum Congregatio, Index ac Status Causarum Beatificationis Servorum Dei et Canonizationis Beatorum. Rome, Typis Polyglottis Vaticanis, 1953.

Annuario Pontifico. Citta del Vaticano, 1956.

Lexikon des Katholischen Lebens. Edited by Archbishop Dr. Wendelin Rauch. Freiburg, Verlag Herder, 1952.

Bruno de Jésus-Marie, O.C.D. (ed.). *Satana*. Milan, Vite e Pensiero, 1953.

—— *Satan*. New York, Sheed and Ward, 1952.

Enciclopedia Cattolica, Ente per L'Enciclopedia Cattolica e per il Libro Cattolico. Città del Vaticano, 1949–1954.

National Catholic Almanac. Paterson, N. J., St. Anthony's Guild, 1956.

The Catholic Encyclopedia. New York, Gilmary Society, 1911– .

A Catholic Commentary on Holy Scripture. New York, Thomas Nelson & Sons, 1953.

Enciclopedia Apologetica Della Religione Cattolica. Pia Società S. Paolo-Alba (Cuneo), 1953.

Butler–Thurston–Attwater. *Life of the Saints*. New York, P. J. Kenedy & Sons, 1956.

Anichini, Guido. *Un Astro di Santità*. Rome, Postulatore. Francescano, 1947.

Andrè, Marie. *Les Visites de la Sainte Vièrge a la France au XIXe Siécle*. Paris, Alsatia, 1946.

Aurelio della Passione, C.P. *Santa Maria Goretti, Martire della Purezza*. Rome, Coletti Editore, 1950.

Barnard, G. C. *Il Supernormale*. Rome, Astrolabio, 1949.

Benedetti, P. Claudio. *San Gerardo Maiella*. Rome, Cooperative Poligrafica Editrice, 1904.

San Giovanni Bosco. *San Domenico Savio*. Turin, Società Editrice Internazionale, 1954.

Branca, Remo. *S. Ignazio da Laconi*. Rome, Postulazione Generale O.F.M. Cap., 1951.

Belleney, Joseph. *Guérisons de Lourdes*. Paris, Centurion, 1955.

303

304   BIBLIOGRAPHY

Blanshard, Paul. *American Freedom and Catholic Power*. Boston, Beacon Press, 1949.

Barnett, Lincoln. *The Universe and Dr. Einstein*. New York, Harper & Bros., 1948.

Brodrick, James, S.J. *Saint Francis Xavier*. New York, Pellegrini & Cudahy, 1952.

Browe, P. *Die Eucharistichen Wunder des Mittelalters*. Leipzig, Diederichs, 1938.

Cassels, Walter R. *Supernatural Religion*. London, Longmans, 1938.

Una Carmelitana, del Monastero di Santa Maria Maddalene de' Pazzi in Firenze. *Un Fiore di Passione della città del Volto Santo (Gemma Galgani)*. Alba, Pia Società San Paolo, 1930.

Caminada, Costantino. *Santa Francesca Saverio Cabrini*. Turin, L. I. C. E.-R. Berutti & C., 1946.

Cassinari, Ernesto, C.M. *Santa Caterina Labouré*. Rome, Postulazione Generale della Congregazione della Missione, 1947.

Contardi, Enrico. *Santa Giovanna*. Rome, Ed. Paoline, 1950.

Cranston, Ruth. *The Miracle of Lourdes*. New York, McGraw-Hill Book Co., 1955.

Compendio della Vita del B. Giovanni Massias. Rome, Tipografia Salviucci, 1837.

Compendio della Vita di S. Clemente M° Hofbauer. Isola del Liri, Tipografia Arturo Macioce, 1909.

Cristiani, L. *Actualité de Satan*. Paris, Centurion, 1954.

D'Arcy, M.C., S.J. *The Mind and Heart of Love*. New York, Henry Holt, 1946.

Doheny, William, C.S.C. *Selected Writings of St. Teresa of Avila*. Milwaukee, Bruce Publishing Company, 1950.

Dolch, Heimo. *Theologie und Physik*. Freiburg, Herder, 1951.

Favini, Sac. Guido. *Santa Maria Domenica Mazzarello*. Turin, Società Editrice Internazionale, 1951.

Fantappiè, Luigi. *Principi di una Teoria del mondo fisico e biologico*. Rome, Soc. Ed. Humanitas Nova, 1950.

Fernandez, C.–Lorente, I. *S. Antonio M. Claret*. Rome, Tip. Poliglotta C. ci M., 1950.

Fonck, L. *I Miracoli del Signore nel Vangelo*. Rome, Pontificio Istituto Biblico, 1914.

Frediani, G. *Il Santo di Ferro*. Rome, Orbis Catholicus, 1951.

Gamow, George. *The Birth and Death of the Son*. New York, The Viking Press, 1940.

Giannini, P. Umberto, S.M. *San Pierluigi Chanel*. Rome, Padri Maristi, 1954.

Gorrës, Josef. *Christliche Mystik*. In *Collected Works of Gorrës*. Cologne, Bachem Verlag, 1936.

de Gourmont, Remy. *De Satan dans la Literature*. Paris, Plon, 1938.

de Grandmaison, L. S.J. *Jésus Christ*. Paris, Beauchesne, 1928.

Guardini, Romano. *The Last Things*. New York, Pantheon, 1954.

Germier, Giuseppe, S.J. *San Bernardino Realino*. Florence, Libreria Editrice Fiorentina, 1942.

Gelin, Albert. *The Key Concepts of the Old Testament*. New York, Sheed and Ward, 1955.

Gemelli, Agostino, O.F.M. S. *Francesco D'Assisi*. Milan, Vita e Pensiero, 1950.

—— *Il Francescanesimo*. Milan, Vita e Pensiero, 1937.

Gillett, H. M. *Famous Shrines of Our Lady*, 2 vols. Westminster, Newman Press, 1952.

Handley, M. L. *Santa Maria Eufrasia Pelletier, Suore del Buon Pastore*. Rome, 1940.

Hellé, Jean. *Miracles*. New York, David McKay Co., 1952.

Howitt, W. *The History of the Supernatural*. London, Longmans, 1863.

Hummeler, Hans. *Helden und Helige*. Siegburg, Haus Michaelsberg, 1954.

Instituto delle Figlie di N.S. della Misericordia. *Santa Maria Giuseppa Rossello*. Rome, Società Grafica, 1949.

Abd-El-Jalil, J,-M., OFM. *Maria im Islam*. Werl-Westf., Dietrich-Coelde-Verlag, 1954.

Kennedy, John S. *Light on the Mountain*. New York, McMullen, 1953.

Knox, R. A. *Miracles*. London, Catholic Truth Society, 1927.

—— *God and the Atom*. New York, Sheed and Ward, 1945.

—— *The Hidden Stream*. New York, Sheed and Ward, 1953.

Lazzarini, A. *Documenti dei Sec. XIII e XIV sul Miracolo di Bolsena*. Rome, Ed. Paolina, 1951.

Legoux, Arsenio Maria. *Vita di S. Maria Maddelena Postel*. Rome, Officina Tipografica Ausonia, 1925.

Lépicier, A. M., O.S.M. *Le Miracle*. Paris, Desclée de Brouwer, 1936.

—— *The Unseen World*. London, Sheed and Ward, 1929.

Leuret, F., and Bon, Henri. *Les Guérisons miraculeuses modernes*. Paris, Presses Universitaires de France, 1950.

Lewis, C. S. *Miracles*. New York, Macmillan Co., 1947.

Lhermitte, Jean. *Mystiques et Faux Mystiques*. Paris, Bloud et Gay, 1952.

de Libero, Giuseppe. *S. Gaspare del Bufalo*. Rome, Curia Generalizia della Congregazione del Prez. Sangue, 1954.

Luigi, P.–Teresa di Gesù Agonizzante C.P. *S. Paolo della Croce, Postulazione Generale PP. Passionisti, SS. Giovanni e Paolo*. Rome, 1952.

Little, George A. *Brendan the Navigator*. Dublin, M. H. Gill and Son, Ltd., 1946.

Lemoyne, G. B. *S. Giovanni Bosco*. Turin, Cura di A. Amadei, S.E.I.

Maraldi, Ugo. *La Scienza Moderna ed i Miracoli*. Turin, Edizione S.A.I.E., 1955.

March, A. *Il Cammino dell'Universo*. Rome, Ed. Casini, 1951.

Maynard, Theodore. *Saints for Our Times*. New York, Appelton-Century-Crofts, 1951.

Merton, Thomas. *The Living Bread*. New York, Farrar, Straus & Cudahy, 1956.

306   BIBLIOGRAPHY

Moberly, C. A. E. and Jourdain, E. F. *An Adventure.* New York, Coward-McCann, 1955.

Molaine, Pierre. *L'Itineraire de la Vièrge Marie.* Paris. Correa, 1953.

Monnin, Sac. Alfredo. S. *Giov. Batt. Maria Vianney, Curato d'Ars.* Rome, Libreria Ecclesiastica Ernesto Coletti, 1925.

Mouly, Abbé. *Des Miracles Revolutionnent l'Amérique.* Paris, Lib. Mignard, 1946.

Occelli, Pierluigi. *Il Papa che Morì Povero.* Rome, Edizione Paoline, 1951.

Papasogli, G. *Santa Maria Anna di Gesù.* Rome, Tipografia Pontificia Università Gregoriana, 1950.

—— *Una Gloria Bresciana, Santa Maria Crocifissa di Rosa.* Brescia, Casa Madre, 1954.

Papini, Giovanni. *The Devil.* New York, Dutton, 1954.

Pecchiai, Lucia. *Santa Emilia de Vialar.* Rome, Suore di S. Giuseppe dell'Apparizione, 1951.

Pfeiffer, E. *Das Wunder als Erkenntnismittel der Glaubwurdigkeit der Offenbarung.* 1936.

Pietromarchi, D. Maria Eugenia, O.S.B. *Santa Emilia de Rodat.* Rome, Suore della Santa Famiglia, 1950.

Planck, Max. *Religion und Naturwissenschaft.* Leipzig, Johann Ambrosius Barth-Verlag, 1953.

Power, Eileen. *Medieval People.* New York, Doubleday, 1925.

Porretta, P. Felice da. *Il Beato Corrado da Parzham.* Rome, Tipografia Poliglotta Vaticana, 1930.

Praz, Mario. *La Carne, la Morte e il Diavolo nella Litteratura Romantica.* Milano, La Cultura, 1930.

Daniel–Rops (pseud.). *Sacred History.* New York, Longmans, Green and Co., 1949.

—— *Jesus and His Times.* New York, E. P. Dutton & Co., 1954.

Rossi, D. Giovanni. *Gesù.* Rome, Pro Civitate Christiana, 1954.

Rougemont, Denis de. *The Devil's Share.* New York, Pantheon Books, 1944.

Rudwig, Maximilia. *Ecrivains Diaboliques de France.* Paris, Figuiere, 1930.

Sala, Felice M. *L'Apostolo di Napoli.* Rome, Lib. Ente Religioso PP. Barnabiti, 1951.

Salotti, Carlo. *San Giovanni Bosco.* Turin, Societa Editrice Internationale, 1934.

—— *La Perla del Clero Italiano–Il Santo Giuseppe Cafasso, La Palatina.* Turin, Tip. G. Bonis, 1947.

Saverio, P. Franceso di S. Teresa. *Storia di S. Teresa del Bambino Gesù.* Milan, Casa S. Lega Eucarista, 1925.

Scatizzi, P., S.J. *Fatima.* Rome, Coletti, 1946.

Schamoni, Wilhelm. *Das Wahre Geischt der Heiligen.* Leipzig, Jakob Hegner, 1938.

Schneider, Reinhold. *Der Fünfte Kelch.* Cologne, Jakob Hegner, 1953.

Seifert, Josef Leo. *Sinndeutung des Mythos.* Vienna, Verlag Herold, 1954.

Selvaggi, F. *Le Leggi Statistiche e il Miracolo.* Rome, Civilta Cattolica, V. IV, pp. 45-56; 202-213, 1950.

Sertillanges, A. D., O.P. *Meditazioni.* Brescia, Morcelliana, 1938.

Sivek, Paul, S.J. *The Riddle of Konnersreuth.* Milwaukee, The Bruce Publishing Co., 1953.

Stocchetti, Agostino. *Le Sante Bartolomea Capitanio e Vincenza Gerosa.* Vicenza, Tip. Pont. Vesc. S. Giuseppe G. Rumor, 1950.

Soloviev, V. *L'Avvento dell-Anticristo.* Milan, Vita e Pensiero, 1951.

Stern, Karl. *The Third Revolution.* New York, Harcourt, Brace, and Company, 1954.

Tesnière, P. Alberto. *Compendio della Vita del Beato Pietro Giuliano Eymard.* Milan, Tip. S. Lega Eucarista, 1925.

Testore, Celestino, S.J. *I Santi Martiri Canado-Americani della Campagnia di Gesù.* Soc. Tip. A. Macioce & Pisani, Isola dle Liri, 1930.

Tonquédec, J. de., S.J. *Introduction a l'Etude du Merveilleux et du Miracle.* Paris, Beauchesne, 1923.

Thurston, Herbert, S.J. *The Physical Phenomena of Mysticism.* Chicago, Henry Regnery Co., 1952.

—— *Ghosts and Poltergeists.* Chicago, Henry Regnery Co., 1954.

—— *Surprising Mystics.* Chicago, Henry Regnery Co., 1955.

—— *The Church and Spiritualism.* Milwaukee, Bruce Publishing Co., 1933.

Trochu, Francis. *Le Curé d'Ars.* Paris, E. Vitte, 1927.

Undset, Sigrid. *Die Heilige Angela Merici.* Freiburg, Herder, 1933.

Vallet, Prof. A. *La Vérité sur Lourdes et ses Guérisons Miraculeuses.* Paris, Flammarion, 1950.

Van Hove, A. *La Doctrine du Miracle chez S. Thomas et son Accord avec les Principes de la Recherche Scientifique.* Paris, Gabalda, 1927.

Vecchi, Alberto. *Intervista col Divavolo.* Rome, Paoline, 1954.

Verardo, R. *Il Miracolo di Fronte alla Scienza.* Turin, L.I.C.E., 1949.

Wehrle, J. *Sous la Lumière du Christ.* Paris, Perspectives, 1934.

Whitehead, A. N. *Science and the Modern World.* New York, Macmillan, 1925.

Zacchi, A. *Il Miracolo.* Milan, Vita e Pensiero, 1932.

Compendium Vitae Virtutum et Miraculorum, necnon actorum in Causa Canonizationis BEATI LUDOVICI M. GRIGNION A MONTFORT Sacerdotis Fundatoris Presbyterorum Missionariorum Societatis Mariae et Instituti Filiarum a Sapientia, ex tabulario Sacrae Rituum Congregationis, Typis Polyglottis Vaticanis, 1947.

Compendium . . . BEATI MICHAELIS GARICOITS Fundatoris Congregationis Presbyterorum a SS. Corde Iesu Vulgo de Betharram, ex tabulario Sacrae Rituum Congregationis, Typis Polyglottis Vaticanis, 1947.

Compendium . . . B. IOSEPHI PIGNATELLI Confessoris Sacerdotis Professi e Societate Iesu, ex tabulario Sacrae Rituum Congregationis, Typis Pont. Universitatis Gregorianae, 1954.

Compendium . . . BEATAE IOANNAE ELISABETH BICHIER DES DESAGES, Virginis, Confundatricis Congregationis Filiarum a Cruce Vulgo

308 BIBLIOGRAPHY

Sororum S. Andreae . . . ex tabulario Sacrae Rituum Congregationis, Typis Polyglottis Vaticanis, 1946.

Compendium . . . Beati Francisci Xaverii M. Bianchi Confessoris Sacerdotis Professi Congregationis Clerr. Regg. S. Pauli Vulgo Barnabitarum, ex tabulario Sacrorum Rituum Congregationis, Typis Polyglottis Vaticanis, 1951.

Compendium . . . Beatae Mariae Dominicae Mazzarello Virginis Confundatricis Instituti Filiarum Mariae Auxiliatricis ex tabulario Sacrorum rituum Congregationis, Typis Polyglottis Vaticanis, 1951.

Compendium . . . B. Joannis De Britto Martyris Sacerdotis Profess e Societate Iesu ex tabulario Sacrae Rituum Congregationis, Typis Pont. Universitatis Gregorianae, 1946.

Compendium . . . Beatae Mariae Crucifixae Di Rosa Virginis Fundatricis Instituti Ancillarum a Caritate, ex tabulario, Sacrorum Rituum Congregationis, Typis Polyglottis Vaticanis, 1954.

Compendium . . . Beati Francisci Xaverii M. Bianchi Confessoris Sacerdotis Professi Congregationis Clerr. Regg. S. Pauli Vulgo Barnabitarum, ex tabulario Sacrorum Rituum Congregationis, Typis Polyglottis Vaticanis, 1951.

Compendium . . . B. Salvatoris Ab Horta, Laici Professi Ordinis Fratrum Minorum, ex tabulario Sacrae Rituum Congregationis, Typis Polyglottis Vaticanis, 1938.

Compendium . . . Beatae Bartholomaeae Capitanio Virginis Fundatricis Institutu Sororum a Caritate, ex tabulario Sacrae Rituum Congretationis, Typis Polyglottis Vaticanis, 1949.

Compendium . . . Beatae Vincentiae Gerosa Virginis Alterius Fundatricis Instituti Sororum a Caritate, ex tabulario Sacrae Rituum Congregationis, Typis Polyglottis Vaticanis, 1949.

Compendium . . . Beati Vincentii Mariae Strambi Confessoris Pontificis e Congregatione Clericorum Exc. SS. Crucis et Possionis D. N. Iesu Christi, ex tabulario Sacrorum Rituum Congregationis, Typis Polyglottis Vaticanis, 1950.

Compendium . . . Beatae Ioannae De Valois Galliarum Reginae Fundatricis Ordinis SS. Mae Annuntiationis B.M.V., ex tabulario Sacrae Rituum Congregationis Typis Polyglottis Vaticanis, 1949.

Compendium . . . Beatae Mariae Annae A Iesu De Paredes Virginis, ex tabulario Sacrorum Rituum Congregationis Typis Polyglottis Vaticanis, 1950.

Compendium . . . Beati Ignatii A Laconi Confessoris Laici Professi Ordinis Fratrum Minorum Capuccinorum, ex tabulario Sacrorum Rituum Congregationis, Typis Polyglottis Vaticanis, 1951.

Compendium . . . Beati Anotnii M. Gianelli Fundatoris Instituti Filiarum B. Virginis ab Horto, Cortonae Stabilmento Tipografico Commerciale, 1951.

Compendium . . . Beatae M. Iosephae Rossello E Tertio Ordine S. Francisci Fundatricis Instituti Filiarum Nostrae A. Misericordia, ex tabulario Sacrae Rituum Congregationis, Typis Polyglottis Vaticanis, 1949.

Compendium . . . BEATAE JOANNAE DE LESTONNAC Viduae Fundatricis Ordinis Filiarum Beatae Mariae Virginis ex tabulario Sacrae Rituum Congregationis, Typis Polyglottis Vaticanis, 1949.

Compendium . . . BEATAE AEMILIAE DE VIALAR Fundatricis Congregationis S. Ioseph ab Apparitione, ex tabulario Sacrorum Rituum Congregationis, Typis Polyglottis Vaticanis, 1951.

Compendium . . . BEATAE MARIAE THERESIAE GORETTI Virginis Rituum Congregationis, Typis Polyglottis Vaticanis, 1950.

Compendium . . . Beatae MARIAE GUILELMAE AEMILIAE DE RODAT, Virginis, Fundatricis Congregationis a Sancta Familia, ex tabulario Sacrorum rituum Congregationis, Typis Polyglottis Vaticinis, 1950.

Compendium . . . BEATI P II PAPAE X, Confessoris, ex tabulario Sacrorum Rituum Congregationis, Typis Polyglottis Vaticanis, 1954.

Compendium . . . BEATI ANDREAE BOBOLA MART. Sacerdotis Professi e Societate Iesu, ex tabulario Sacrae Rituum Congregationis, Typis Polyglottis Vaticanis, 1938.

Compendium . . . BEATI GASPARIS DEL BUFALO, Fundatoris Congregationis Missionariorum Pretiosissimi Sanguinis D.N.I.C., ex tabulario Sacrorum Rituum Congregationis, Typis Polyglottis Vaticanis, 1954.

Compendium . . . BEATI COMINICI SAVIO, Confessoris Adolescentis Laici Alumni Oratorii Salesiani, ex tabulario Sacrorum Rituum Congregationis, Typis Polyglottis Vaticanis, 1954.

Compendium . . . BEATI PETRI ALOISII M. CHANEL, Sacerdotis e Societate Mariae Oceaniae Protomartyris, ex tabulario, Sacrorum Rituum Congregationis, Typis Polyglottis Vaticanis, 1954.

Compendium . . . BEATI NICOLAI DE FLUE, Anachoritae Helvetici, ex tabulario Sacrae Rituum Congregationis, Typis Polyglottis Vaticanis, 1947.

Compendium . . . BEATI IOSEPHI CAFASSO, Confessoris Sacerdotis Saecularis Collegii Ecclesiastici Taurinensis Moderatoris, ex tabulario Sacrae Rituum Congregationis, Typis Polyglottis Vaticanis, 1947.

Compendium . . . B. BERNARDINI REALINO, Confessoris Sacerdotis Professi e Societate Iesu, ex tabulario Sacrae Rituum Congregationis, Typis Pont. Universitatis Gregorianae, 1946.

ARTICLES:

Siegmund, Georg. "Wunderheiligen in Lichte der Modernen Heilkunde," Stimmen der Zeit, (Munich) II (August, 1951).

Guardini, Romano. "Das Wunder und das Bild Vom Menschen und Von Der Welt," Die Schildgenossen, (Würzburg) (1932).

Conrad-Martius, Hedwig. "Wissenschaft, Mythos und Neues Testament," Hochland, (Munich) (October, 1955).

Index

Aaron, 18, 117
Abraham, 114
Achatius, St., 157
Adams, Henry, 215
Aegidius, St., 158
Agnes, Mother, 185-186
Ahriman, 35, 43
Aix-en-Provence, Archbishop of, 237
Alacoque, Mary Margaret, 186
Albigensianism, 42, 47
Alchemy, 49
Alexander III, Tsar, 29
al Hallag, Mohammedan prophet, 29
Aloysius Gonzaga, St., 173
Ambrose of Milan, St., 181
André Hubert Fournet, St., 23, 89
Angela de Foligno, St., 95
Angela Merici, St., 181
Angels, Church doctrine on nature of, 64-65
Anthony of Padua, St., 186
Anthony the Hermit, St., visions of, 44
Anti-Christ, 33, 37, 257-260
Apocrypha, miracles related to, 30, 133, 154
Apollo, temple of, at Delphi, 74
Apollonius of Tyana, 29-30, 154, 257
Apparitions, 158-181, 215-260
  see also Blessed Virgin; Vision
Apporte, 75
Arnold, Matthew, 291
Asclepius, 29
Assumption, dogma of, 125
Astrology, 49, 73
Athanasius, St., 45
Atomic energy, 270-271
Attwater, Donald, 16, 24, 25, 45
Augustine, St., 11, 30, 130, 147, 159-160
Automatic writing, 78
Avesta, 35

Baal, 124
Babylon, destruction of, 127
Bacon, Francis, 76
Bahram, King, 42
Baltasar, King, 24
Banneux, Belgium, apparitions at, 8-9, 24, 254

Baptism, as form of exorcism, 38
Barbara, St., 158
Beatrice Mary of Jesus, Mother, 97
Beauraing, Belgium, apparitions at, 8-9, 24, 250-254
Benedict XIV, 73, 79
Benedict Joseph Labre, St., 94, 177-178, 193
Bernadette Soubirous (Bernadette of Lourdes), St., 26, 63-64, 95, 190, 204-205, 216, 225-226
Bilocation, 110-11
Black Magic, 45
Blaise, St., 157
Blanshard, Paul, 244
Blasphemy of the Spirit, 40
Blavatsky, Mme. Helen Petrovna, 76
Blessed Virgin, apparitions at Banneux, 8-9, 24, 254; Beauraing, 9-10, 24, 251-254; Lourdes, 204, 225-226; to St. Catherine Labouré, 191-193, 217-221; at Fatima, Portugal, 244-250; to St. Genna Galgani, 100; at Knock, Ireland, 242-243; at La Salette, 220-225; at Lourdes, 204, 225-226; at Pellevoisin, 241-242; assumption of, 125; devotion to, 215; dialogues with St. Mary Magdalen de' Pazzi, 175; Immaculate Conception, 138-139; Motherhood of, 138-139; as Queen of Angels, 243; see also Our Lady
Blood, miracles of, 97, 112, 182-183
Bodily elongation, 90
Body, incorruption of, 23, 181-185
Bogomili sect, 47
Bolsena, Church of, miracle of Eucharist at, 27-28, 149-150
Boniface, St., 184
Bosch, Hieronymus, 49
Braga, Council of, 47
Brahe, Tycho, 140
Bread and fishes, Christ's multiplication of, 23, 280
Breughel, Peter, 49
Bridget of Sweden, St., 184
Bronze serpent, miracle of, 122
Buddha, 29-30, 42
Burning bush, miracle of, 122
Burning phenomena, 79

Severus, Sulpicius, 30, 161
Signorelli, Luca, 33
Signs, vs. miracles, 19
Simon Magus, 45, 48, 74, 88
Skepticism, 3, 11
Sobieski, Jan, 287
Society of Jesus, 173
Society for Psychical Research, 71
Sodom and Gomorrha, destruction of, 116
Solovyev, Vladimir, 257
Sorcery, 45-46; see also Magic
Soubirous, Bernadette, see Bernadette Soubirous, St.
Space, multidimensional, 276-277
Spicer, H., 77
Spirit, in theosophy, 76
Spiritism, 71, 76
Sprenger, Jacob, 49
Star of Bethlehem, miracle of, 139
Stephen of Hungary, St., 184
Stern, Karl, 93, 95, 178
Stigmata, 19, 81, 96-97, 103, 107, 109, 162-163 172, 176
Sufism, 29
Supernatural, vs. modal supernatural, 263-264
Superstition, encouragement of, 11
Supreme Sacred Congregation of the Holy Office, 22, 31, 72, 110
Swedenborg, Emanuel, 75-76, 78, 81
Sybilline oracles at Cumae and Tibur, 74
Syracuse, vision at, 24

Table rapping and moving, 80
Telekinesis, 5-6, 55, 75, 81, 86-87
Telepathy, 29, 55, 74-75, 79, 81-85
Teleplasm, 87
Teleplasty, 75, 81
Telesthesy, 75
Temptation of Christ by Satan, 37-38
Ten Commandments, 114
Teresa, St., see Teresa of Avila, St.
Teresa of Avila, St., 24, 88-89, 93, 169
Teresa of Jesus, see Teresa of Avila
Tertullian, 44
Theosophy, 76
Thérèse of the Child Jesus (Thérèse of Lisieux), St., 25, 102, 110, 190, 205
Thermodynamics, second law of, 282

Thomas Aquinas, St., 17-18, 67, 149, 186
Thomas More, St., 25
Thought reading, 55
Thurston, Herbert, S.J., 6, 48, 50, 77, 87, 90, 96, 98, 163, 183
Tonquedec, Joseph de, S.J., 52, 55-56, 67
Toynbee, Arnold, 262
Transiturus, Urban IV, 150
Transubstantiation, 148; and modern physics, 272-275
Trent, Council of, 153
Truth, deliberate resistance to, 40
Turks, defeat of, by John, 287-288

Universal Spirit, in theosophy, 76
Universe, end of, 282
Ural-Altai, belief in Satan among, 34
Urban IV, Transiturus, 150

Vatican Council, 17, 64, 262
Veronica Guiliani, St., 176
Vincent de Paul, St., 202
Vincent Ferrer, St., 164
Virgin, Blessed, see Blessed Virgin
Virgin birth, 17
Vision(s), 24-27, 106-107; see also Banneux; Beauraing; Fatima; Knock; La Salette; Lourdes; Pius XII; St. Michael; Syracuse; Our Lady
Vitus, St., 157
Voyage to Lourdes, 231

Walburga, St., 184
Water into wine, miracle of, 23, 140-141, 279
White Magic, 45
Willibald, St., 185
Witchcraft, 47-49, 75, 154
Woman taken in adultery, 38
Wonders, vs. miracles, 19
World wars, suffering connected with, 288

Xenoglossy, 72, 78

Yawveh, 119, 124

Zarathustra, 35, 45

About This Book

This book is part of a series we call ARKive Editions: exact photographic reproductions of books published in previous decades or centuries. In them, you find undiluted by modern notions or passing fads the words and ideas of good and thoughtful souls who preceded us in this life.

In this, there is great value: it helps free us from the myopia that afflicts souls drowning in the words and images flooding forth from our modern media, with its attention focused so intently on that which is new and popular today.

Our age is less than perfect and ARKive Editions help us see that, enabling us to measure our own day by the often better standards of other times and places.

At the same time, previous ages and other cultures had their faults: and even in good books from earlier times we often find language, ideas, or values that were once deemed acceptable even by honorable souls, but are now seen clearly to be wrong.

We exclude from ARKive Editions books that have in them as significant themes ideas that are wrong. When, however, books that are overwhelmingly good are tainted by unfortunate peripheral remarks or occasional wrongheaded judgments, we have chosen to publish them intact. For we judge that the good to be done by such books far outweighs the harm done by occasional remarks which good men and women these days can (and should) dismiss as the unfortunate products of an age as flawed as our own, albeit in different ways.

If you disagree with our judgment, please understand, nonetheless, that we have sought to act in goodwill. Let your disagreement be an occasion for you to pray that our generation will soon come to see our own errors as clearly as we see the errors of earlier times; and then turn your attention back to the true riches that are to be found in each of our ARKive Editions, presented here exactly as they appeared to readers in earlier times.

An Invitation

Reader, the book that you hold in your hands was published by Sophia Institute Press.

Sophia Institute seeks to restore man's knowledge of eternal truth, including man's knowledge of his own nature, his relation to other persons, and his relation to God.

Our press fulfills this mission by offering translations, reprints, and new publications. We offer scholarly as well as popular publications; there are works of fiction along with books that draw from all the arts and sciences of our civilization. These books afford readers a rich source of the enduring wisdom of mankind.

Sophia Institute Press is the publishing arm of the Thomas More College of Liberal Arts and Holy Spirit College. Both colleges are dedicated to providing university-level education in the Western tradition under the guiding light of Catholic teaching.

If you know a young person who might be interested in the ideas found in this book, share it. If you know a young person seeking a college that takes seriously the adventure of learning and the quest for truth, bring our institutions to his attention.

www.SophiaInstitute.com
www.ThomasMoreCollege.edu
www.HolySpiritCollege.org

SOPHIA INSTITUTE PRESS

THE PUBLISHING DIVISION OF

 THOMAS MORE COLLEGE *of* LIBERAL ARTS   HOLY SPIRIT COLLEGE